AF581091
LOVE
ALWAYS

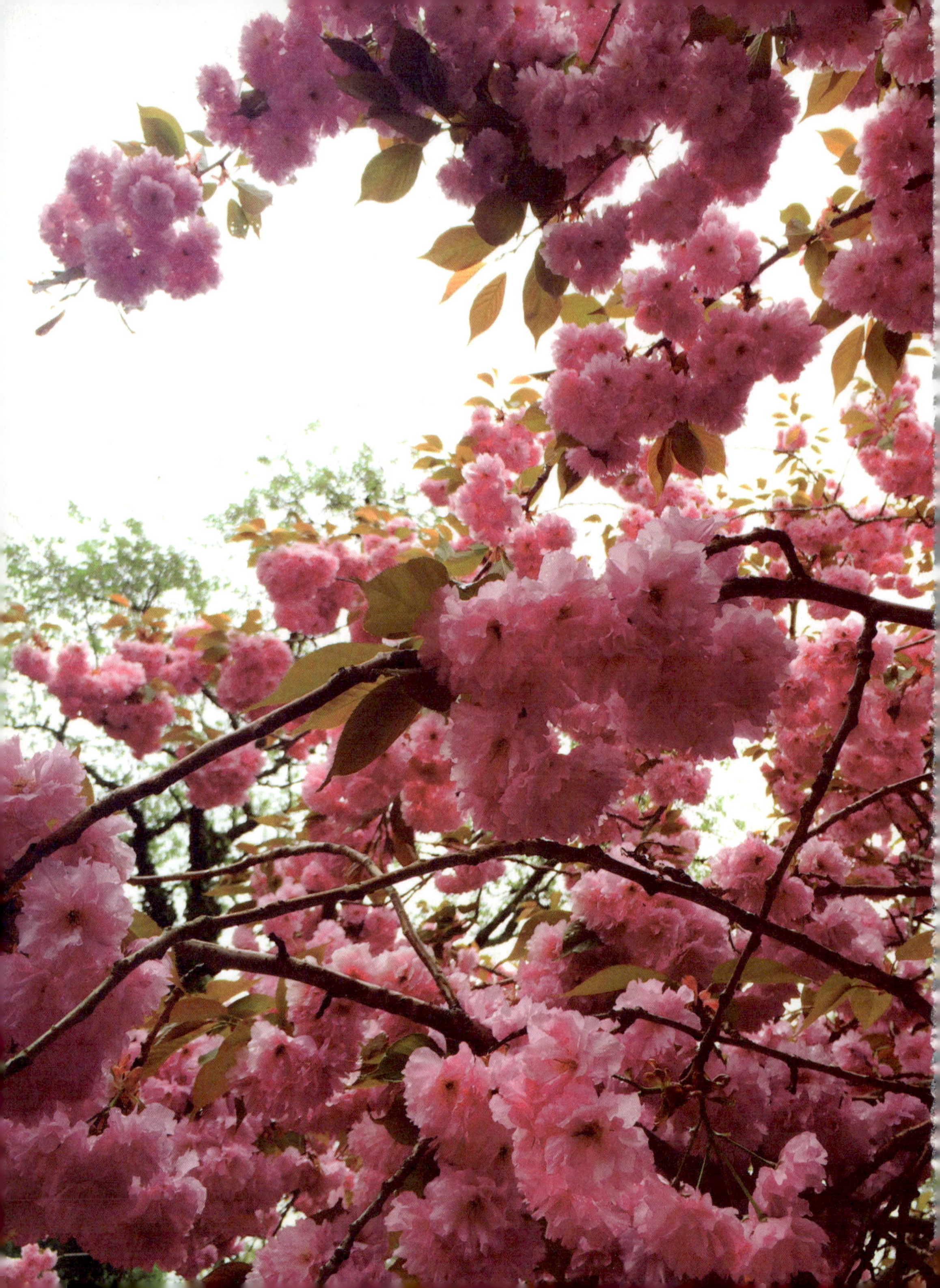

”

Radiate boundless love towards the entire world.

-BUDDHA

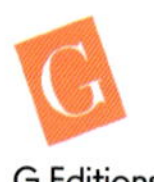

G Editions

www.geditions.com
media@geditions.com

FIRST EDITION, 2022

Library of Congress Cataloging-in-Publication data is available from the publisher.

Hardcover Edition ISBN: 978-1-943876-23-5

Design: Janine Seelen
Printed and bound in China

10 9 8 7 6 5 4 3 2 1

RADIANCE

WORTH REIMAGINED

ROBIN BAKER LEACOCK

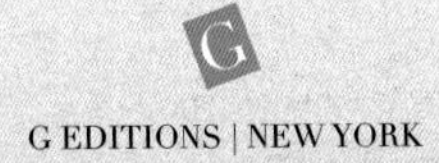

G EDITIONS | NEW YORK

DESI
ABIL

RE

ITY

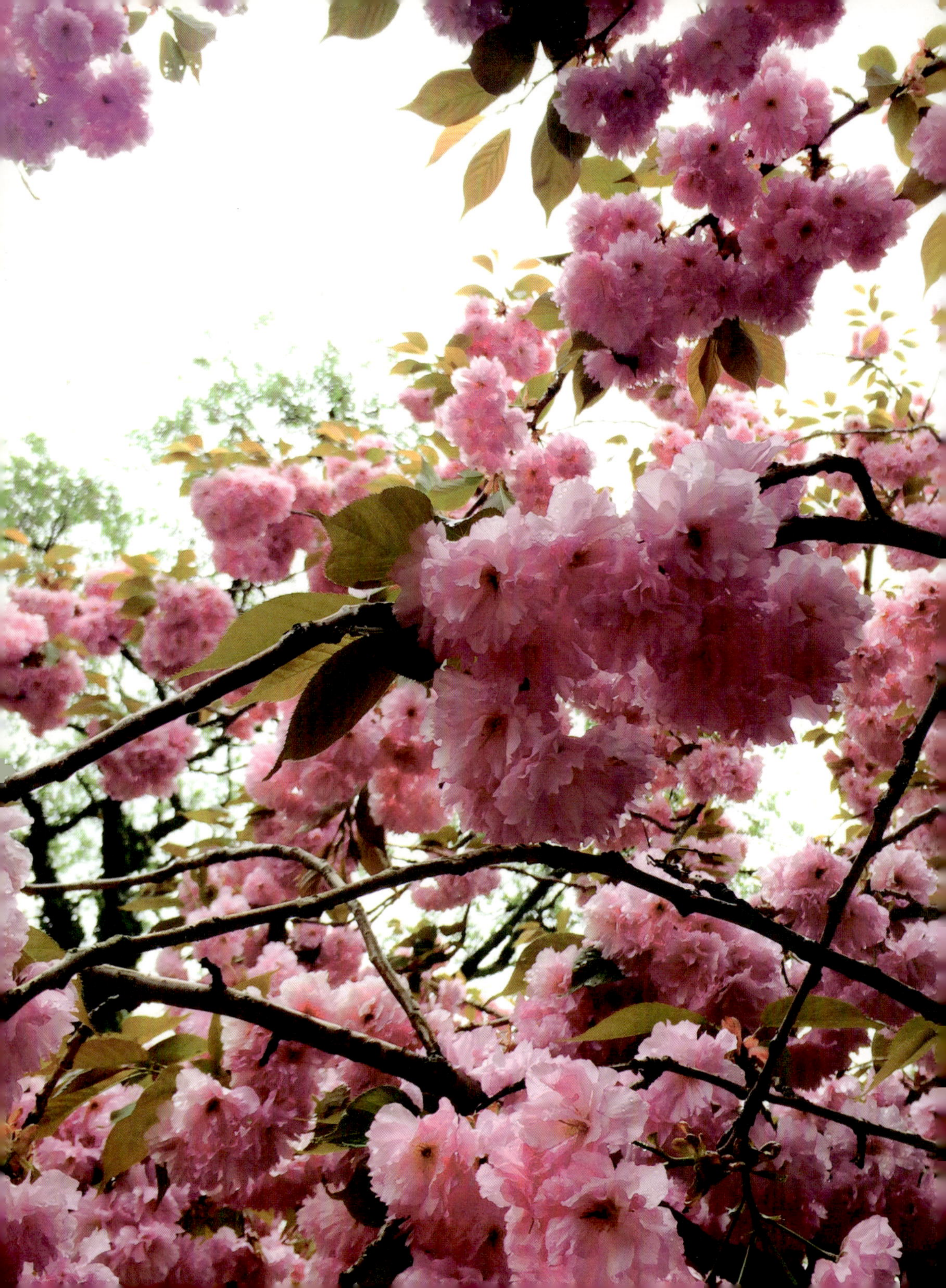

The whole point of this book is to question what we value! It's not a book about self-worth, there are plenty of those. That's why it's called

Worth Reimagined.

It's about what we value as a culture.

I wrote a lot of this book when I was younger and much more idealistic and carefree.
Yet I feel that it resonates now more than ever.
I still believe beauty and worth come from a radiance that shines from within.

We are all seeking, even chasing, beauty and significance in our lives—finding it in a lovely new house, through wonderful memories, sharing online, thriving in health, or even in a feeling, a sense of belonging, a unique sense of self. We're content to live in a beautiful world radiant with love and care. All happy in our cozy place—delicious food and a comfy home often with good friends, family, and pets.

And somehow this has all become upside down, with the relentless desire and chase for more, to be more important, to be bigger in life, to be seen as grand. Our esteem has become based on worth, and our ideas of worth have been conceived by someone other than ourselves, with admiration looking outside ourselves and applause projecting back at us. Images dictating or diminishing who we are, blinding us to what we already have. Some of us have already given ourselves away to that misplaced concept, hopefully not to be put off by future cynicism.

I'm wishing to bring back home the idea that worth is entirely up to the individual: What they are worth, others are worth, objects are worth; the value of our inner self, that we are enough and more than enough and already have what we are running around seeking. Just like in The Wizard of Oz, there's no place like home . . . or from T.S. Elliot:

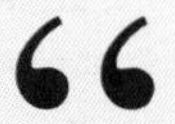

We shall not cease from exploration
And the end of all our exploring
Will be to arrive where we started
And know the place for the first time.

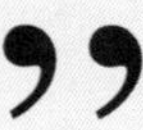

Sometimes we can see that we are already worth everything. And each moment of our lives contains the exquisite beauty we are all seeking and of which we want to be a part.

Desirability is awakened in each instant. Gaze out through your eyes and see that exquisite radiance is everywhere.

—Robin Baker Leacock

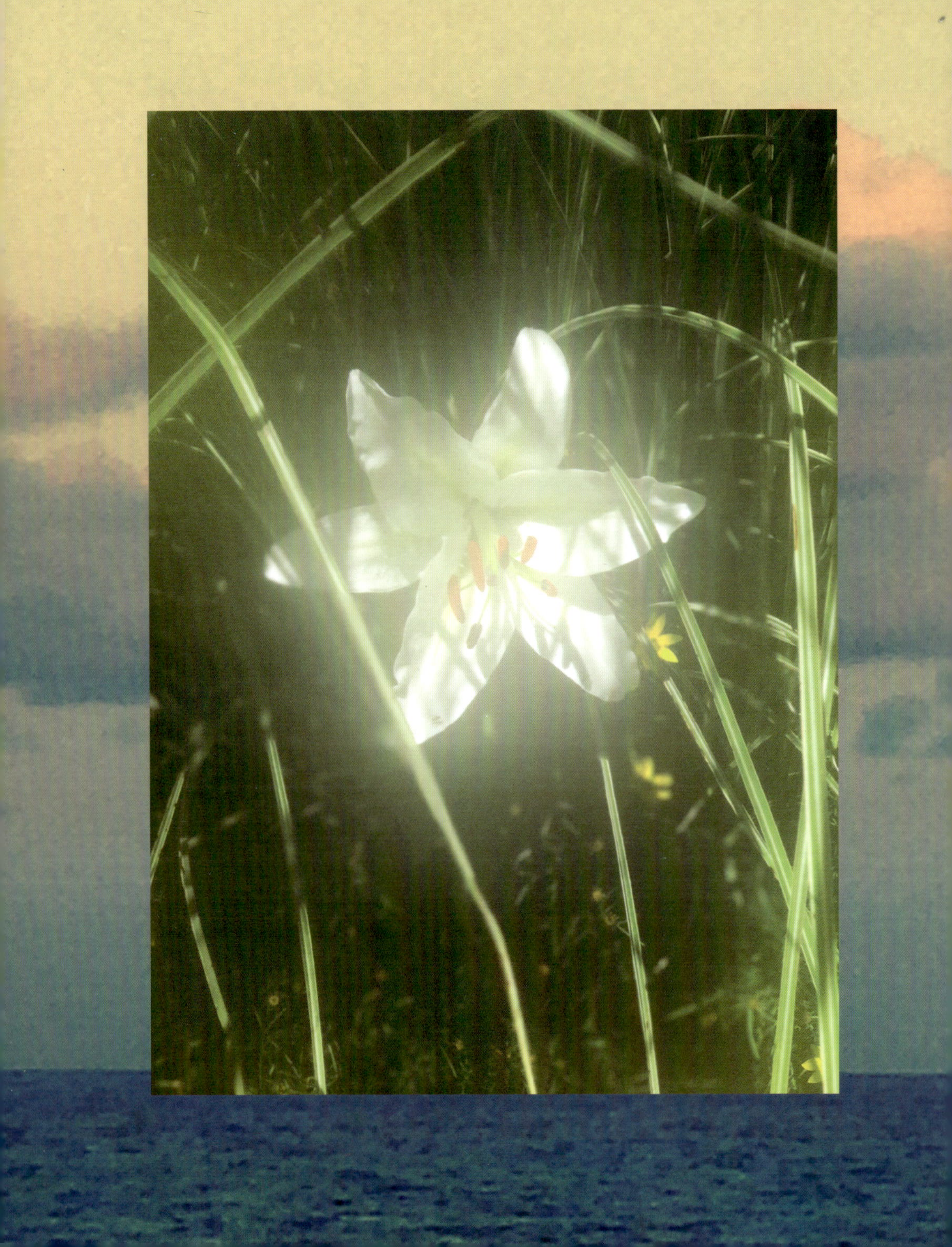

THE PRESENT

When something has worth, you KNOW IT.
You know in your soul that it's something you value and value above all else.
It's real—not based on someone else's idea of value and not something you have to convince yourself to like. It's just a wonderful moment—experience/flavor/music/book/love—in your life that makes life WORTH LIVING.

Look around and see that you now have everything in this moment.
Sky, clouds, air, love, sound, sight, breeze, thoughts, sensations surrounding you. . . .
You're fully alive.

Life is an extraordinary gift, containing all sorts of moments, full of all sorts of things.
It's only our judgement of these moments that makes some worth more than others.
Every moment is as perfect and balanced as can be.
There's no such thing as an empty moment!
Every moment is complete with vision, sound, fullness.

All you can ever do is be absolutely alive and aware in each moment. Absorbing the frequencies of light, sound, and air surrounding you and knowing that this present is what is being presented to you. . . . The PRESENT!

And if you can be fully alive in that instant—each instant—you will come to value each and every moment and have the heightened experience of a life fulfilled.

Life wholly lived is a gift of incalculable value.
We are here on earth, a magical environment that has endless possibilities . . . and being alive is all you really need to feel grateful.

(The approval of others seems really small and unimportant now, doesn't it?)

In this culture, and now all over this planet, we value money more than anything else.
I'm often amazed by this, because sometimes money, to me, is a crumpled up bill in my pocket that I can lose very easily if I reach in to find

something else, like a notepaper, and it falls to the ground unnoticed by me until some concerned citizen (often an older woman) chases after me to tell me WHAT I'VE LOST! But I haven't lost my life, or a precious poem written to me by someone special, or my favorite glasses. There are many, many, many of these dollar bills around, and often very hard-earned. Yet they're all of abstract value; there is just one bottle of water in an emergency, quenching my thirst with a cool sip of fresh spring water if I need it.

Now I understand that these dollars buy all kinds of things. And I truly understand that people work very, very, very hard all their lives to buy food and shelter and healthcare and education for their families.

But what I am saying is the worship of this money and the people who have accumulated a lot of it, by whatever tricks they had up their sleeve, has become very distorted on this planet. Money is a tool of exchange but not of endless admiration. Kindness and giving and loving are to be admired. Money is to be used to make your life and the lives of others better, easier, and happier.

Being envious of someone with a shiny red car or a bright gold watch or a big, big house is as silly as wanting another child's toys.

Please keep the chasing of money in perspective. It closes the door on so much else in life that is worth SO MUCH MORE.

Like . . . a good conversation, an amazing moment of synchronicity, nature, delicious food, the ocean, the desert, the mountains, a good friend, the scent of jasmine in the air, a crisp blue sky, perfect leaves on a tree, the morning sun, the evening sunset, the sounds of songbirds, a sighting of a beautiful bird, a lovely animal, someone you love laughing, a smile from a stranger, a walk down a dreamlike lane on a lovely morning, running for joy, jumping for joy, running down a hill, a somersault, a cool drink on a warm day, a warm drink on a cool day, something sweet, the feeling after exercise, accomplishment, helping someone, being positive, being loving, warm balmy air, springtime, summertime, autumn, white snow, lemons, coconuts, fruit, delicious vegetables, water, happiness.

If we could value what really matters and

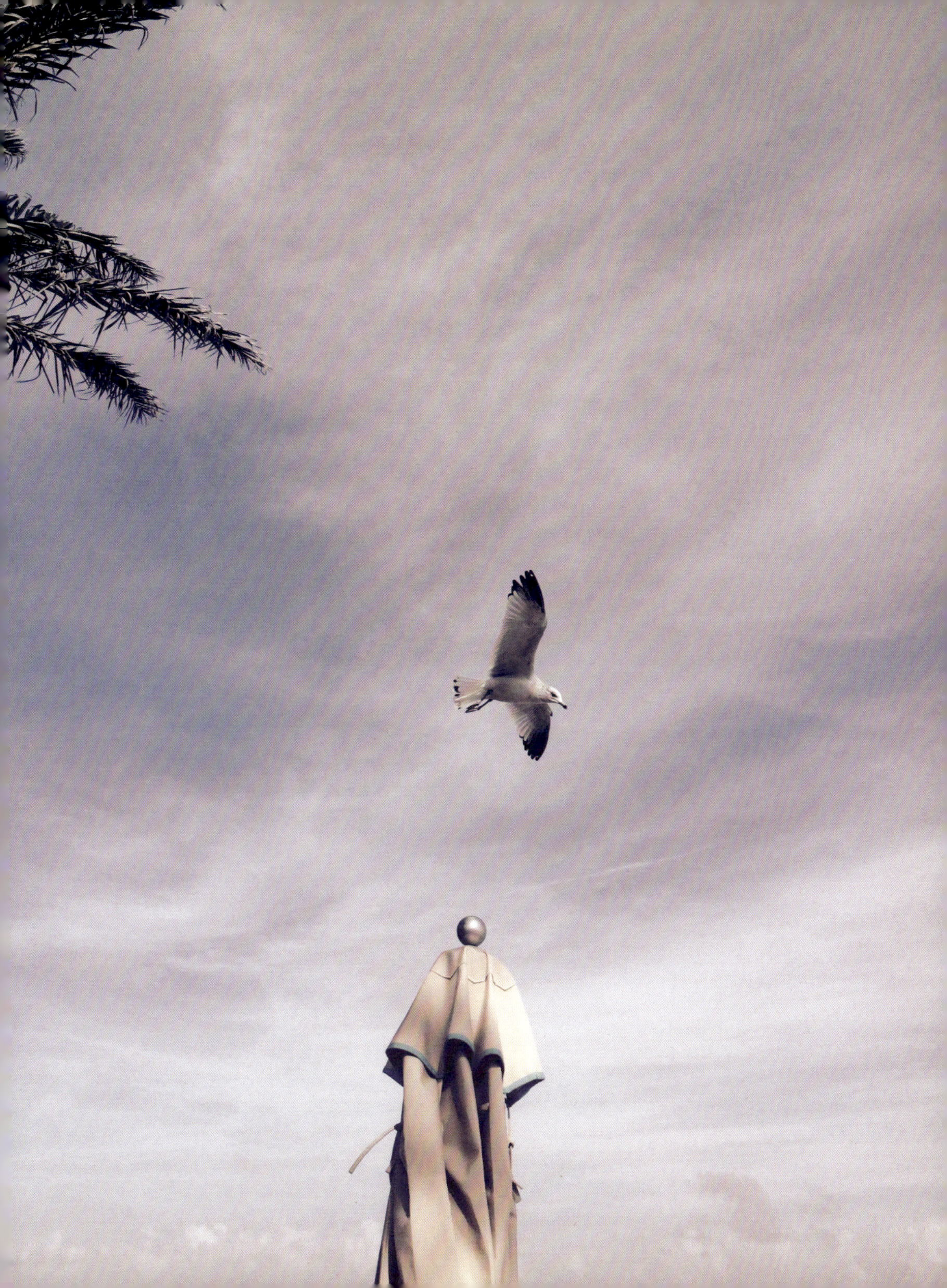

appreciate the worth of all that is around us, then we would not need to put certain items on a pedestal, inflating their desirability, and creating what is an unattainable dream to so many.

Chasing after those "expensive items" is an illusion of importance.
It's really just a mirage. Those items create a longing that can never be fulfilled, and they're not that valuable in the end anyway.

Can you imagine if we made water or an apple or a needle and thread or a light bulb as expensive as a car or a gold watch?
I mean, we could, because if you need something and demand for that product is high and it becomes rare, then it is valuable.

I'm always amazed what we call valuable.
The things I get excited about are often free, yet I see people aiming their whole lives at achieving "material success" like the newest fashions, the blingiest jewelry, the most out-there cars and houses.

I see it all the time, everywhere I turn, in magazines, on TV shows, on social media, and they often look really silly to me, really insecure, and often quite lost in their values.

In contrast, I see people from other spheres of life who seem to have a real handle on what's worthwhile.
I see taxi drivers from all kinds of cultures, landscape workers, cleaning people, all sorts of people from all over the world, and when I am with them, I often hear people with clear values and goals: they want to help their family and friends and enjoy life. I'm sure, if given a chance, they might pursue the same ridiculous desires, but their work is so important to them and those desires go nowhere because they're not real. Just made up by other people, with the same ridiculous goals, to make you think you're not enough.

If you're not happy and alive RIGHT NOW IN THIS MOMENT, you might never be, because this moment is ALWAYS NOW. And you can come alive right now if you'd like!

Pretty much anything

you don't think

you already have,

---

that you now think
you need,
is always worth a lot!

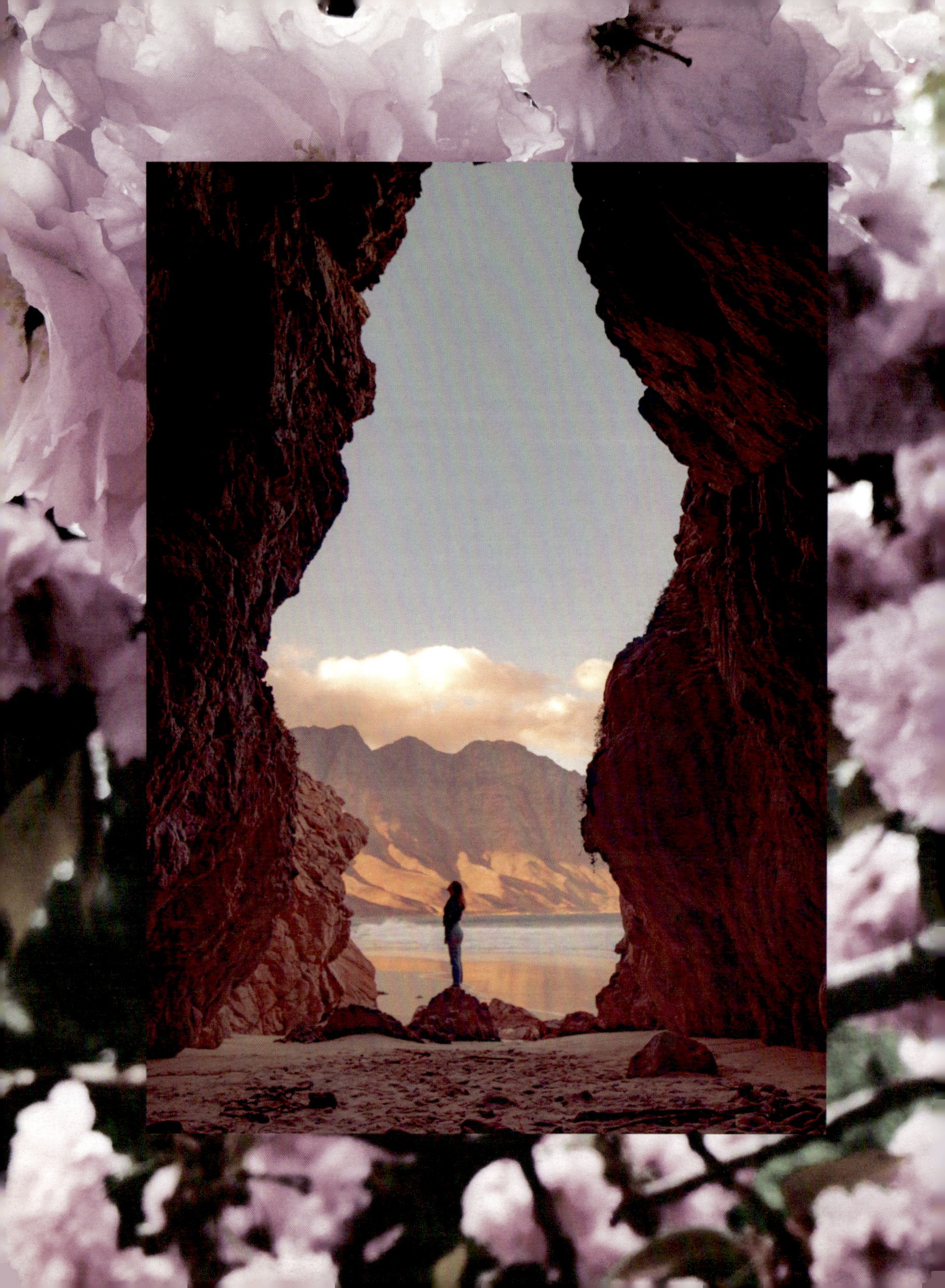

A HEART-BASED SOCIETY

What a fantastic world it would be if, every day, people focused on what truly matters and has meaning.

If we could just remember what actually meant something, when we were feeling humble or desperate or sick, but without having to go through all that sadness or pain.

From good food, to good love, to good smiles, to good thoughts.

The ability to walk to lovely places, smell delicious food, have a nice conversation, and feel happy just to feel happy, without depending on something specific happening outside of you. Just to feel happy because this is our time on this planet, and that is very special.

If only we had one day left to live at the end of life, I think our senses would heighten and all the little things would become magical.
This is how life can be all the time!

This is our time, here and now, and what a true waste to spend it on ridiculous stuff, like what you look like or how much money you have.

If you want the important things to count, let's see how many times you can be kind, or cheer

someone up, or give someone a helping hand,
or let someone know you are there for them.
That's what true wealth really is.

Our time on this planet is a gift to each of us.
It has a beginning, a middle
And, sure enough, an end.
How much you appreciate and give to
EACH moment is the true value of your life.

Not how much you think you are admired
and envied.
Because the truth is not many can really see
you—only you see yourself.
Most people just see a reflection of what they
want to be.

What they might be admiring or seeing in you
is sometimes just a misplaced mirror-image
of themselves.
But lives spent self-cherishing, just trying to look
"cool" or "hot"—
The truth is that's not really hot!

It's just a waste of very special time.

I know the world can move on from these
empty achievements,
and eventually know that what's real is really
what's in your heart and soul.

That's not a money-based society; that's a
HEART-BASED SOCIETY.

SUN

NOW THIS IS WHAT'S REALLY HOT:
THE BRILLIANCE OF THE SUN,
IN ALL ITS RESPLENDENCE,
REFLECTS YOUR RADIANCE.

If You Appreciate It with Love
It Will Reflect Love to You.
So Look to the Light.

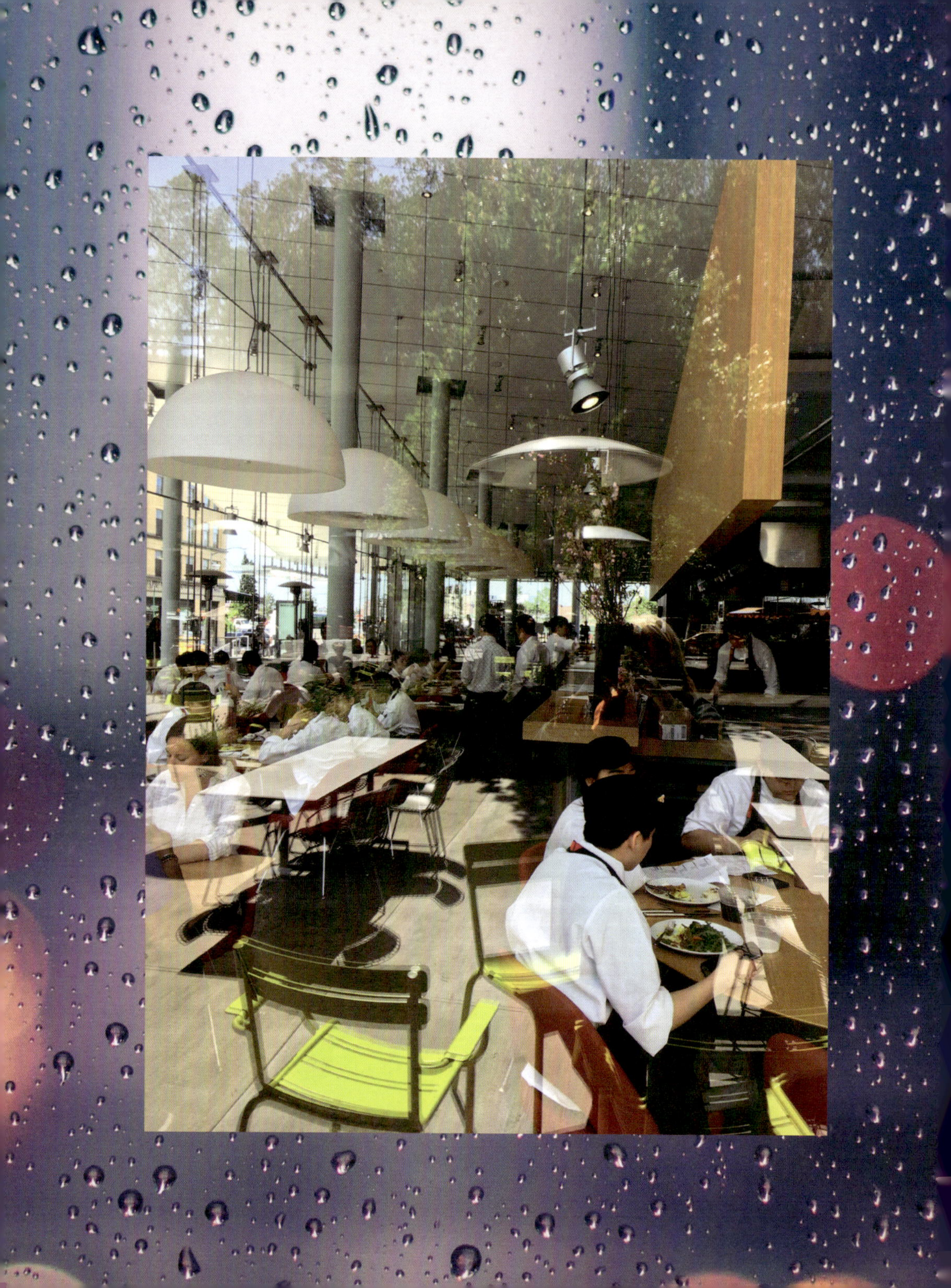

REFLECTIONS ON WORTH

So this book is a discussion of worth,
of what really has relevance
in our lives, in our culture
and on this planet Earth.

Love is the most valuable thing
in the universe.
Without love, this would be a gray,
lonely, and empty place to live.

All things have worth in this world,
although, at times, some things
seem more valuable than others.

In these times that
we are living in now, the things
that seem to have the most value
are not always the things that
have the most meaning.
For instance, paper money, jewelry,
fancy cars, big houses are the
most coveted items.

But if you are hungry or cold,
or tired or lonely, all those things
have absolutely no worth at all!
If you want to be warm and
sheltered and you have no support,
or you are isolated and
lonely and human warmth is
eluding you, all the things that
people spend a lifetime chasing
and coveting have absolutely
no meaning.

And this book is a look at what has
significance in this world, and what we
have come to value.
Wealth and possessions,
status and fame, have become
the most coveted items in our
universe.
But love and kindness
and caring are often undervalued
and overlooked.

I hear people say that some things
or people are "hot," and I hear
people say that some things are
"cool." But I never hear people say
that things are "warm."
To me, the highest form of flattery
is to say that someone is warm!
I just have to imagine what the
world would be like if everyone
were warm.

Let me put my cards on the table.
I'm not someone who is living on air.
I have a nice home and a nice life.
Good things have come to me, and
I often, of course, have to remind
myself to appreciate everything.

The most important thing in
the world to me is to try and
participate in making the world
a kinder and happier place to live.
I, of course, make mistakes or
become too sensitive.
But more than anything else,
I do not worship selfishness,
ego, greed, or control for the
sake of power.

Clearly one can see that those
attributes only lead to negativity,
loneliness, and bitterness.
If you can exist in the realm of
kindness, humor, light, giving,
and love, you can see that the
rewards are much more amazing.

So why pursue negative emotions?
Why dedicate your life to what
money can buy, if it's only
buying emptiness?
And if you have a family to support,
it would seem to me,
you might want to bring them
up in light and love.
A gift of radiance.

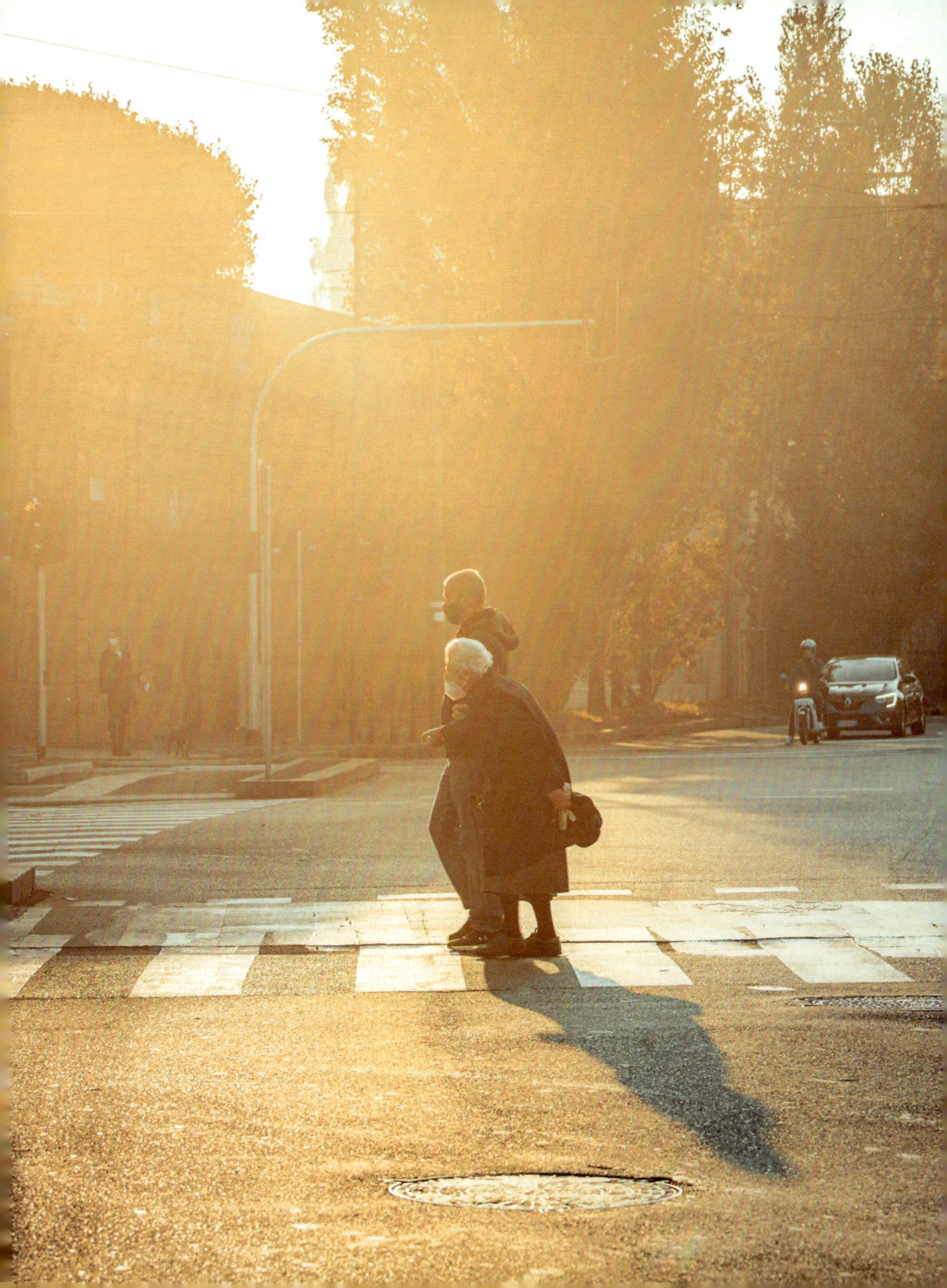

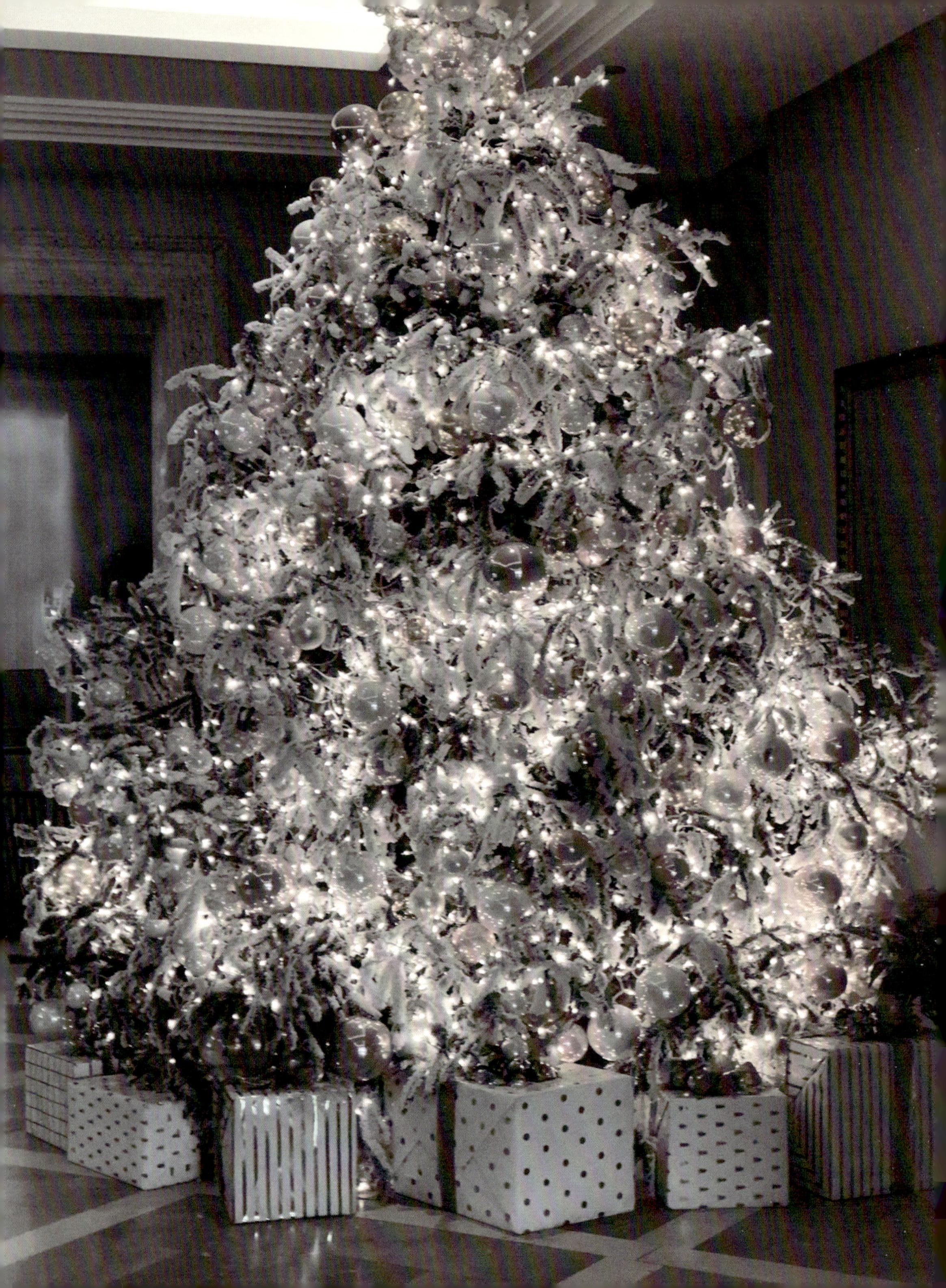

YOU GET WHAT YOU PAY FOR

What someone treasures is an individual concept.

What is priceless to one person may be worthless to the next.

So to have a generalized set of values for objects is ludicrous.

For people to work their entire lives to acquire these objects,
that someone else has highly appraised, is just incredible to me.

Buying a pocket watch a century ago may not have the merit of a gold Rolex today.

Yet that was a big aspiration for many.

Not often do you see giving love as a goal instead.

So how can you dismiss someone's love, and spend countless hours within your ambition,
buying an item of status?

The value of those items fluctuates with the style of the time and era—it is relative.

What is fancied now is transitory.

Real desirability is timeless and meaningful.

Sometimes the things
you don't do
are the most important.

Like not being hurtful.
Or not participating in someone's sadness.
Or not being anyone's source of pain.

Only contributing toward
someone's love,
warmth, and
sense of security.

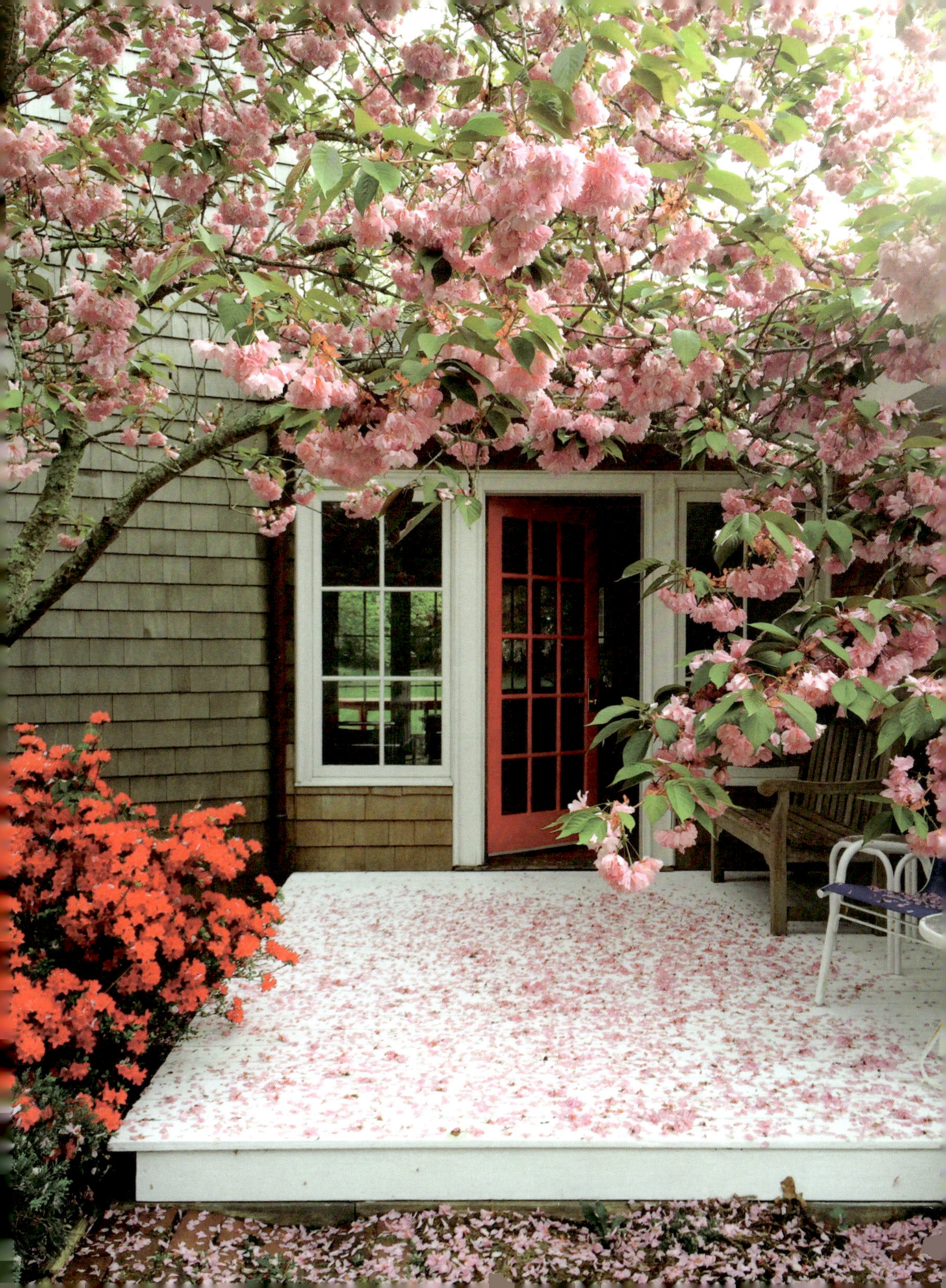

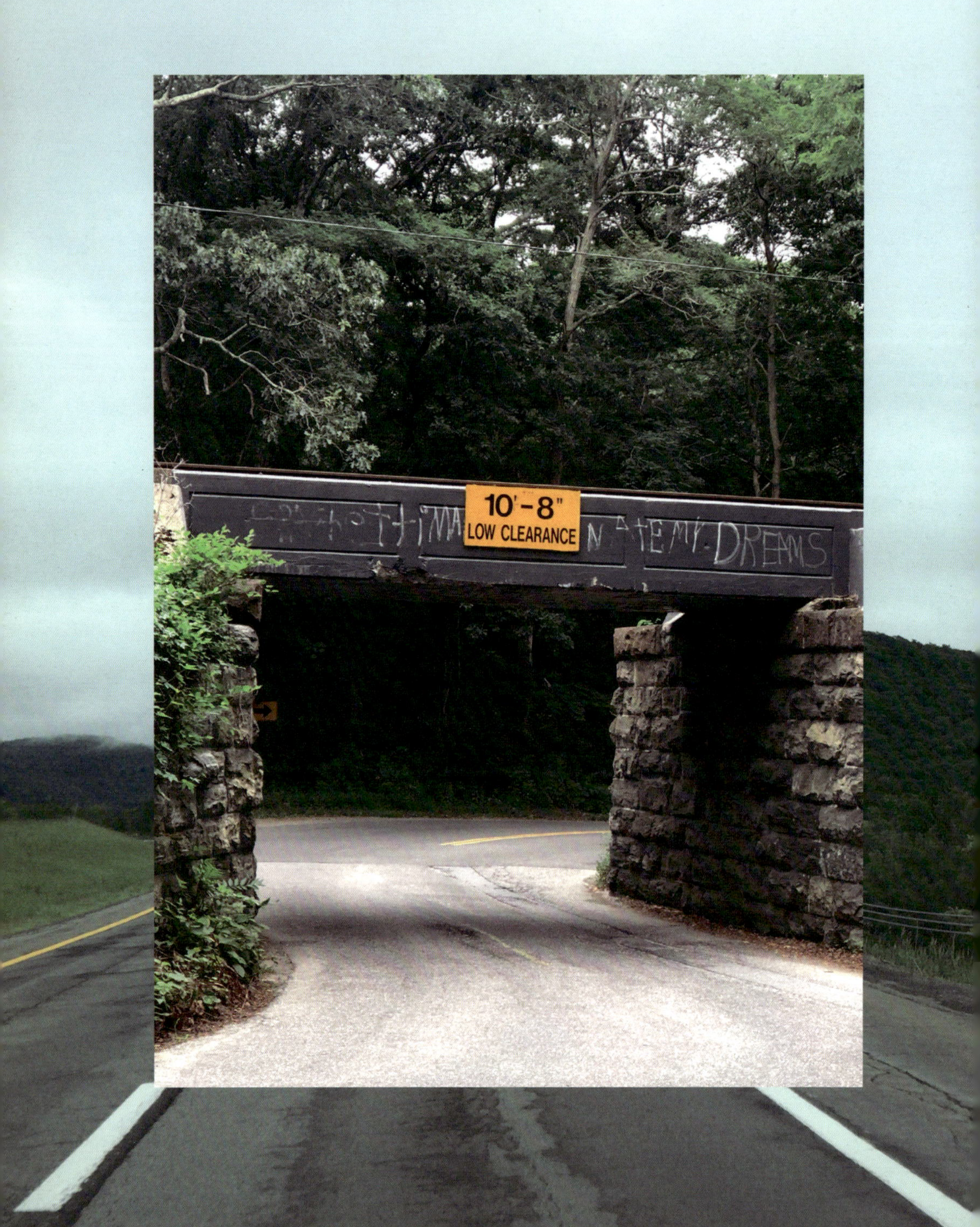
10'-8"
LOW CLEARANCE

THE SPAGHETTI MAN ATE MY DREAMS

I used to drive under a bridge in Long Island that had this graffiti scrawled across the arch. I was struck by these words and wanted to remember them always.

I feel like the Spaghetti Man has eaten many of our dreams. He is the one that swoops down at a moment's notice and scoops up our treasures and our dreams.

So maybe, sometimes, we have to value what can't be taken away:
Our ability to love, our generosity and our kindness.
Anything we give can't be taken away.
Love is an invisible shield that protects us from the Spaghetti Man.

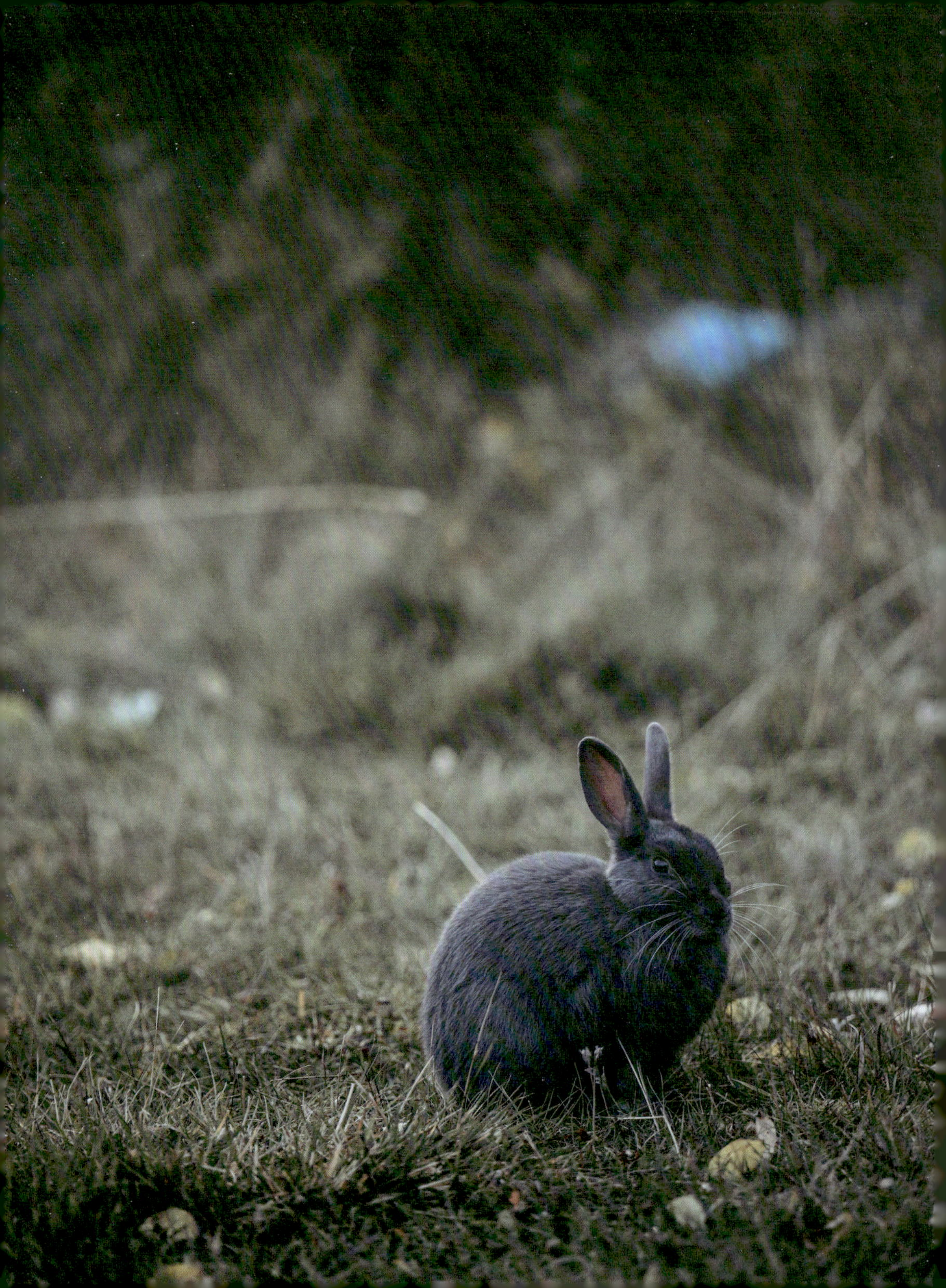

I live entwined in a web of synchronicity.

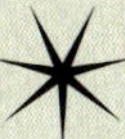

When I'm in synchronicity, I know it.

My energy is in tune with the universe and
extraordinary things begin to happen.

I see beautiful birds and amazing animals arrive.

I meet people who have relevance in my life,
and things move about like magic.

This usually happens when I am in a state of creativity or altruism.

When I'm out of synch, when I'm angry or annoyed,
then nothing ever works.

It's hard to get out of that cycle sometimes.

But when you can stop and breathe and know and love,
then you can become immersed in a web of synchronicity
~
The trick is to stay in that energy.

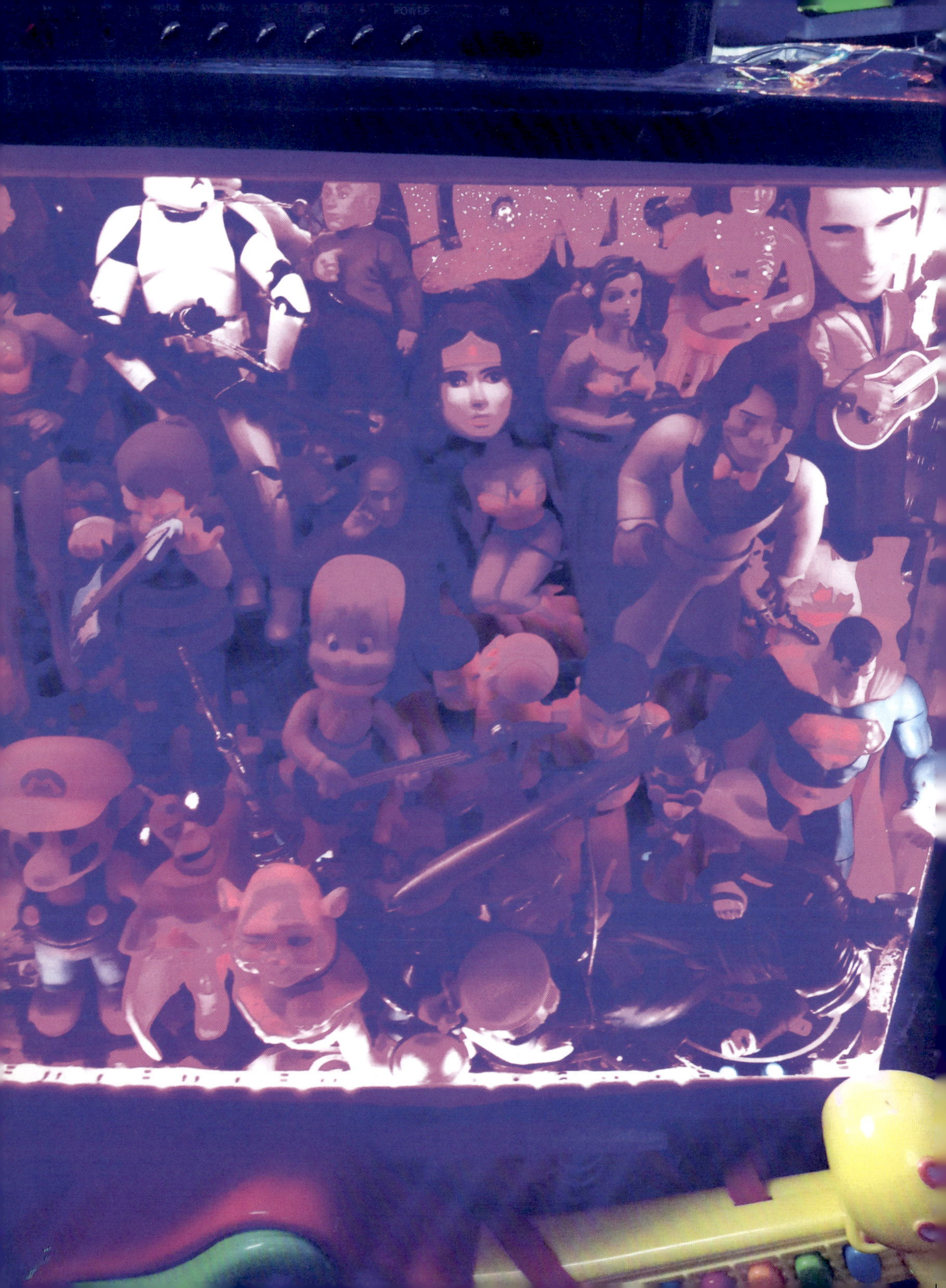

ARTISTS ARE SELF-CONTAINED EMOTIONAL MACHINES.
THEY ARE INDEPENDENT OF EVERYDAY CONCEPTS.
THEY ARE A TERMINAL FOR HIGHER
POWER.

AND SO THEY FIND OUT
COMMUNICATING YOUR ESSENTIAL NATURE IS THE HIGHEST FORM OF ART.

ARTISTS ARE CONDUITS OF MANY DIFFERENT KINDS OF REALITY.

AND BY THE WAY–

you do become your
thoughts

WAITING FOR GREATNESS

A QUALITY THAT'S
CONSIDERED GREAT OR
INTERESTING IN ONE ERA
ISN'T ALWAYS CARRIED
OVER INTO THE NEXT TIMEWAVE.

THAT'S WHY SOME PEOPLE
ARE ONLY
IN THE SPOTLIGHT
OF OTHER PEOPLE'S EYES
FOR JUST A LITTLE WHILE.

PEOPLE WITH PROFOUND AND
BRILLIANT QUALITIES WILL BE REMEMBERED
FOREVER
IT'S JUST A MATTER OF KNOWING THEIR REAL WORTH.

THAT'S WHY RECOGNIZING OLDER PEOPLE'S VALUE IS SO IMPORTANT;
THEY'VE HAD TIME TO FIGURE OUT WHAT IS REALLY OF WORTH.

So wait for greatness. It's worth waiting for.

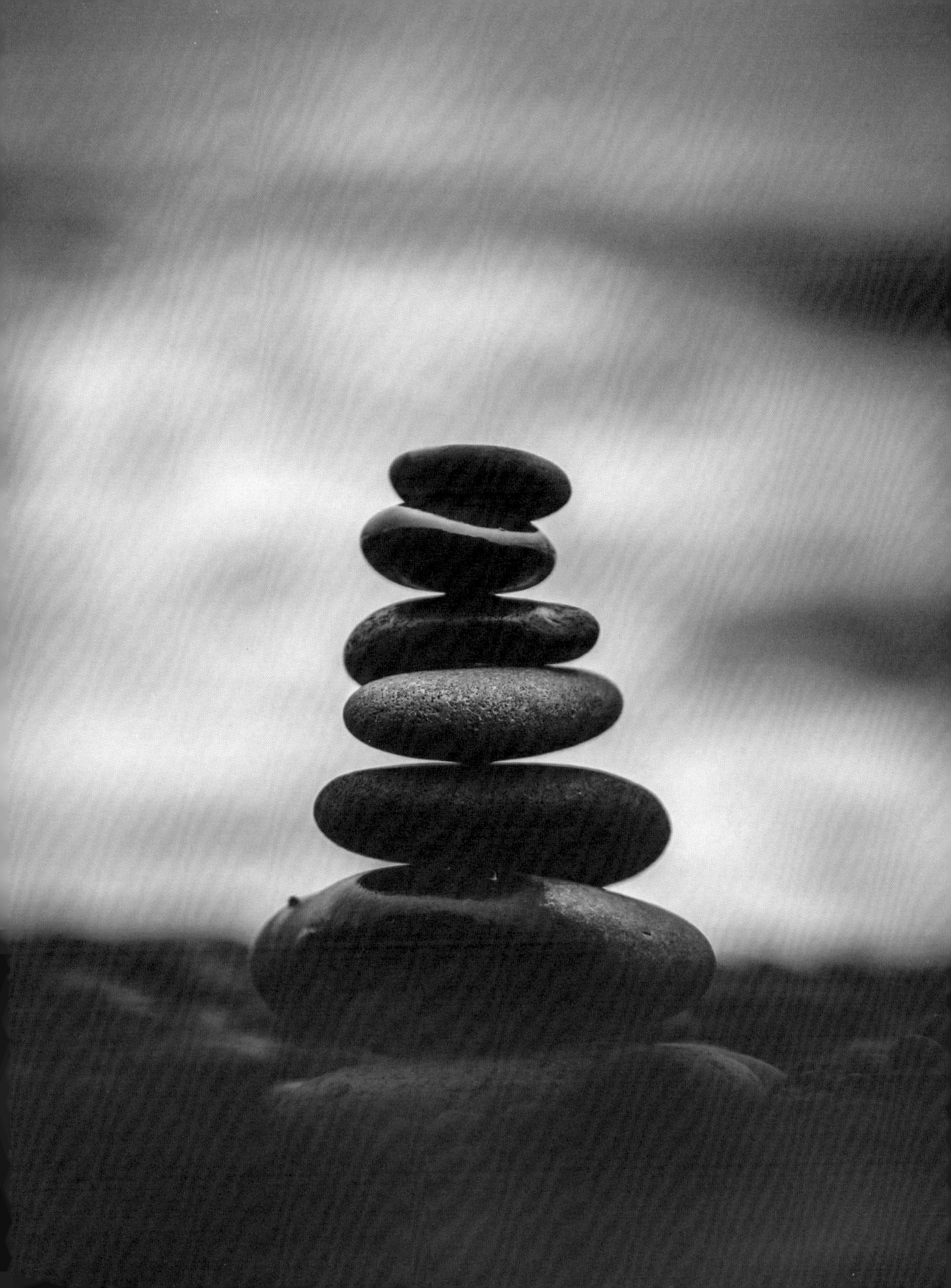

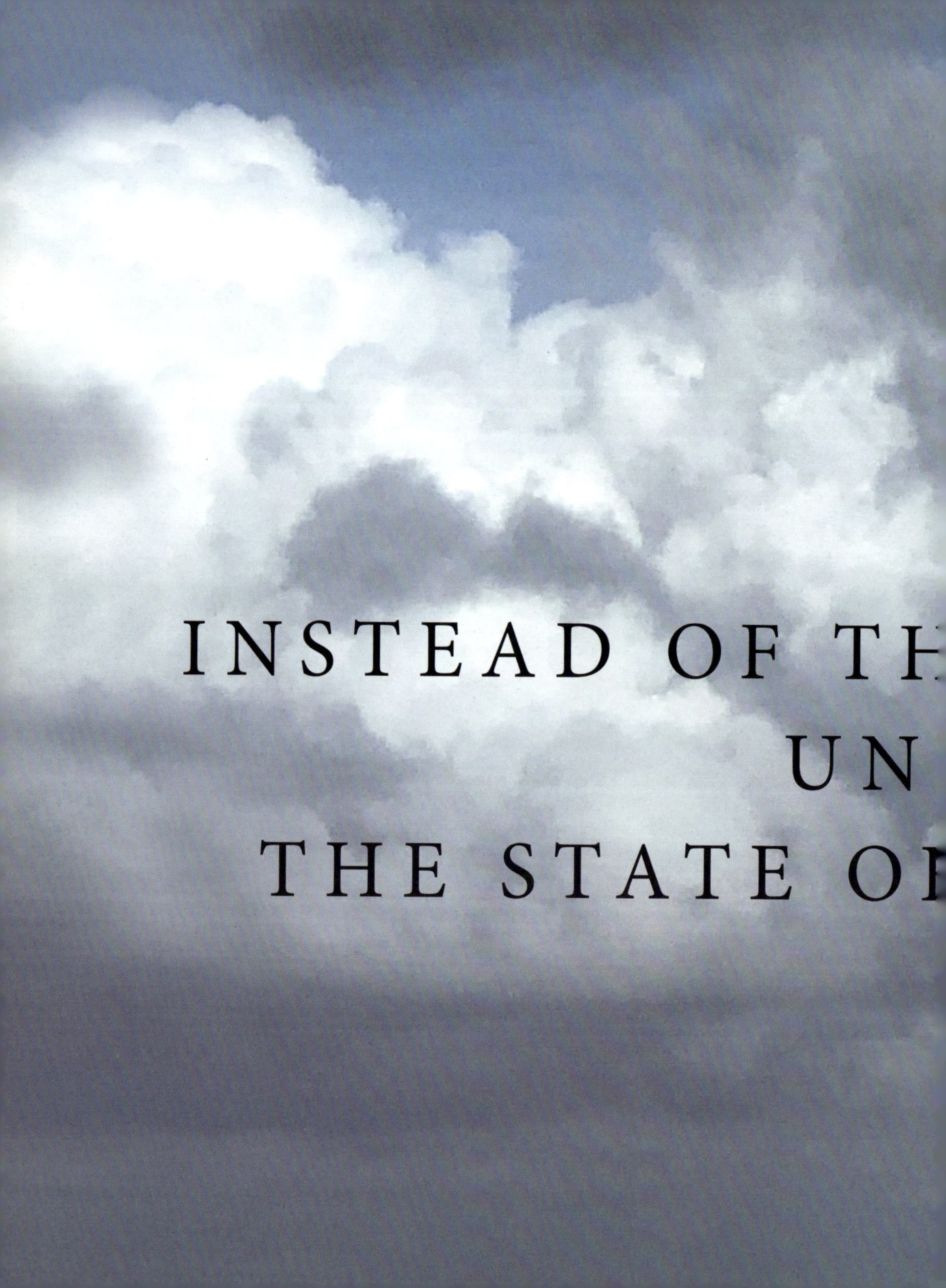

INSTEAD OF TH

UN

THE STATE OF

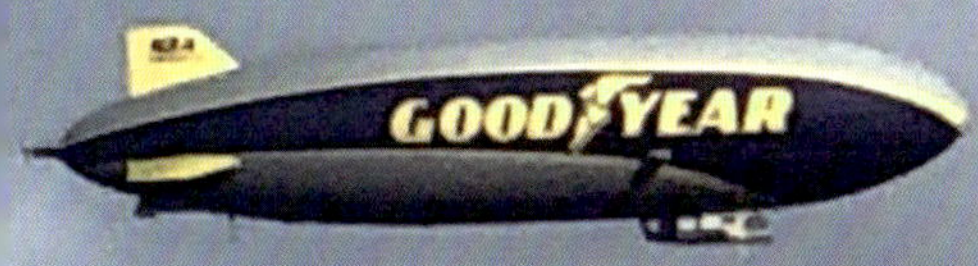

E STATE OF THE

ON:

THE UNIVERSE

Watching the politicians makes me think about getting active.
I can be very articulate sometimes, but it seems to me that, these days, politics is a politics of anger.
So many things need to flip and change for the better.
But acting out of combative rage and self-motivation is acting in darkness.
Wouldn't it be wonderful if our politics actualized out of wisdom and light?

When our society has fallen into a sick or difficult time, then only a bold, forward shift will effectively sort it out—just like a prescription drug.
But when times are calm and smooth, then a natural approach is possible—
like a boost of nutrients.

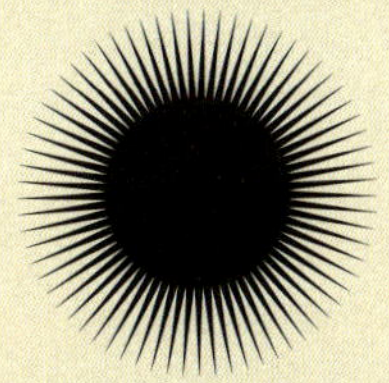

LEARN

TO LOVE WHAT'S HEALTHY.

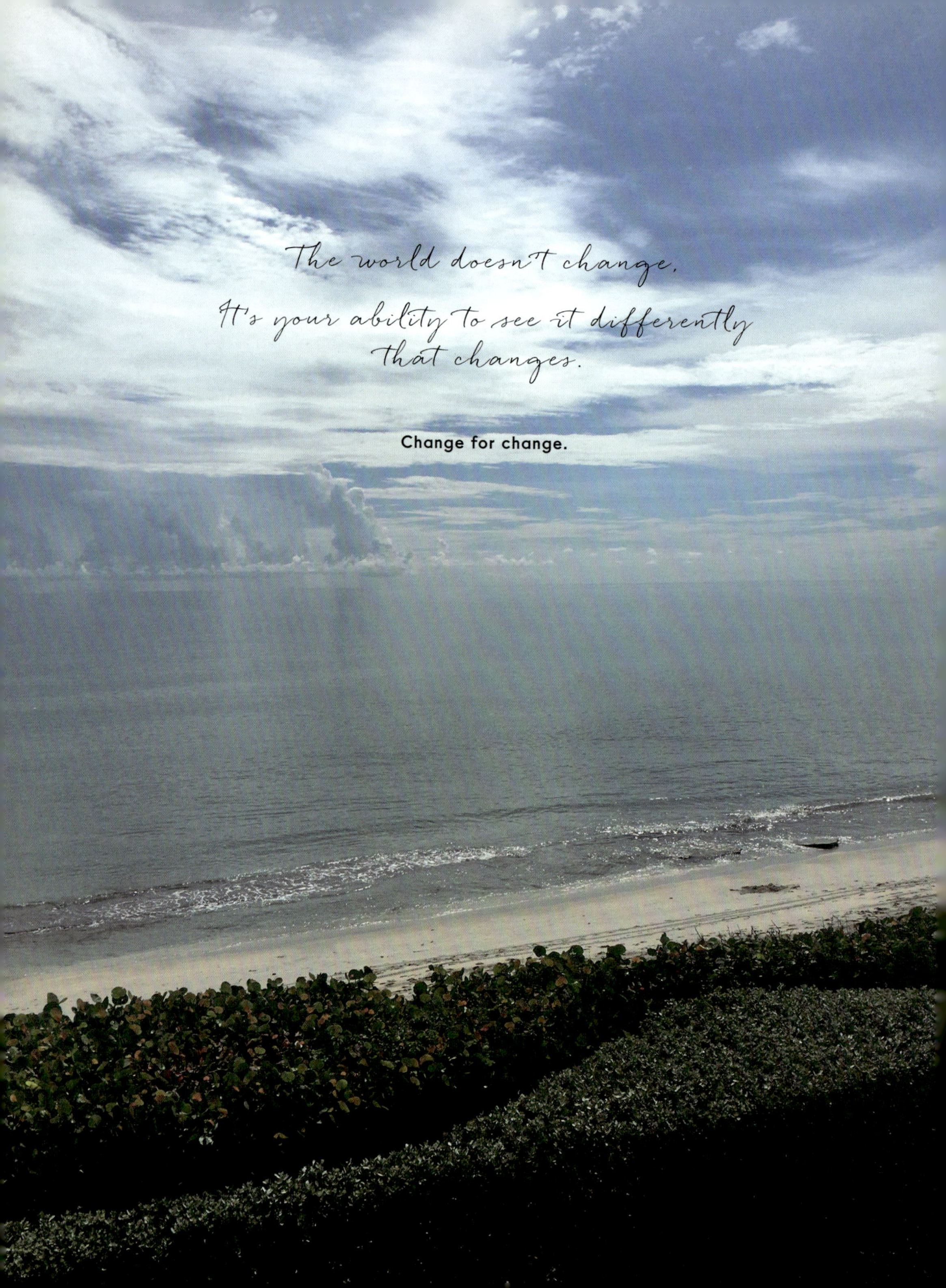

The world doesn't change.

It's your ability to see it differently that changes.

Change for change.

BEING KIND

GIVING INSTEAD OF TAKING

TO ME, THAT IS ABSOLUTELY THE MOST VALUABLE WAY TO HAVE SIGNIFICANCE.

NOTHING ELSE COMES CLOSE TO COMPASSION,FOR MEANING IN OUR EXISTENCE.

AND OF COURSE, BECOMING FULLY VIBRANT IN EVERY MOMENT,
SO THAT EACH INSTANT IS INFUSED WITH RADIANCE.

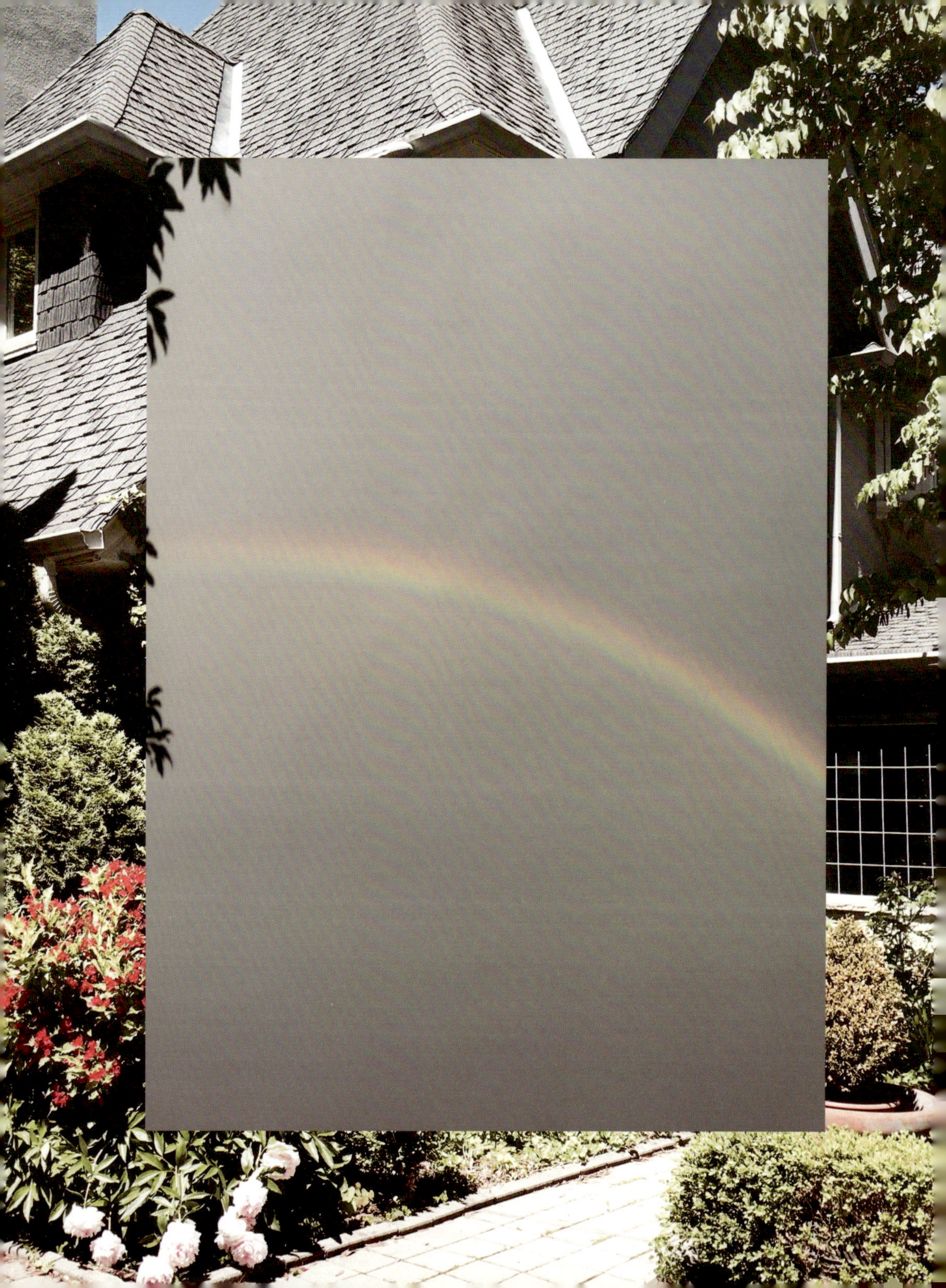

A CULTURE BASED ON KINDNESS

Well, if we lived in a culture based on kindness, can you imagine what life would be like on our planet?
If only children were taught the inestimable worth of kindness—more than the worth of money and acquisition or display.
We live in a time of showing off—like on Instagram—and showing off can be born of insecurity.
If people were thoughtful and compassionate to each other, there would be no reason to show off your latest purchases or experiences or contacts, except to share the love.
Because you should be loved anyway.
No matter what your life looks like.

Visuals have gained prominence in our culture.
We have many senses, as well—feeling, hearing, sensing, knowing.
Yet seeing and appearance dominate. What things look like. Not what things really are.

In a society based on compassion,
our children would be encouraged to give,
and things would be very different.
We would be there for each other in kindness.
And that would be the ultimate "like."

WHAT IF YOU COULD SEE
HUMAN SOULS AND SPIRITS?

WHAT WOULD THAT BE WORTH?

YOU WOULD KNOW EXACTLY
WHOM YOU WERE SPEAKING TO!

AND THAT WOULD SAVE A LOT OF FOOLING AROUND.

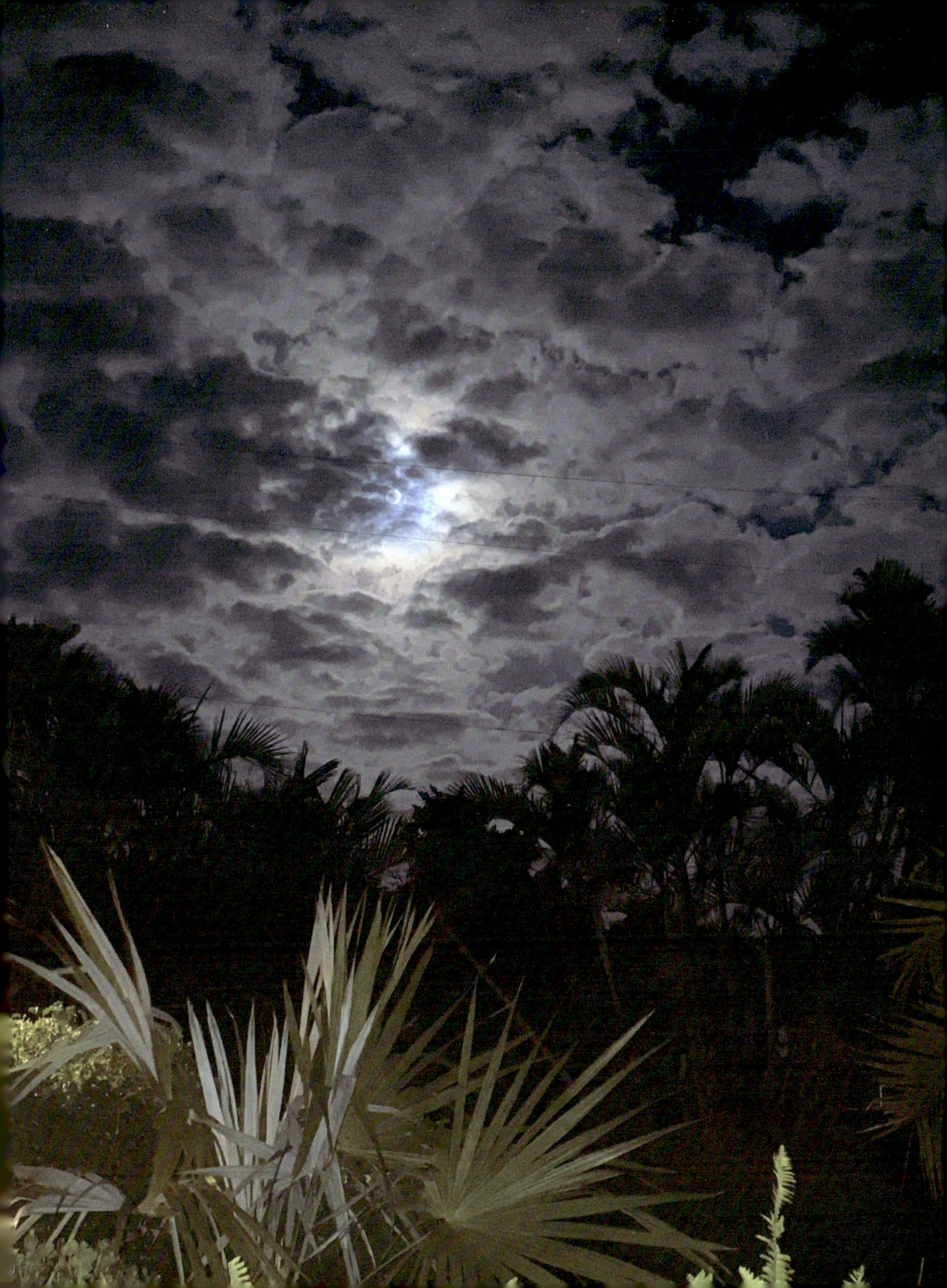

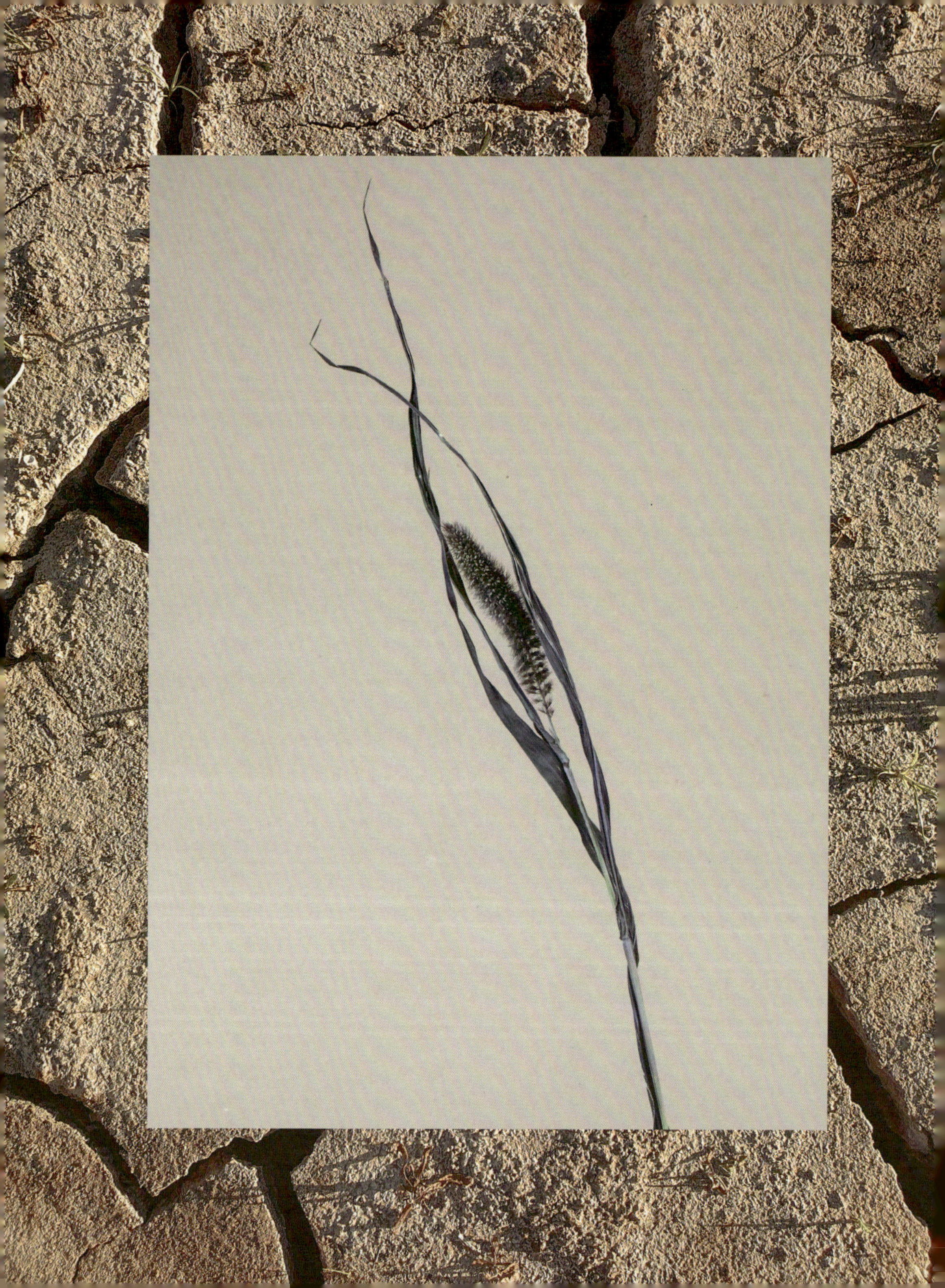

THINGS ONLY COME TO YOU IF THEY'RE YOURS

As we all know, if you have to force something to happen, it might not be meant for you.

Yet our modern culture forces so many things from the Earth. And the Earth is resisting this force with a force bigger than us, and that is the climate changing.

In your life, if you make a person, animal, or circumstance, be for your benefit only, there is often resistance.
If there is a shared and honest benefit and respect for all then everything seems to fall into place. And you might find more things come to you, often and easily.

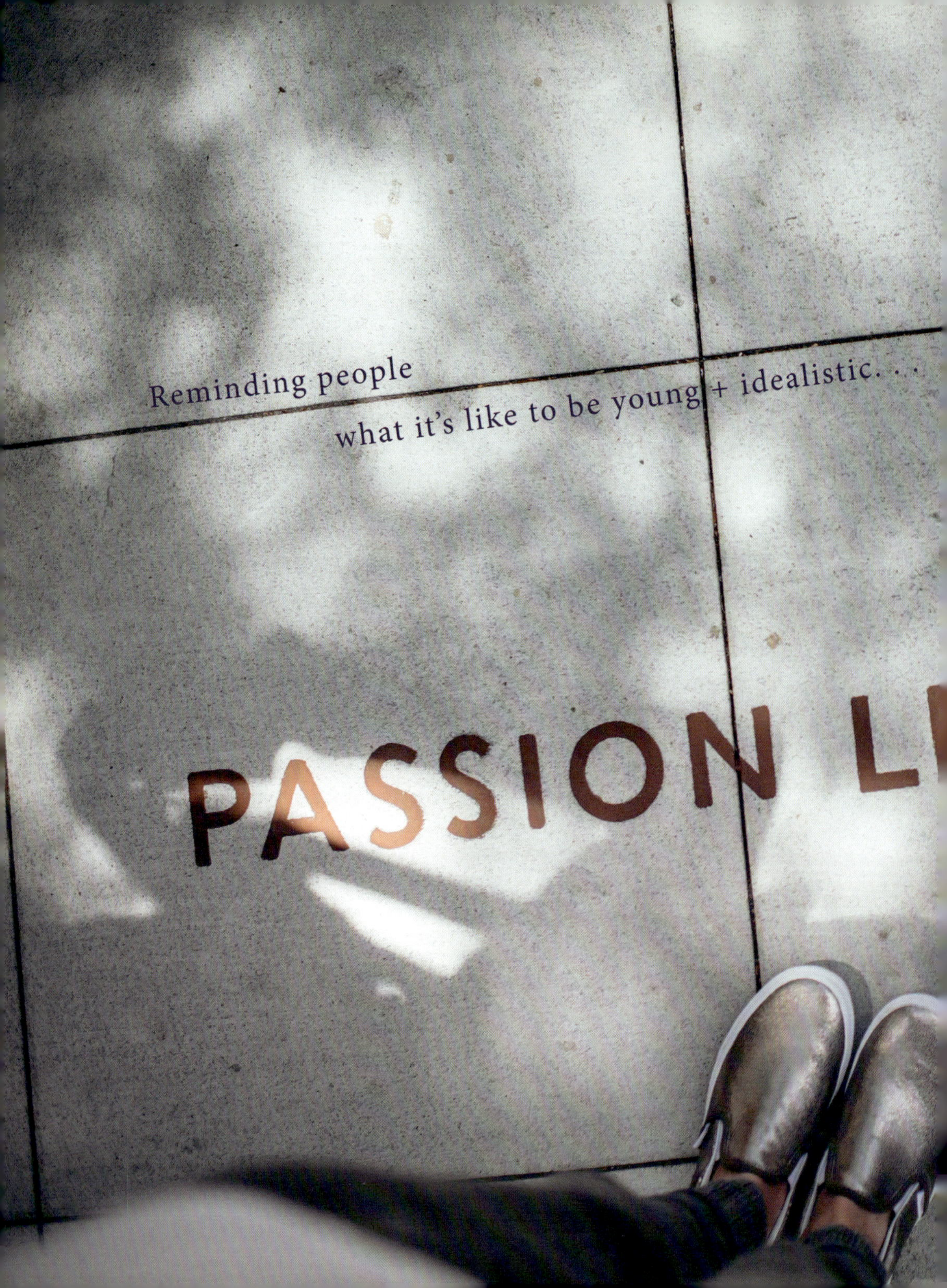

Reminding people
what it’s like to be young + idealistic. . .

Or hopefully inspiring the young + idealistic

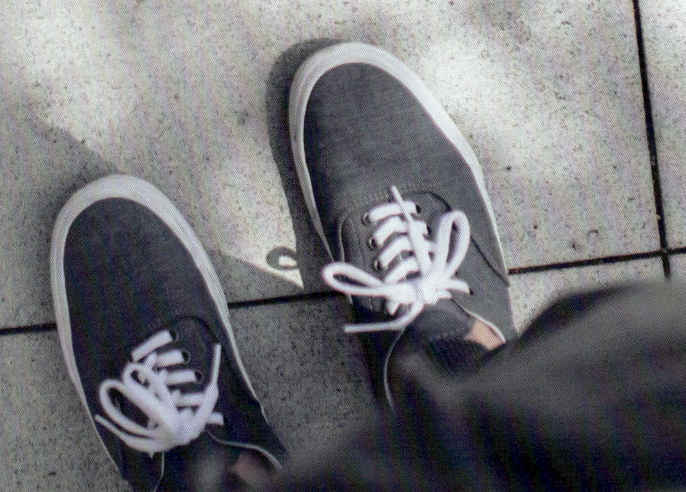

For love to be in the air!
DREAM:

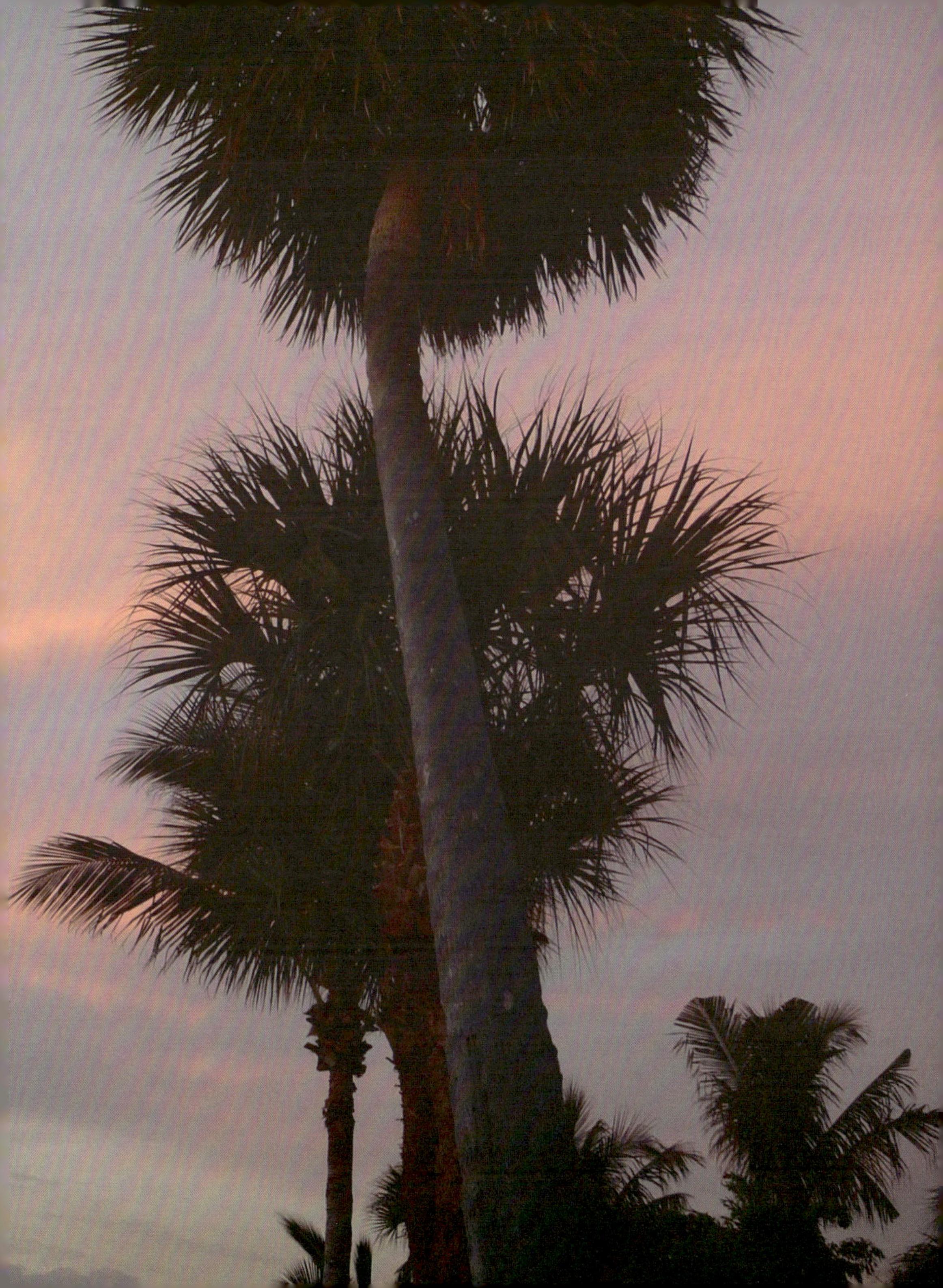

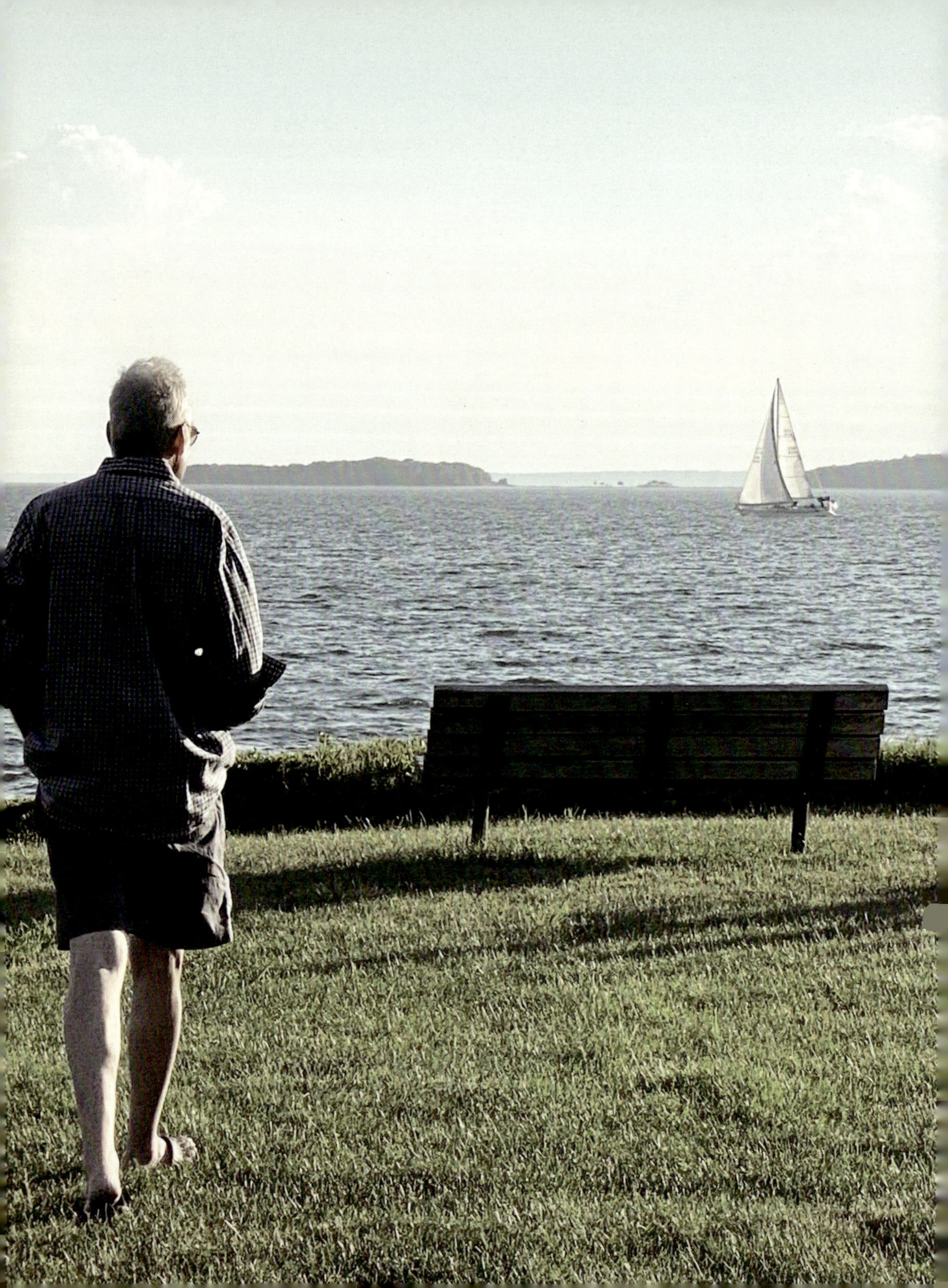

TIME

THERE IS NO SUCH THING
AS TIME!

ALL THINGS COEXIST AT
ONCE AND ALWAYS HAVE . . .

IT'S JUST A MATTER OF
DISCOVERING AND WAKING
UP TO SIMULTANEOUS EXISTENCE

THIS IS WHAT WE CALL EVOLUTION OF PERCEPTION

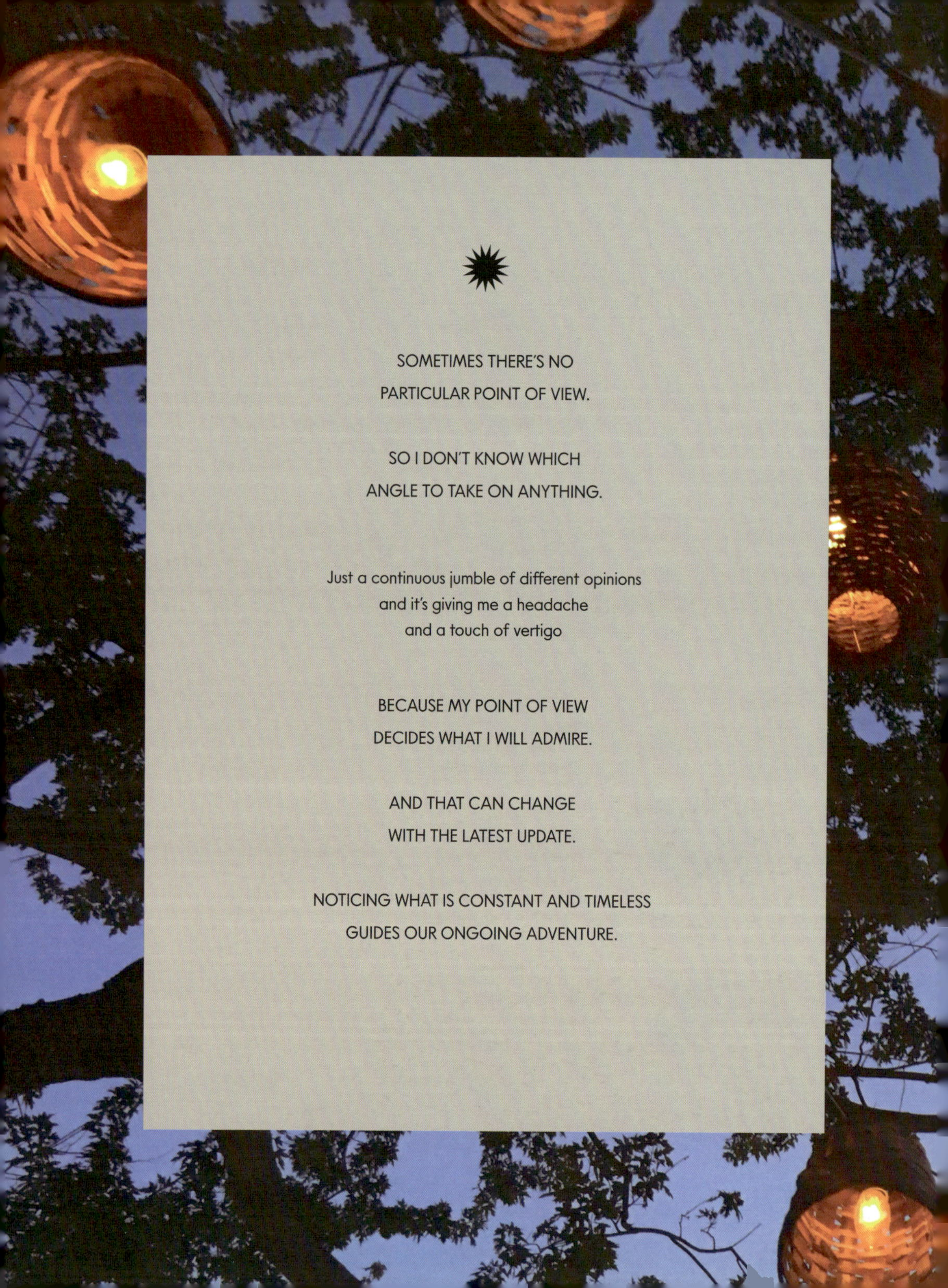

SOMETIMES THERE'S NO
PARTICULAR POINT OF VIEW.

SO I DON'T KNOW WHICH
ANGLE TO TAKE ON ANYTHING.

Just a continuous jumble of different opinions
and it's giving me a headache
and a touch of vertigo

BECAUSE MY POINT OF VIEW
DECIDES WHAT I WILL ADMIRE.

AND THAT CAN CHANGE
WITH THE LATEST UPDATE.

NOTICING WHAT IS CONSTANT AND TIMELESS
GUIDES OUR ONGOING ADVENTURE.

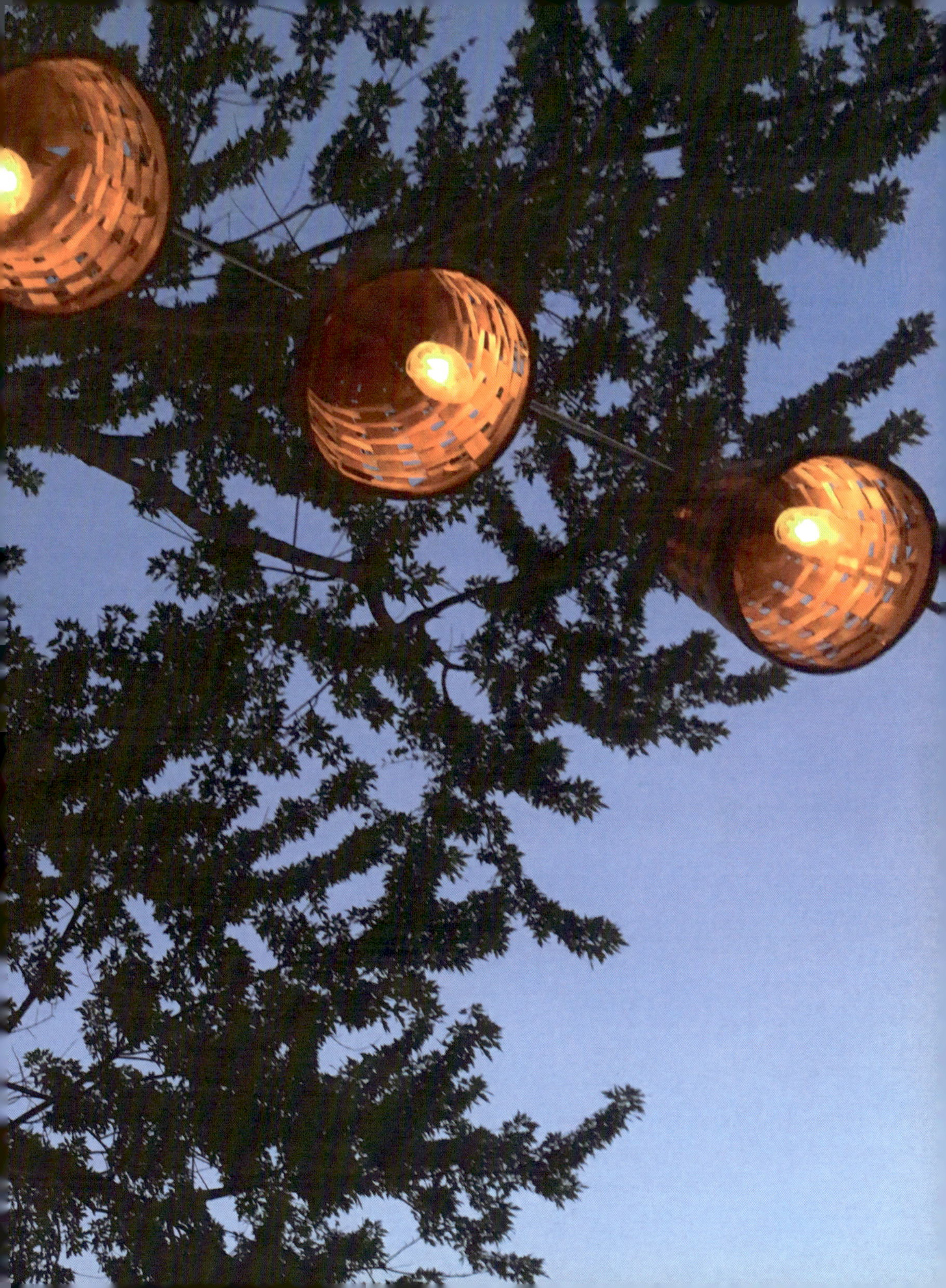

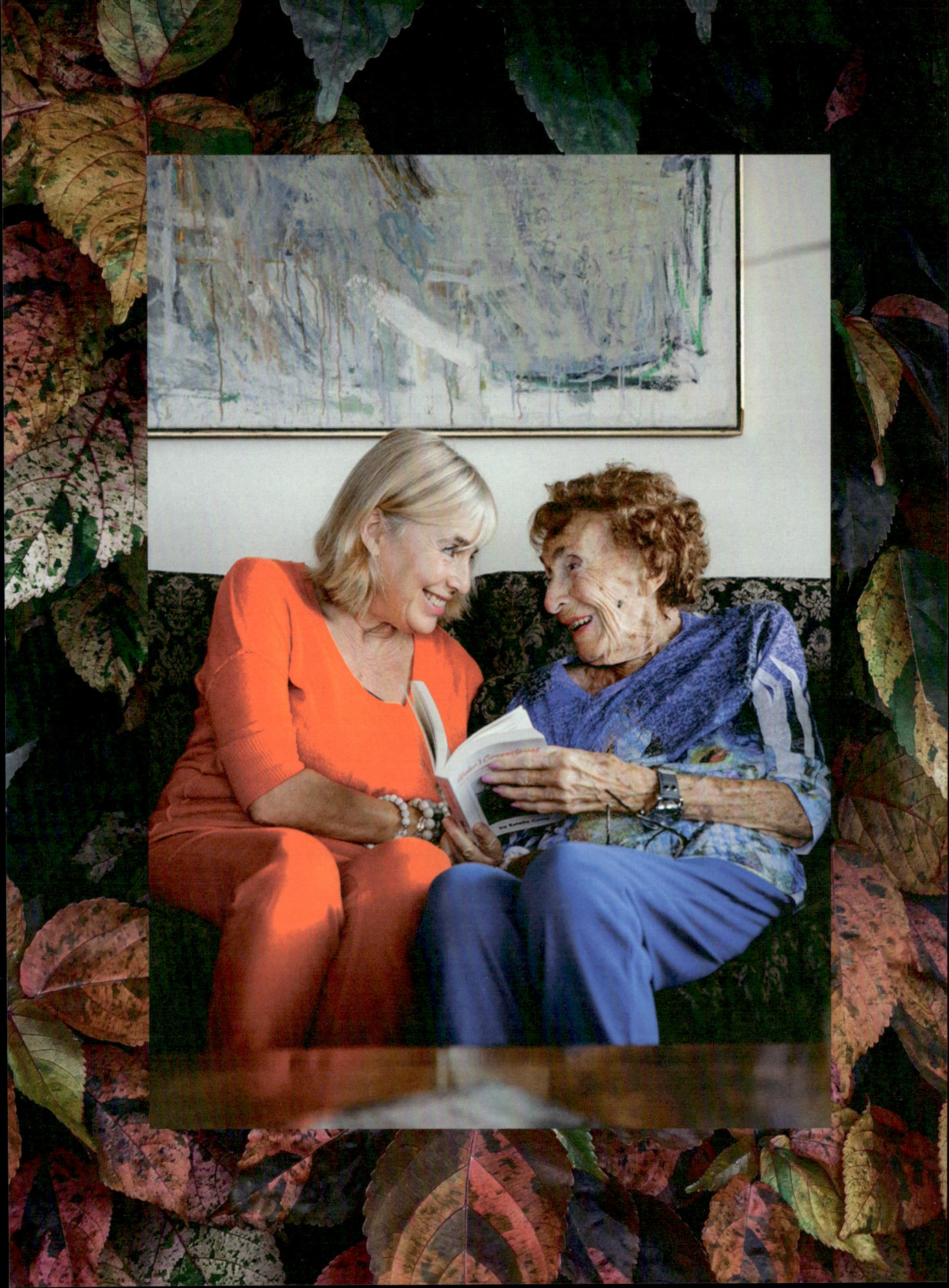

MY DUET WITH MY MOM

WHAT I VALUE: OLD AGE

I'M DOING OLD AGE WITH
MY MOTHER, STEP-BY-STEP.

She's not alone.

Giving my Mom nutrients and exercise therapy
and constant love and care every day.
She's so funny and smart and witty and charismatic.

Her impressive spirit constantly surprises me.
Aging beautifully, she's my role model.

MOM IS VERY
CONTEMPORARY.AT THE AGE OF 100 YEARS,
SHE SAYS:
"I FULLY INTEND TO CONTINUE
THE GREAT ADVENTURE THAT
IS MY LIFE."

AND I WILL HELP HER AS SHE AGES, JUST
LENDING HER A HAND CONSTANTLY ALONG
THE WAY.

MY MOM PASSED ON RECENTLY.
I HELD HER HAND AND I NEVER LET IT GO.

MOM'S OPTIMISTIC VIEW OF LIFE

”

OF COURSE EVERYONE
HAS A GLASS OF CHAMPAGNE
IN THEIR HANDS IN NEW YORK CITY.”

Mom is very groovy!

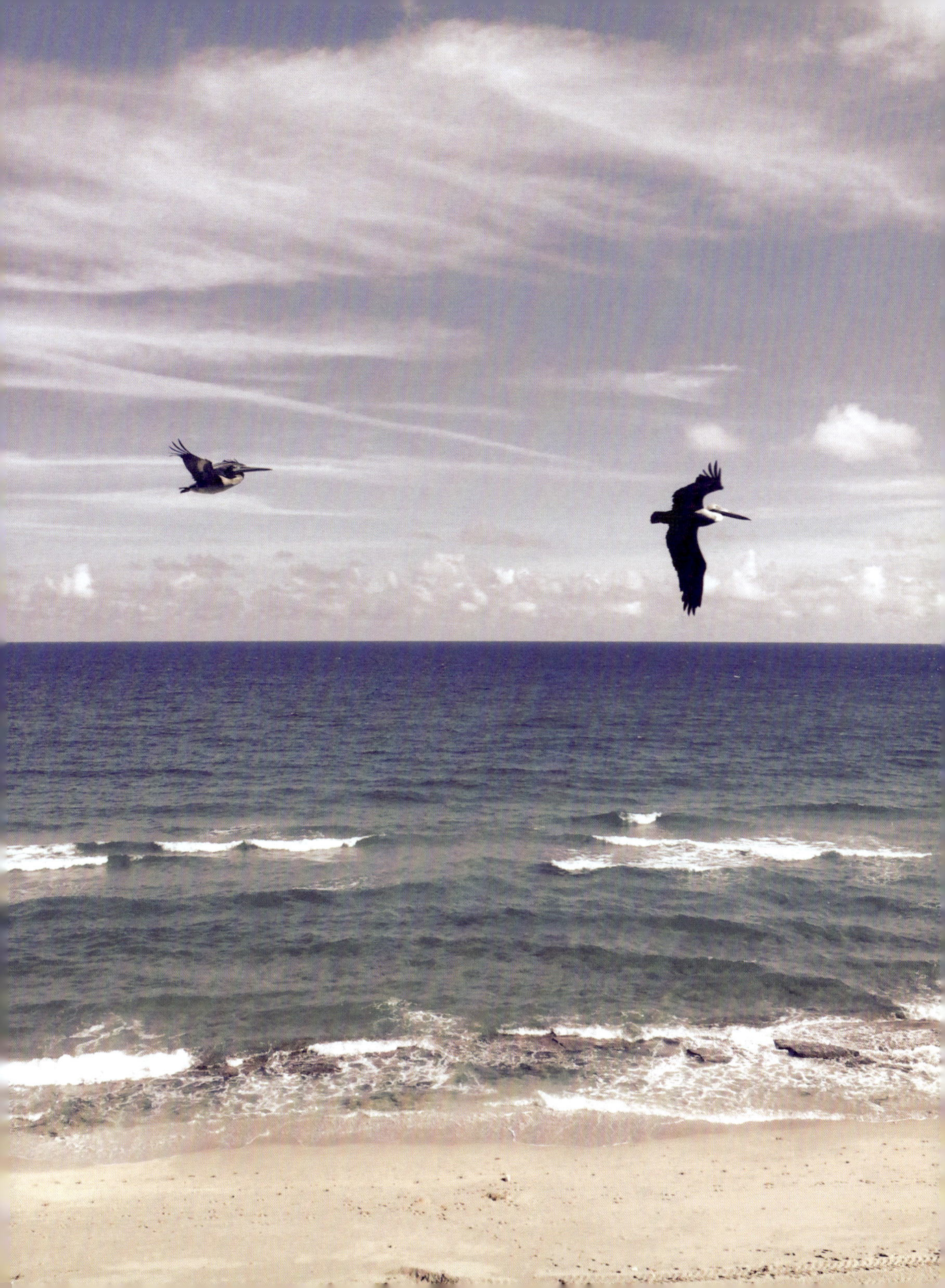

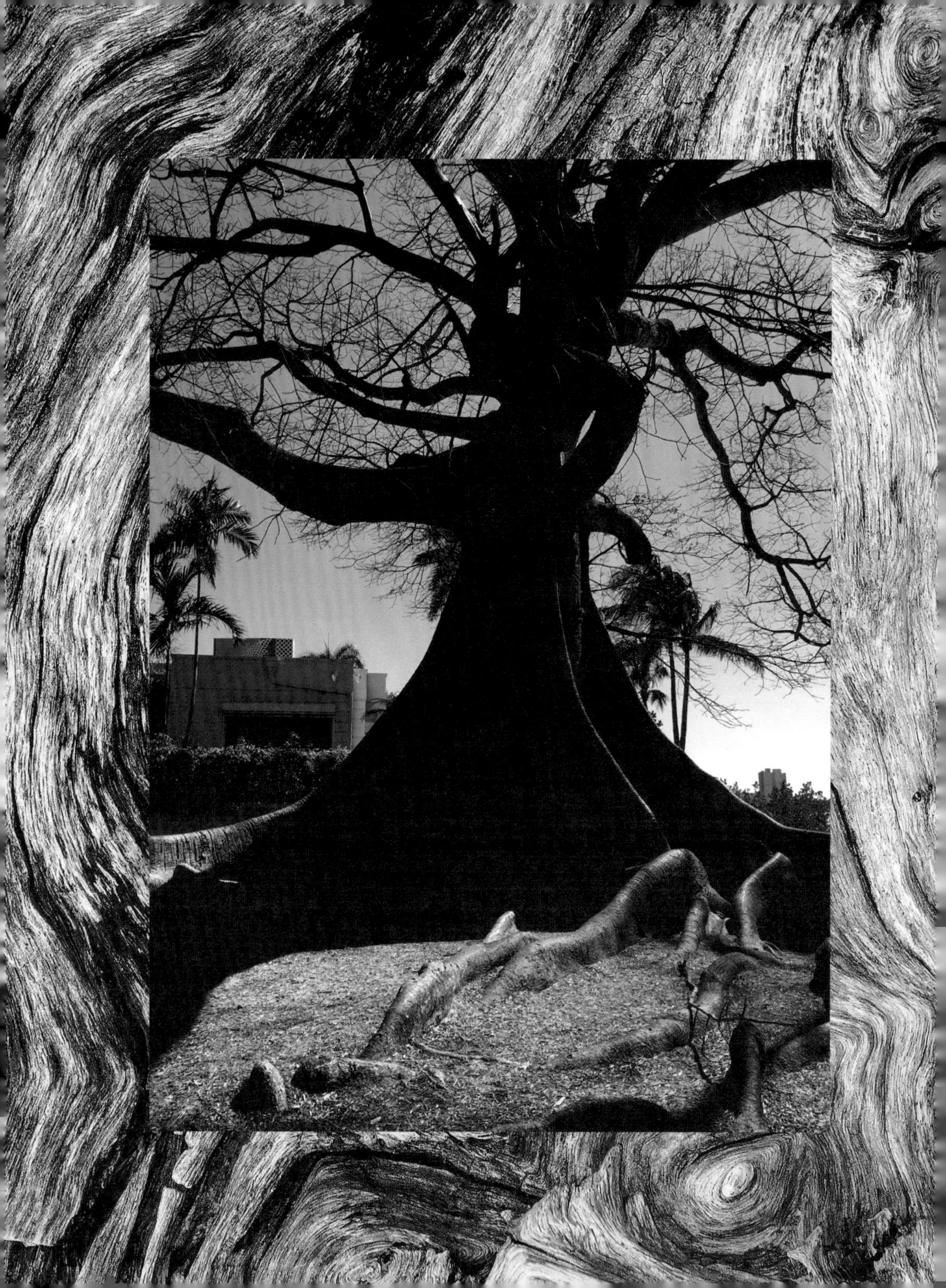

WHEN YOU'RE OLDER

I DISCOVERED THAT
IT'S NOT WHAT YOU DID THAT
MATTERS—
BUT WHAT YOU THINK
YOU DID—
WHEN YOU'RE OLD AND LOOK BACK AT
YOUR LIFE.

And it's not always what you thought then—
it's also what you think now.

IF YOU THINK THAT YOU DRANK CHAM-
PAGNE ALL YOUR LIFE,
BECAUSE YOU LOVED YOUR LIFE.
THEN YOU DID!

ALL YOUR ACCOMPLISHMENTS
ARE HOW OPTIMISTICALLY YOU VIEW THEM,
IN TWILIGHT
MEMORIES, THROUGH METAPHORICAL
ROSE-COLORED GLASSES.

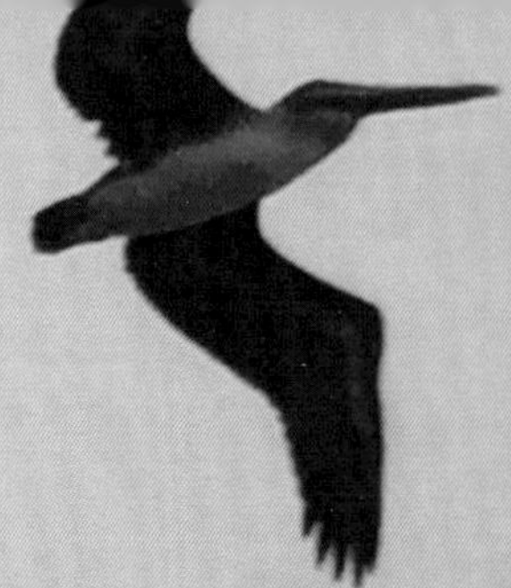

Don't judge people by their age.
or judge them at all—
They're still the same person.

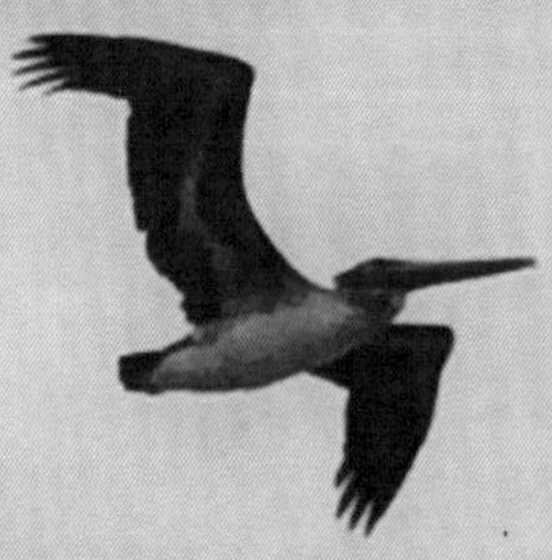

It's not people's appearances.
It's people's enthusiasm and vibrancy that intensifies their vitality!!

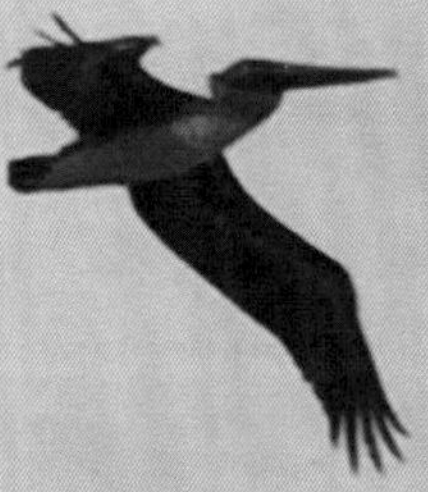

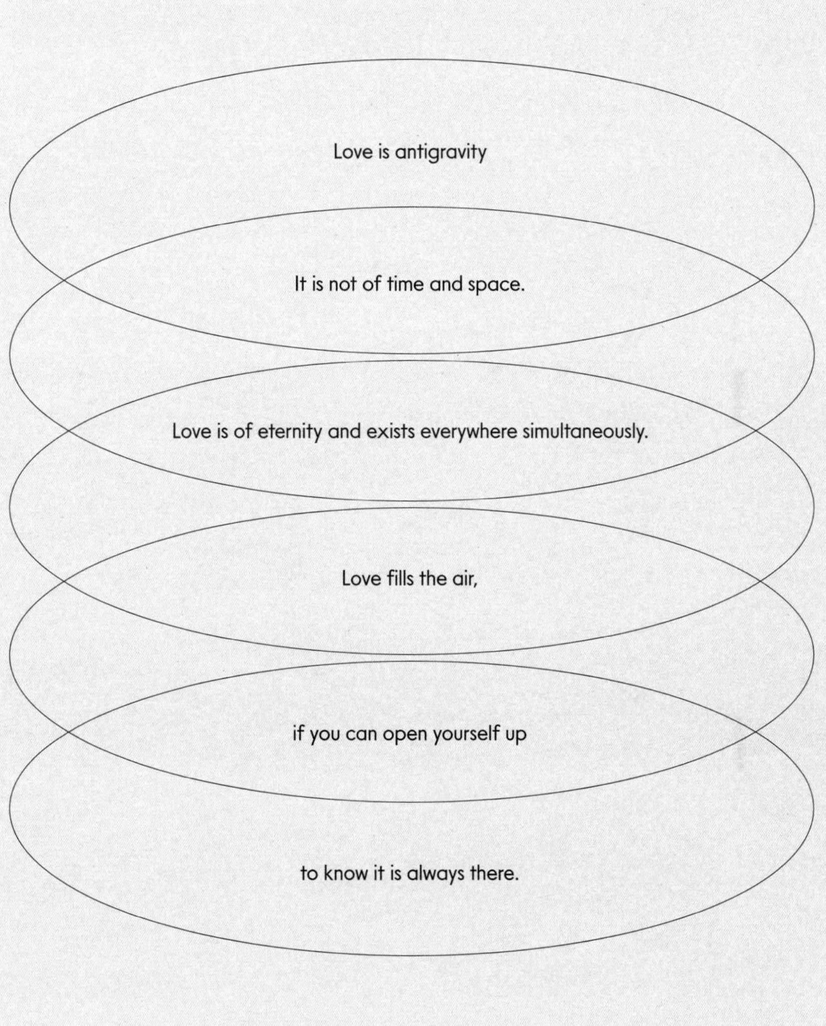
Love is antigravity
It is not of time and space.
Love is of eternity and exists everywhere simultaneously.
Love fills the air,
if you can open yourself up
to know it is always there.

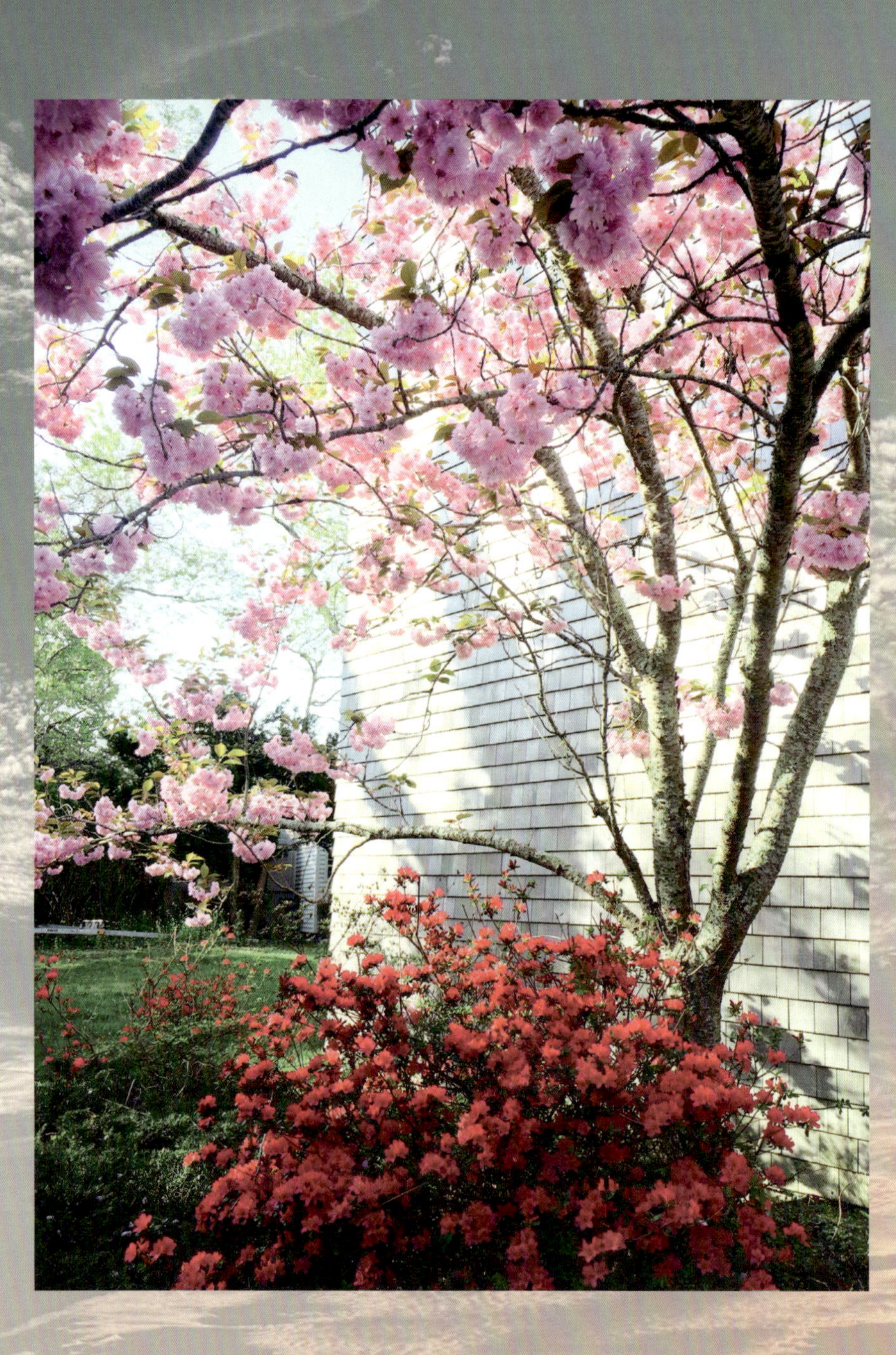

ROBIN UNPLUGGED (FROM THE WORLD)

I'm lying outside in the shade on a hot sunny day.
Feeling so lucky for the beautiful weather.
I see birds and butterflies and trees, and I feel an occasional breeze.
To have this time and place is an incredible gift.
As long as I am open enough and attentive enough to feel every sacred moment in this reality.

Wouldn't it be amazing to have glasses that let you see more than our visible reality?

That would be Super-reality.

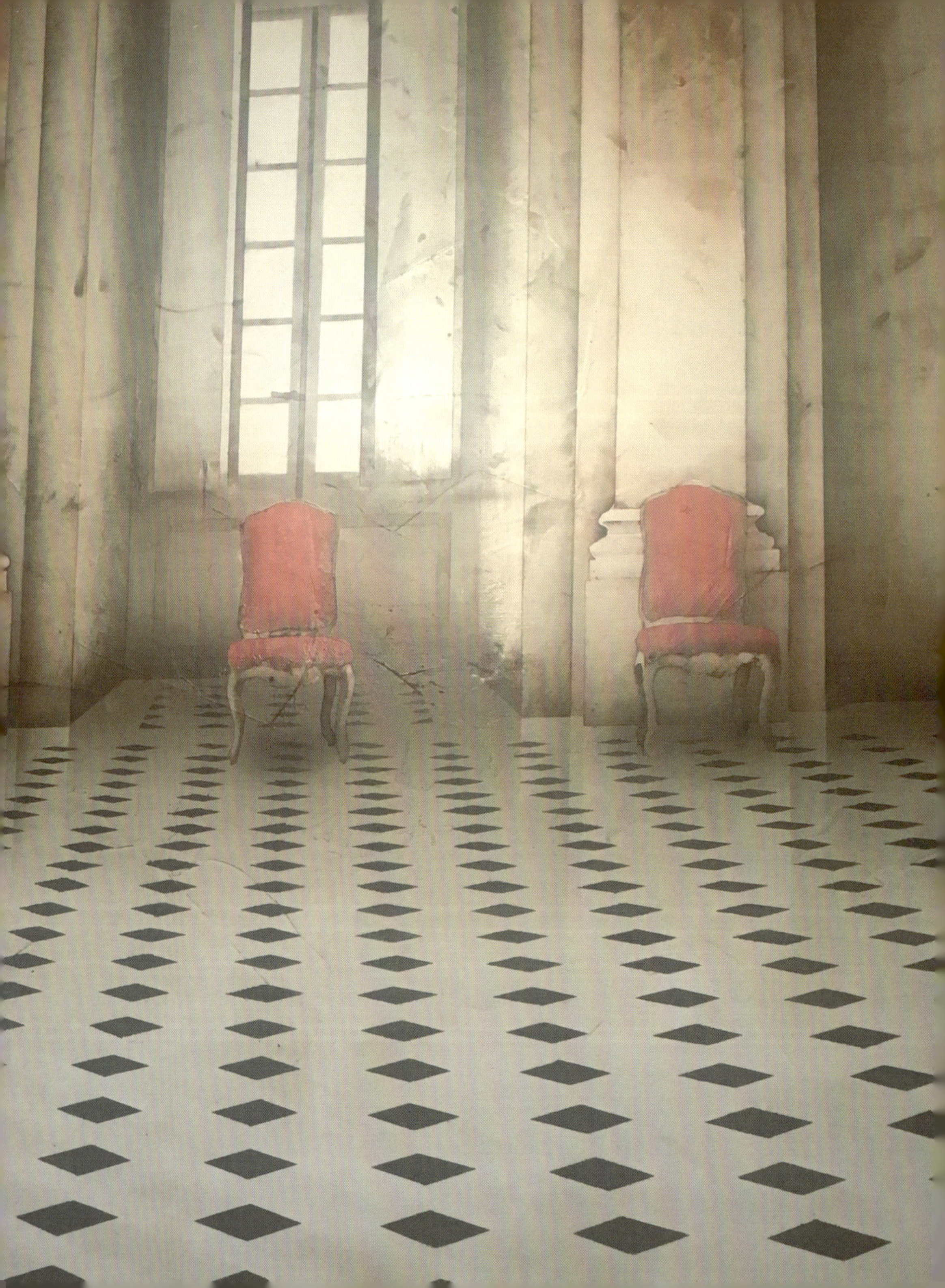

INTERVIEW WITH MYSELF

1. What has Worth??

A chair, when you need to sit down.

A needle and thread, when you have a hole in your favorite top.

A hug, when you're sad.

A wink, when someone connects to you.

A bird, when it sings.

The beauty of nature.

A glass of water, when you're thirsty.

A massage to make you feel better, when you need one.

A nice conversation, when you're feeling alone.

Humor, when you're feeling sad.

Music and dancing, to lighten you up.

Beautiful photos, memories, and documenting the energy of the moment.

All these things have tremendous merit.

And I wouldn't trade any of them for a fancier car or more expensive clothes.

Style is how you carry yourself, anyway.

2. What's more important: Looking for love or loving yourself?

Love is wherever you look, and the amazing thing is that you can see love anywhere, always.

Because we live in a sea of love. We just have to open our hearts and SEE it with our hearts.

Loving yourself is a powerful way to open your heart.

It took me a long time to learn that.

Some people seem to be born with the ability to love themselves and others easily.

I find that, now, the more I can clear myself of any conflict or negative emotions or responses,
The more my heart can open.

The way that I am clearing is, whenever anything disagreeable occurs to me or takes me over,
rather than trying not to feel it, I embrace the anxiety, fear, sadness, and anger.
I let that feeling rise to the top of my consciousness and I dive in and send it some love (just send the feeling some love), and ALWAYS within moments, the feeling has dissipated and cleared and whatever was gripping me was JUST A FEELING.

The best way to release our negative thoughts is to feel them, live through them, and love them; don't suppress them or they will stay below your consciousness.

Once I have let it disappear and drift off, I am lighter, much freer, and whatever was holding on to me was just, and only just, A FEELING.

And then I am free for positivity to fill me up, if I let it (nature abhors a vacuum), until, of course, the next sensation arises.
Then I do it again.

And it becomes kind of fun, the clearing process.

And I feel SO GOOD once I tried it a few times! Clear and good! Just know that any negativity in your immediate vision is only coming from your own heart, so acknowledge it, love it, and release it.

3. What took you so long to realize that you have everything you could possibly want?

I've spent a lot of my life looking and found that every second of life, every moment, is as complete as the next.

Every breath, every sight, and every sound is quite perfect. As soon as we are able to see that, then we have found what we are looking for.

So, there's no point in searching. (Easier said than done, of course, when you're young.)
Life is sometimes an amusing game of exploration, but as I get older, I can see that everything exists in every moment and the glue of every moment is love.

4. There's no place like home?

To find out that there's no place like home, you have to go on a journey, like Dorothy in The Wizard of Oz.

To understand what is worthwhile in your life, you need to see what is not, or you will always wonder.

And often, if you're lucky enough to meet your soulmate, you must first connect to many who are not.

People who buy a lot of clothes will often tell you that their favorite thing to wear is what they already have—an old pair of shoes, jeans, or jacket.

So if you're smart, you'll open your heart from the start and appreciate what you already have.
Although, here and there, memories make the journey worthwhile.

5. What is my journey?

My journey, up to now, seems to have been living in a swirling energy, meeting creative and colorful people, and being in the center of the center.

Growing up, I had to always be where the dynamic excitement was.

But now, I have retreated to the outskirts, only to see, surprisingly, that no one really misses me, and I guess I don't really miss the ride.

Now I can reflect objectively that the ride is everywhere.
Looking all around at the sky, birds, ocean, and trees,
my heart perceives the intrinsic peace and tranquility of all that surrounds me, bathing in THAT glow.

I am happy to have had my journey, as all young people should.
But I am so lucky now to have serenity and inner happiness, because that
is where the seeds of life truly lie and that is WORTH everything.
To see with a clear heart.

6. What is life's adventure worth to you?

Authentic experience is ALL that has certain worth;
what you own, or who you know, or who knows you, or any of that is just your ego and your ego is a three-dimensional mirage.
Life's ride, in every vibrant moment, is what makes you alive.
And how present you are to each moment, how much you savor each moment, is what, at the end of your life, will be that which has the most WORTH.

7. Is celebrity a longing for significance in our culture, with so many people chasing fame and riches?

We are made to feel that a simple life has little value, and a life lived loud, projected on a big screen, with words echoed in the media, makes a more valuable life.

But that fact is really only for simple-minded people who only see "red," like a bull.

With any subtlety of vision, one can see that a truly beautiful life is one lived enchanted with all our blessings.

That's true celebrity!

It's so easy to compare our lives to another.

But if we open our eyes, we'll see that every existence, including our own (and all animal life, too) is unique and special.

8. What do you love about a summer day?

A beautiful breeze, to me personally, is everything. On a hot day, or even a cool day, a light, gentle wind is so lovely to bask in.

I'd rather a lovely, balmy breeze than a vodka, but I'm sure there are many who would disagree with me on that.

9. What's a day made of?

Love is the fiber of the universe, the molecules and atoms and cells.
Days, nights, and the bubble of time we live in,
are all made up of love.

Our job is to clear our eyes enough to see all that.
Because once we do, then every second of life is pretty amazing
and worthwhile.

10. Is happiness sustainable?

Complete happiness exists in every instant.
So if we can learn to appreciate the frequency of every moment,
the good and not-so-good,
knowing that it's only your own vision coming your way.

To have empathy for other's intentions,
and then as day follows night,
one moment of happiness follows the next,
and then yes, happiness CAN be sustainable.

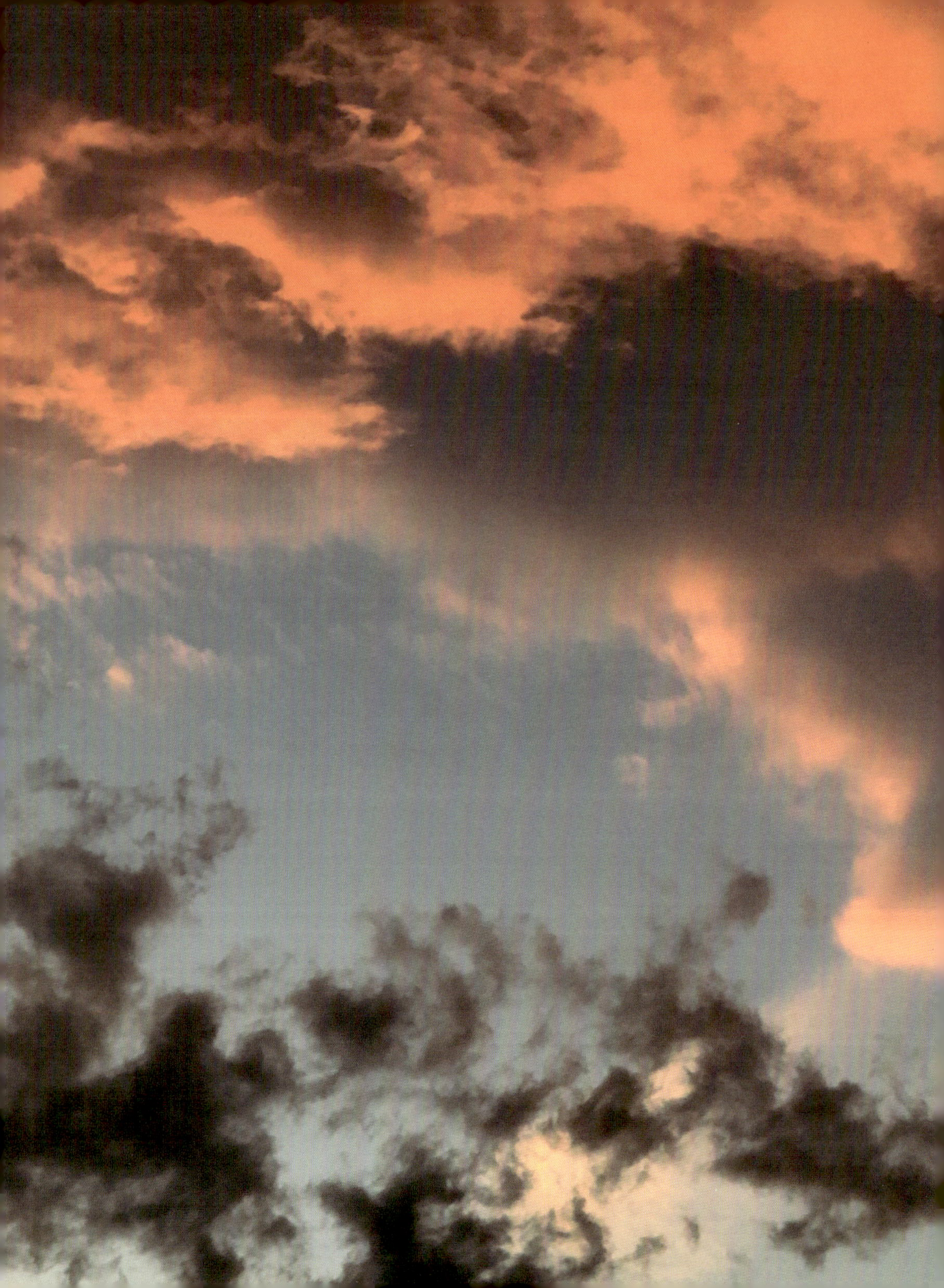

Lying in the shade, with a warm breeze and the sun shining—

or

on a cloudy day with beautiful music and laughter

and good food from your garden.

I'll take it.

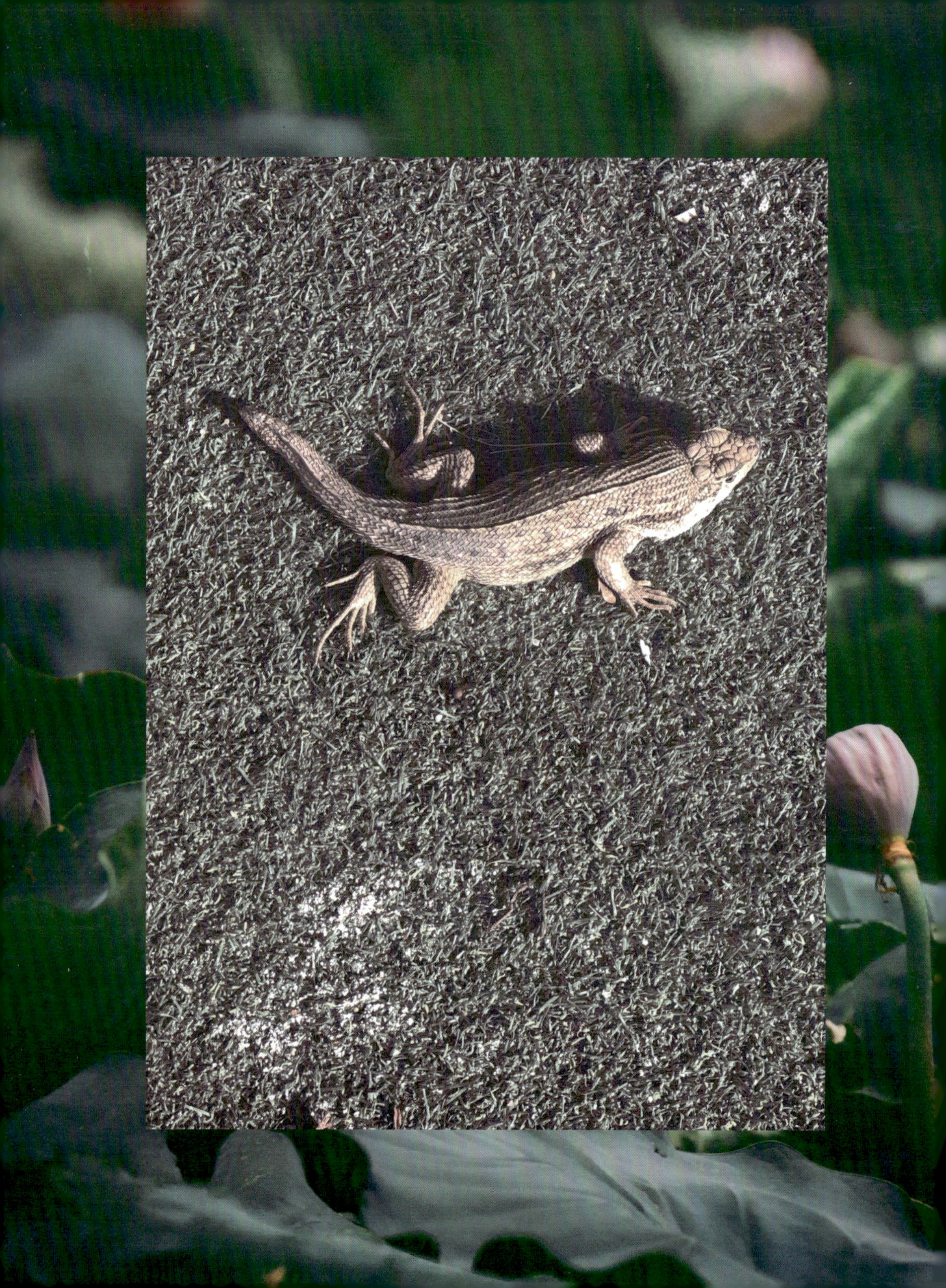

COMPASSION

Nothing, but nothing, but nothing is more amazing than to be absolutely in the moment. It's the intensity of your time that matters.

That's what memories are made of, and memories become your life.

If you know how to be bright and naturally vivacious, then you have given yourself the biggest gift that any money can buy.

Because the more you graciously give, the more enthusiasm you feel. Philosophers call that compassion.

Giving is getting. Any good Buddhist knows that.
Because the more you do and feel for others, the more cheerful, contented, and sunny you will be.

The fewer negative emotions you have toward others, the greater your ability to live an upbeat, idealistic, and clear life.

It's not what you have, but how you spend your time, thoughts, and emotions.
Kind thoughts and altruism make you truly an extraordinary person.

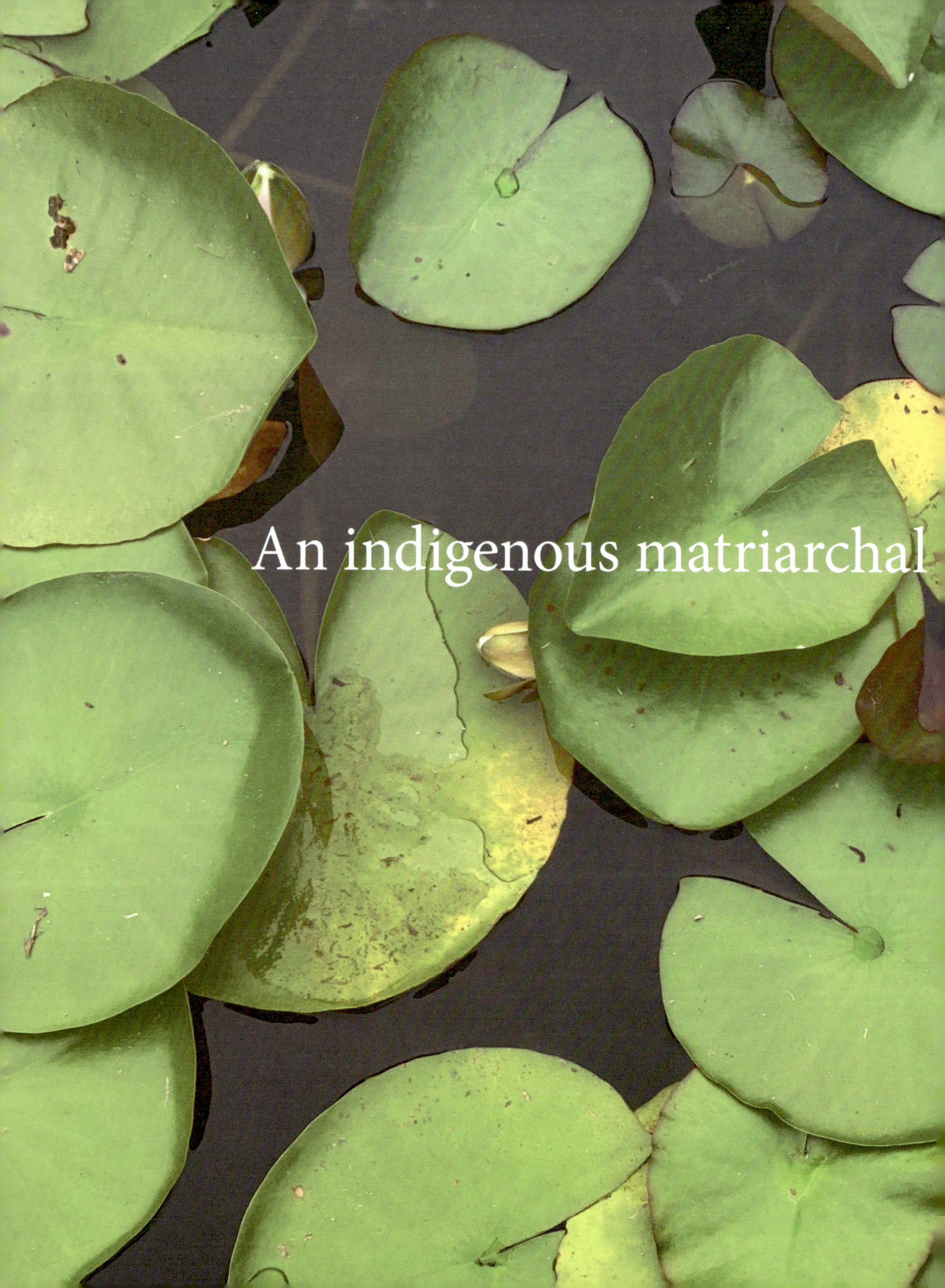
An indigenous matriarchal

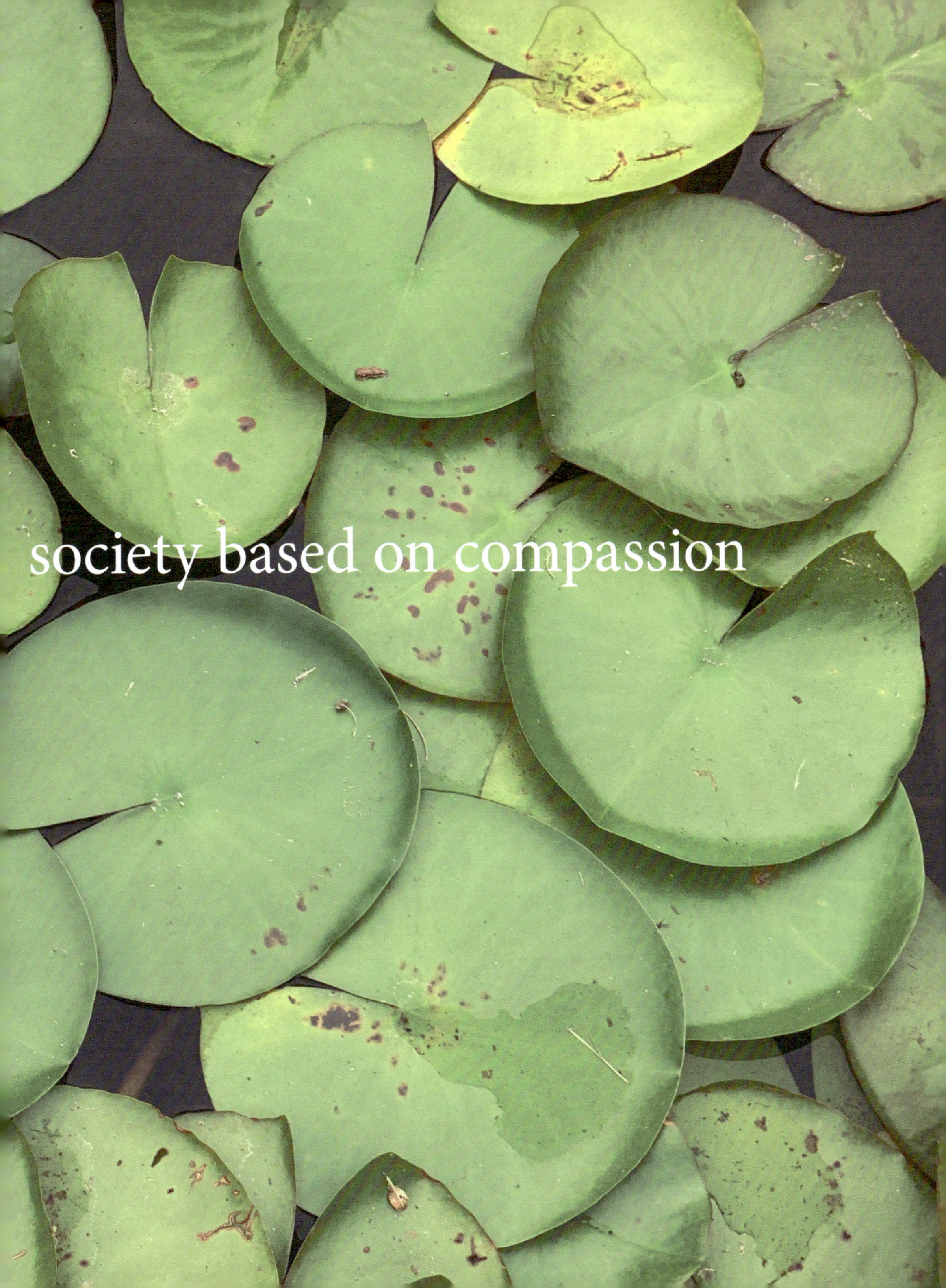
society based on compassion

Desire can often confuse us,
because seldom are we content with the siren call of longing.

✸

We only really feel complete when we are already complete.

✸

By meditating and releasing our negative thoughts,
we can just love them and let them drift off on their way.

✸

Acting on a negative idea, any negative concept,
brings it into physical reality.
Whatever intention we put our attention on becomes larger.

✸

But if you just let it pass on, like anything else,
it will go on its merry way
and leave you feeling cleaner and lighter.

✸

Don't engage with negativity and it will not engage with you.

✸

Obsessing over sensational stories,
whether it be in the media, videos, or just gossip . . .
While it gives us a temporary charge to witness this aspect of existence,
it is truly a distorted sense of what really matters.

✸

Ask your child or your pet what is authentically meaningful.
You will see that reality is made of a hug and a sunny afternoon.

✸

Not someone's projected view into negativity or their own ego.

✸

Fulfilling your ego is like trying to fill a glass with a hole in the bottom.
It will never be whole.

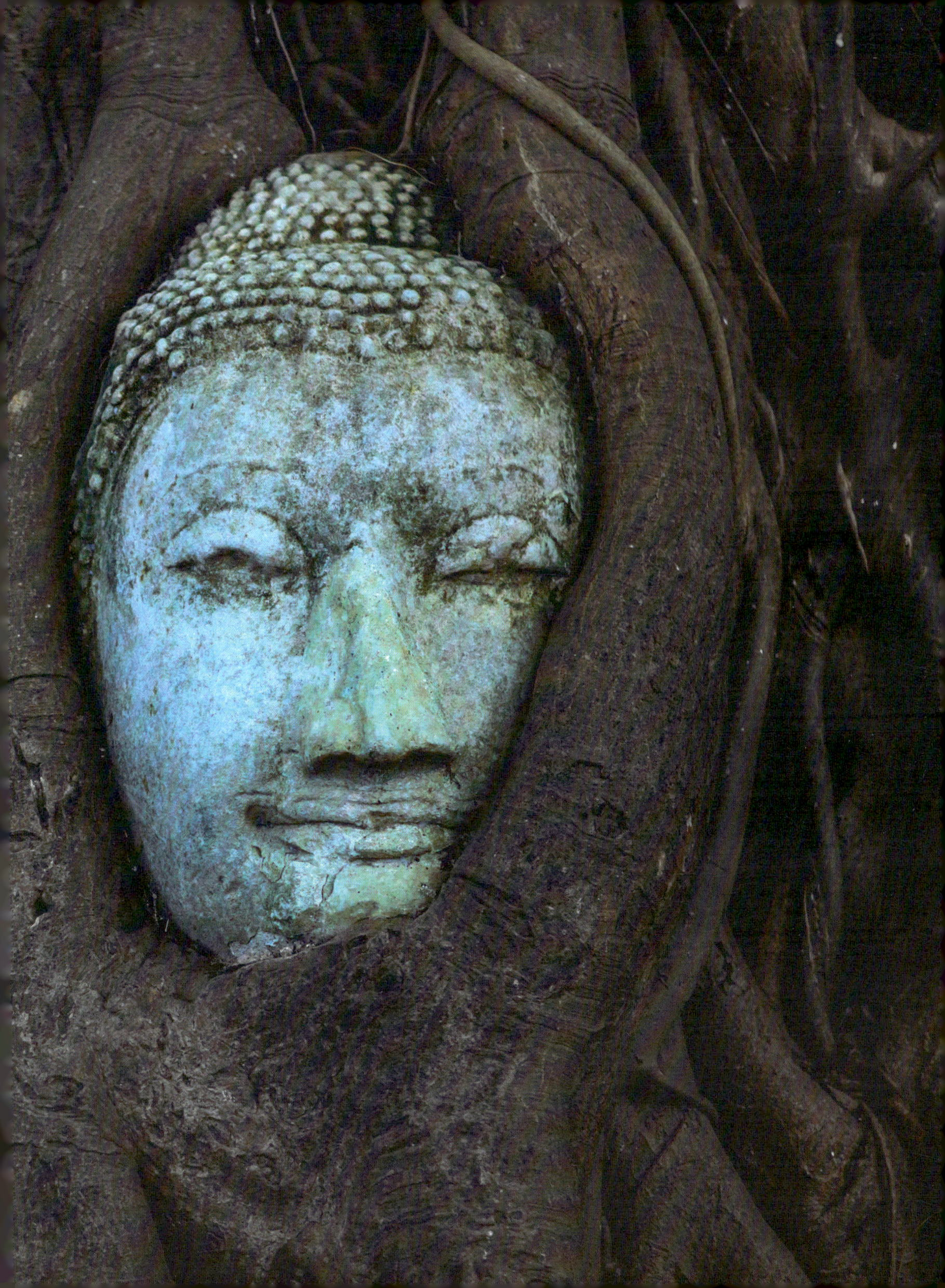

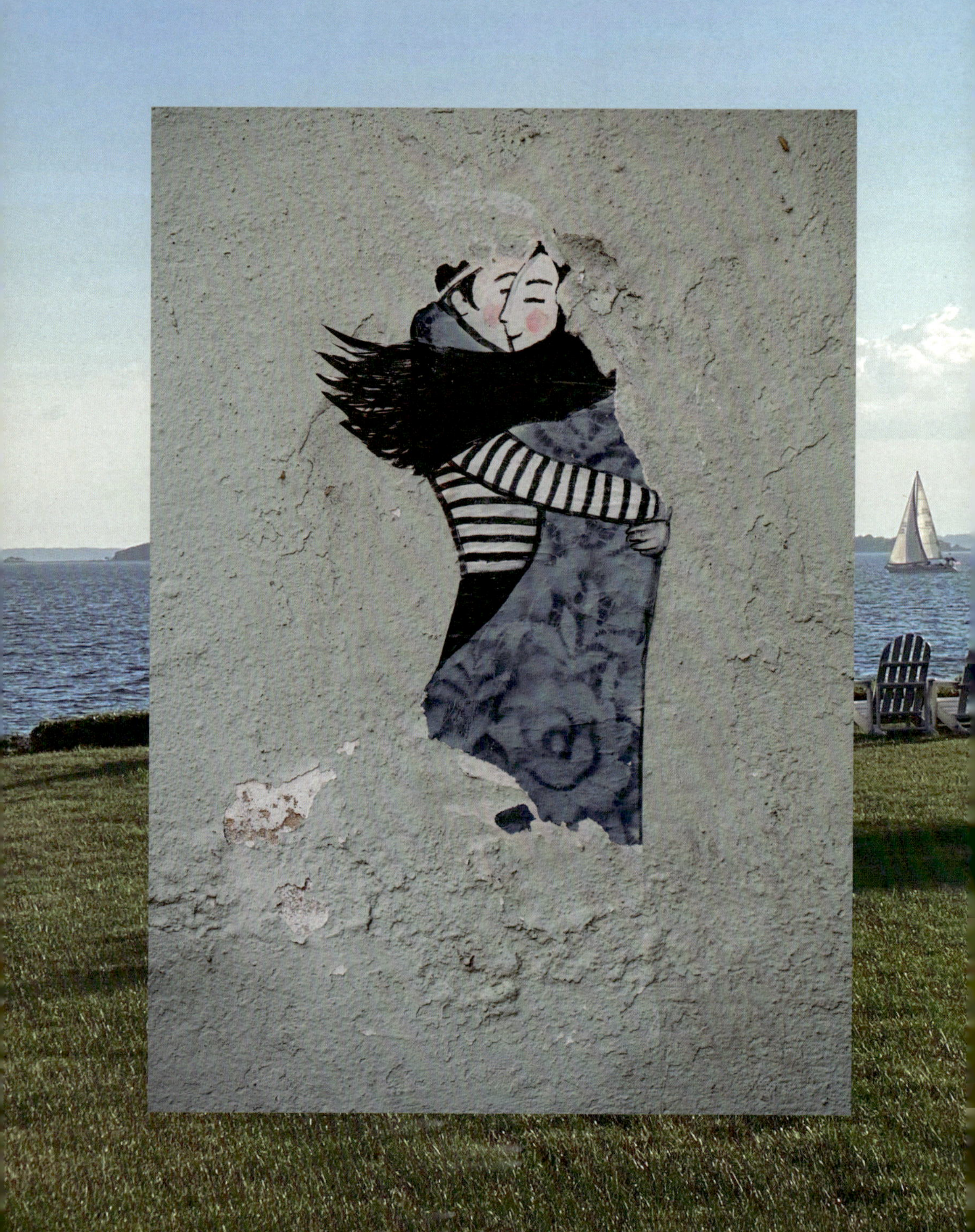

WHAT MATTERS MOST TO YOU?

Is a piece of paper, called a dollar, crumpled up in your wallet, worth the same as a refreshing glass of water to you, when you're thirsty and alone with no access to a gratifying sip?

Is your gold jewelry that you've accumulated worth more than a comfortable chair to sit in when you're really tired—or even better, a comfy bed or a nice lawn of green grass to lie on?

What REALLY matters to you?

Is your photo, seen on the internet, the same as a warm hug from someone you love?

WHAT'S IMPORTANT TO ME

I would rather have dinner
in a shack with warm friends
than dinner
in an elegant restaurant
with cold friends.

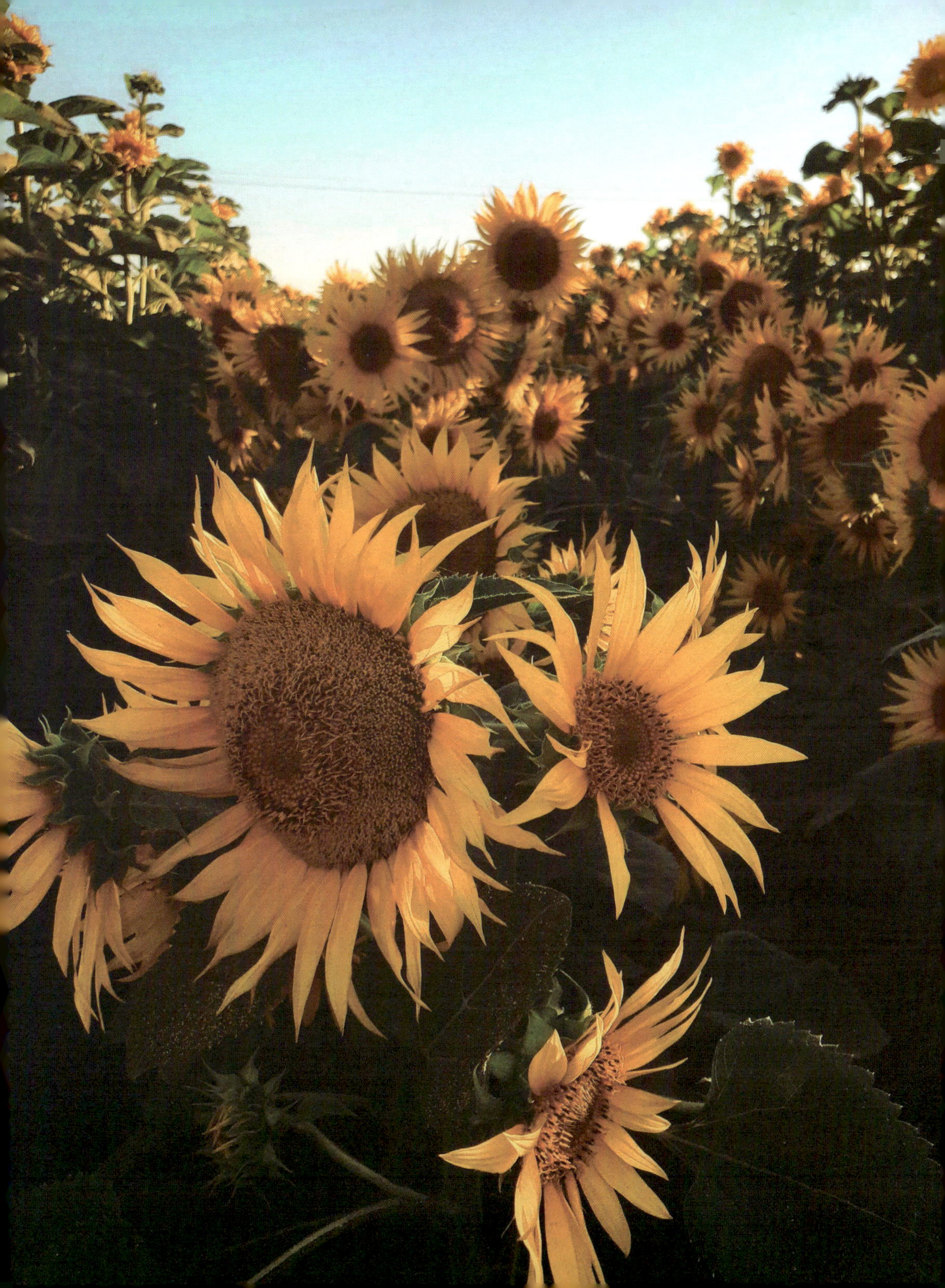

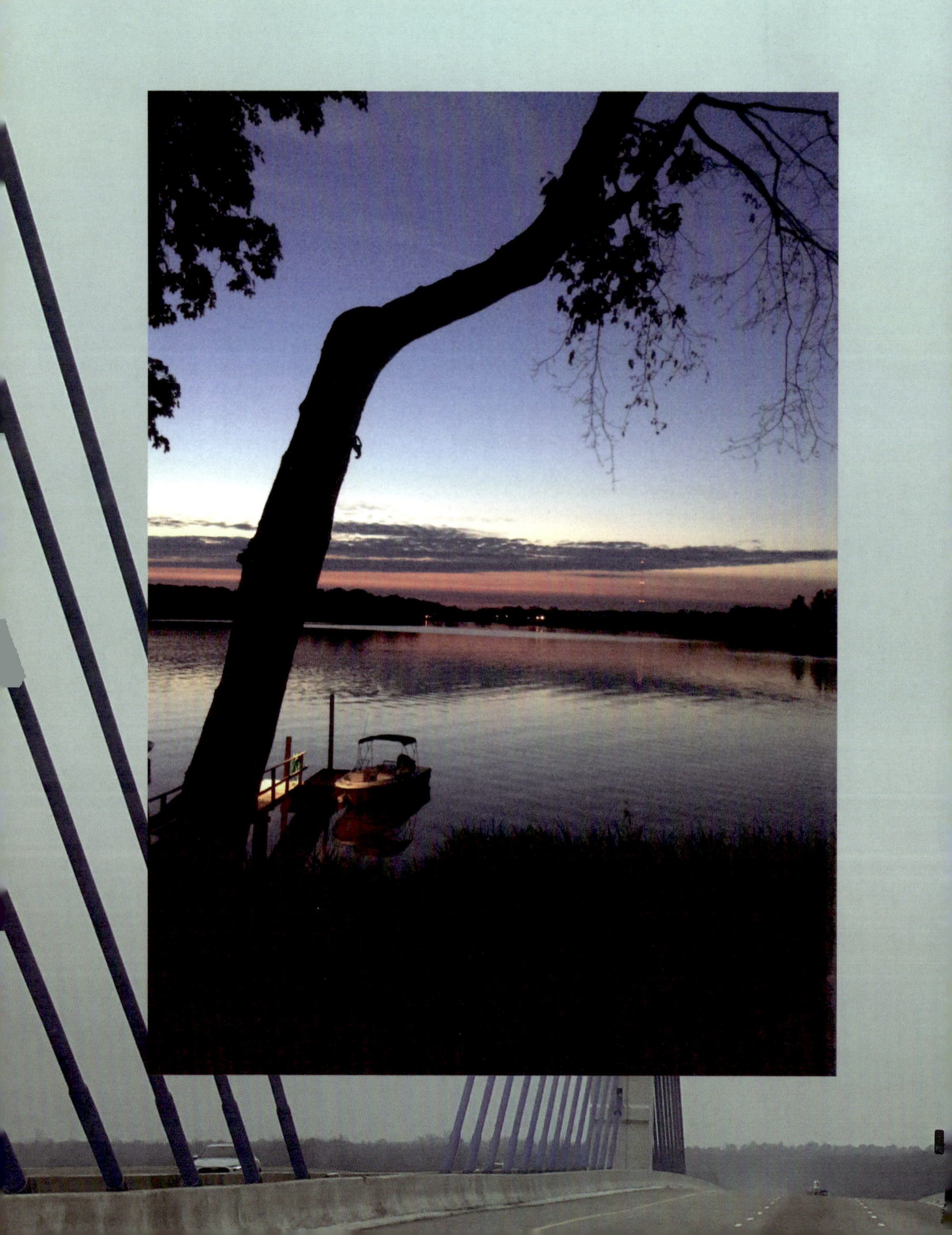

SOUNDS OF CIVILIZATION

I'm sitting here under a beautiful tree in
my garden.

Thinking how lucky I am that I even have a
garden and a tree . . .

except,

Now I've moved and I'm by the beautiful water,
escaping the sounds of civilization so I can write.

All around me are loud leaf blowers and sitting
diesel trucks running noisily,
and very hardworking people--where are the
quiet tools?

Drilling and sawing and clipping,

So here I sit pondering the sounds of
modern life,
not really understanding the lack of gentleness
and consideration of noise.

Isn't that the key to a wonderful, thoughtful,
and kind life, after all?

Careful, loving actions.

I'd rather be surrounded by considerate people
right now (of course) than clipping trees or a
noisy construction site.

I feel like a sound refugee.
People can always ask carefully of others:
What works best for those surrounding them?
Kindness and Thoughtfulness.

A lot of people acquire a lot of things to be liked.
(Cars, clothes, jewelry, houses, and more.)
I put it out there that all you need to do, where
you live, is to be good to people and be as
helpful as possible.

KNOWING

1.
It's all about a person's energy.
It doesn't matter if they're rich
or not.
Life's about communicating warmth
and being grateful for being in such a beautiful world.

2.
The true path to beauty is radiating kindness.

3.
Not eating meat or hurting animals is an expression of love for all creatures. Intelligence comes in many different forms.

4.
Whoever invented the gun should be shot.

5.
The world COULD have evolved to be just about anything:
Vegetarian, Spiritual, Happy,
Natural, Anything.
Look how it turned out.

6.
Time to make my own music.
Detach.

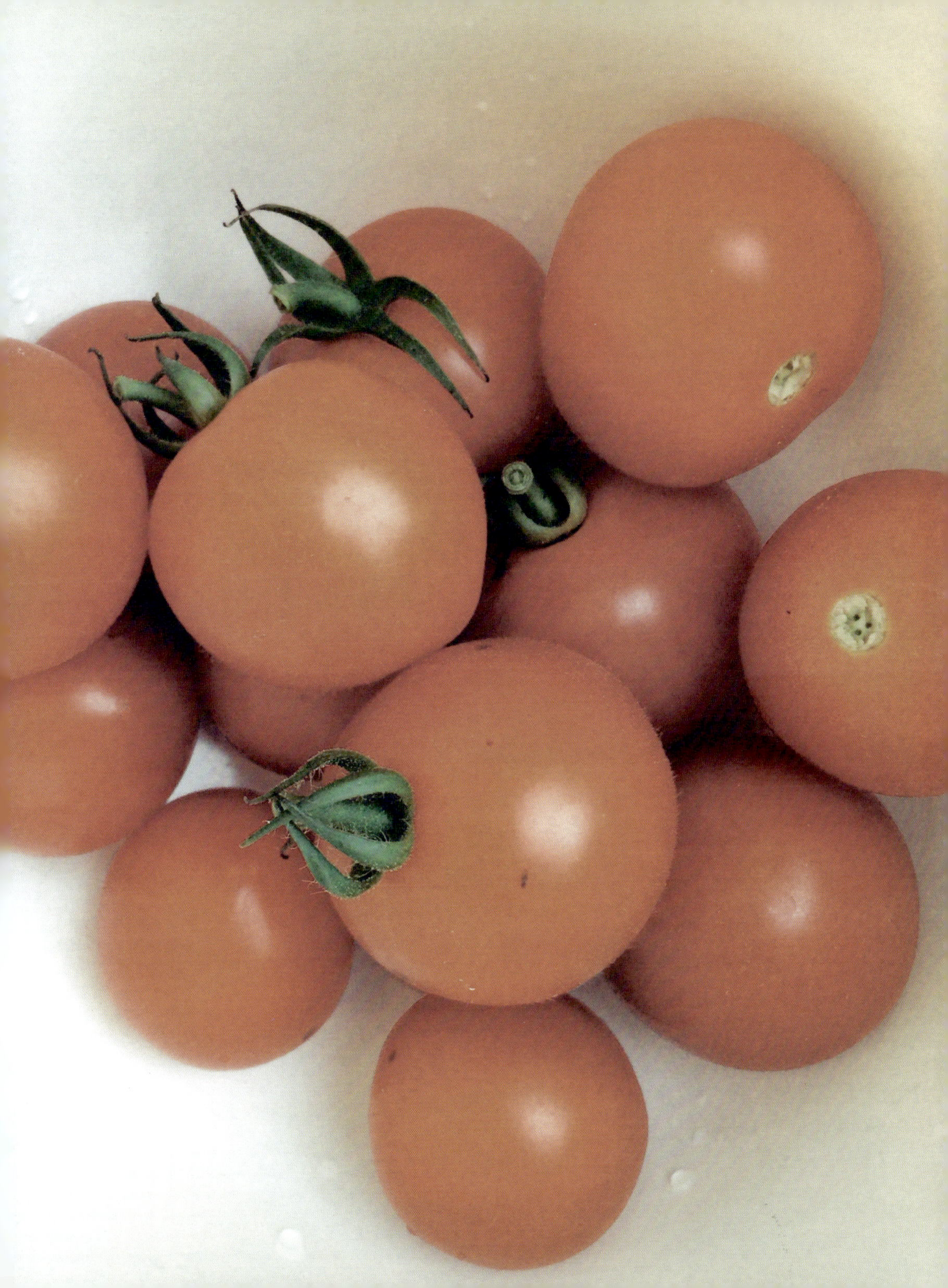

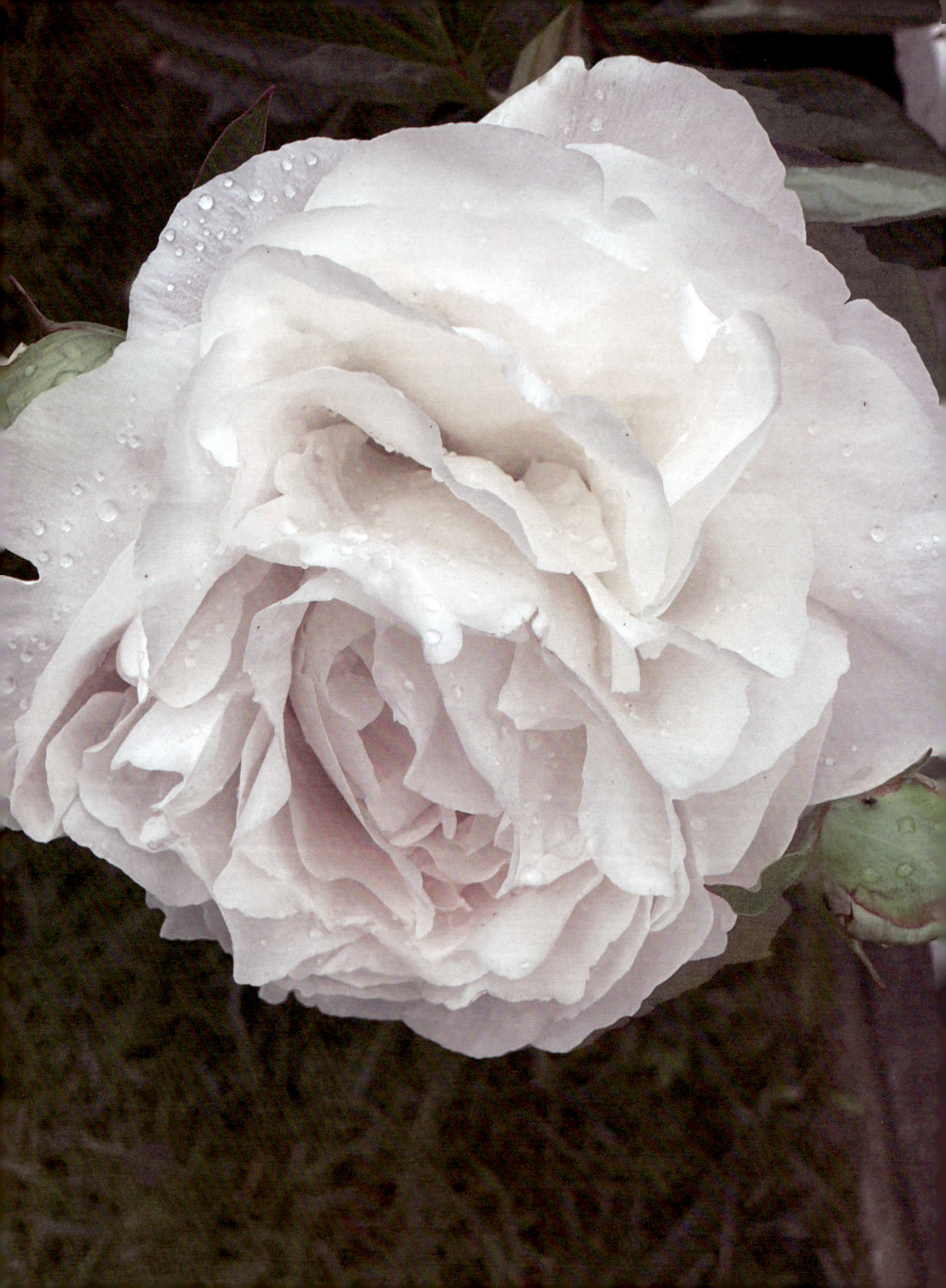

QUESTIONS FOR MY "A PASSION FOR GIVING" DOCUMENTARY

Q. Why are you so passionate about giving?

A. Giving can change the world.
Giving enriches your life, so when you give, you receive.
It makes you part of the bigger picture and connects us all and everyone wins.

Q. What are you hoping to achieve in life?

A. To treat others the way I would like to be treated. It's called the "golden rule."

Q. Why do you give your time and energy?

A. When you give, you are developing the deeper parts of yourself, like compassion, empathy, and generosity.

Q. What is important to you?

A. To live a meaningful, appreciative life, with no regrets.

Q. What drives you to try to help people?

A. Giving can take you out of yourself and your own story and connect you to the larger world and what really matters. Even the smallest act of giving can create a ripple effect around the world.

Q. What would you like to see other people trying to do to help others?

A. A quote from the Dalai Lama: "Be kind whenever possible. It is always possible."

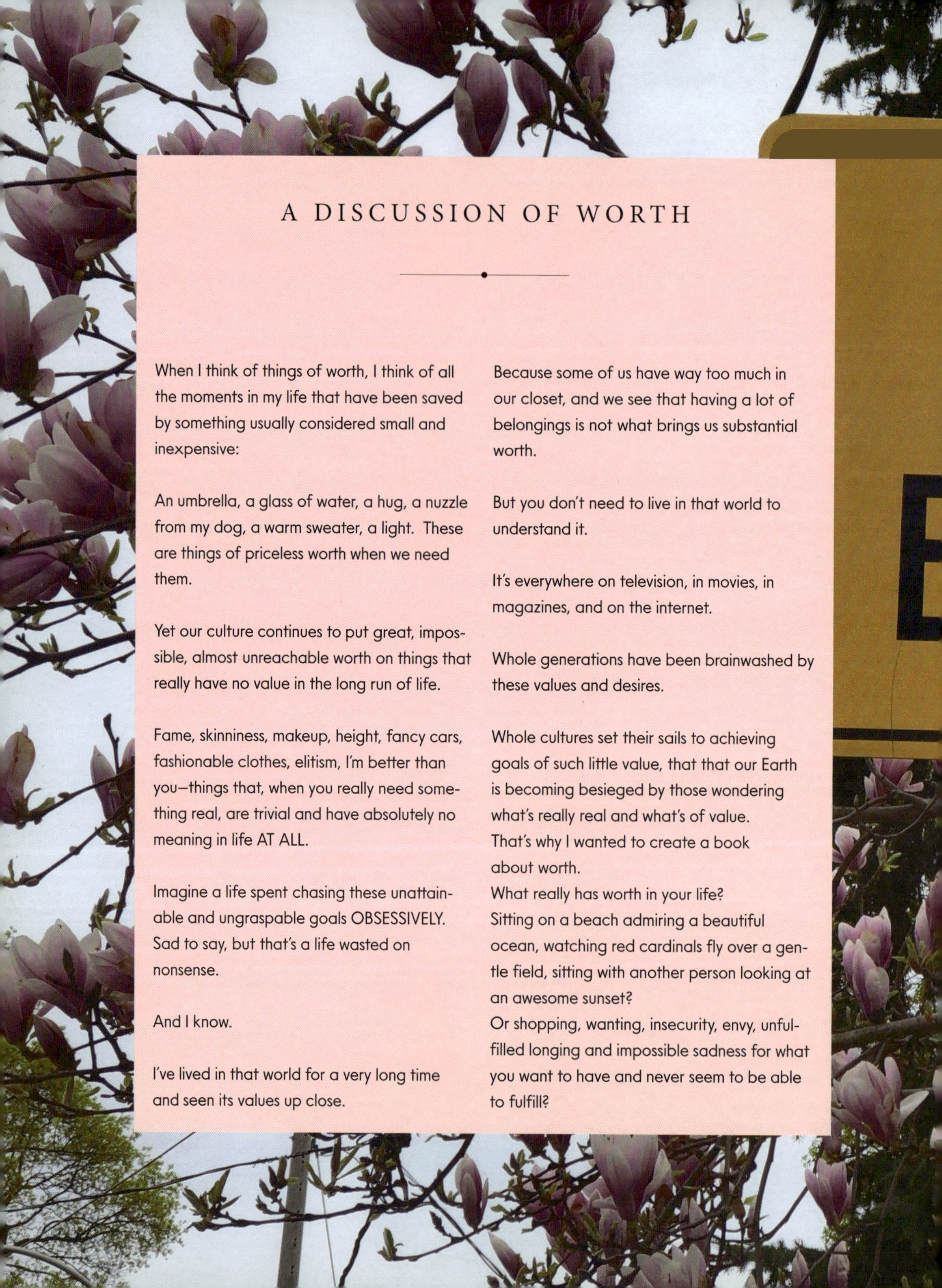

A DISCUSSION OF WORTH

When I think of things of worth, I think of all the moments in my life that have been saved by something usually considered small and inexpensive:

An umbrella, a glass of water, a hug, a nuzzle from my dog, a warm sweater, a light. These are things of priceless worth when we need them.

Yet our culture continues to put great, impossible, almost unreachable worth on things that really have no value in the long run of life.

Fame, skinniness, makeup, height, fancy cars, fashionable clothes, elitism, I'm better than you—things that, when you really need something real, are trivial and have absolutely no meaning in life AT ALL.

Imagine a life spent chasing these unattainable and ungraspable goals OBSESSIVELY. Sad to say, but that's a life wasted on nonsense.

And I know.

I've lived in that world for a very long time and seen its values up close.

Because some of us have way too much in our closet, and we see that having a lot of belongings is not what brings us substantial worth.

But you don't need to live in that world to understand it.

It's everywhere on television, in movies, in magazines, and on the internet.

Whole generations have been brainwashed by these values and desires.

Whole cultures set their sails to achieving goals of such little value, that that our Earth is becoming besieged by those wondering what's really real and what's of value.
That's why I wanted to create a book about worth.
What really has worth in your life?
Sitting on a beach admiring a beautiful ocean, watching red cardinals fly over a gentle field, sitting with another person looking at an awesome sunset?
Or shopping, wanting, insecurity, envy, unfulfilled longing and impossible sadness for what you want to have and never seem to be able to fulfill?

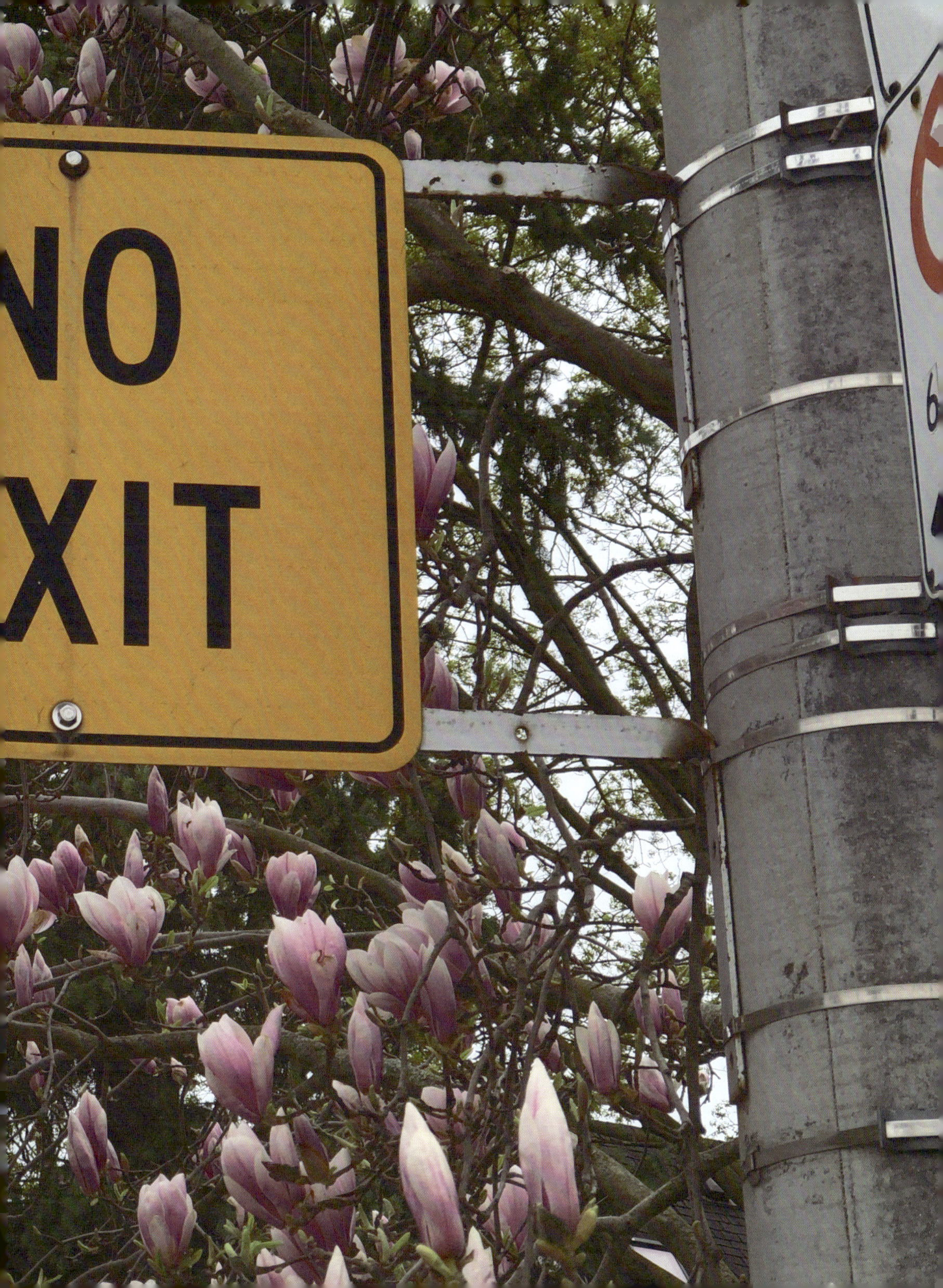
NO
XIT

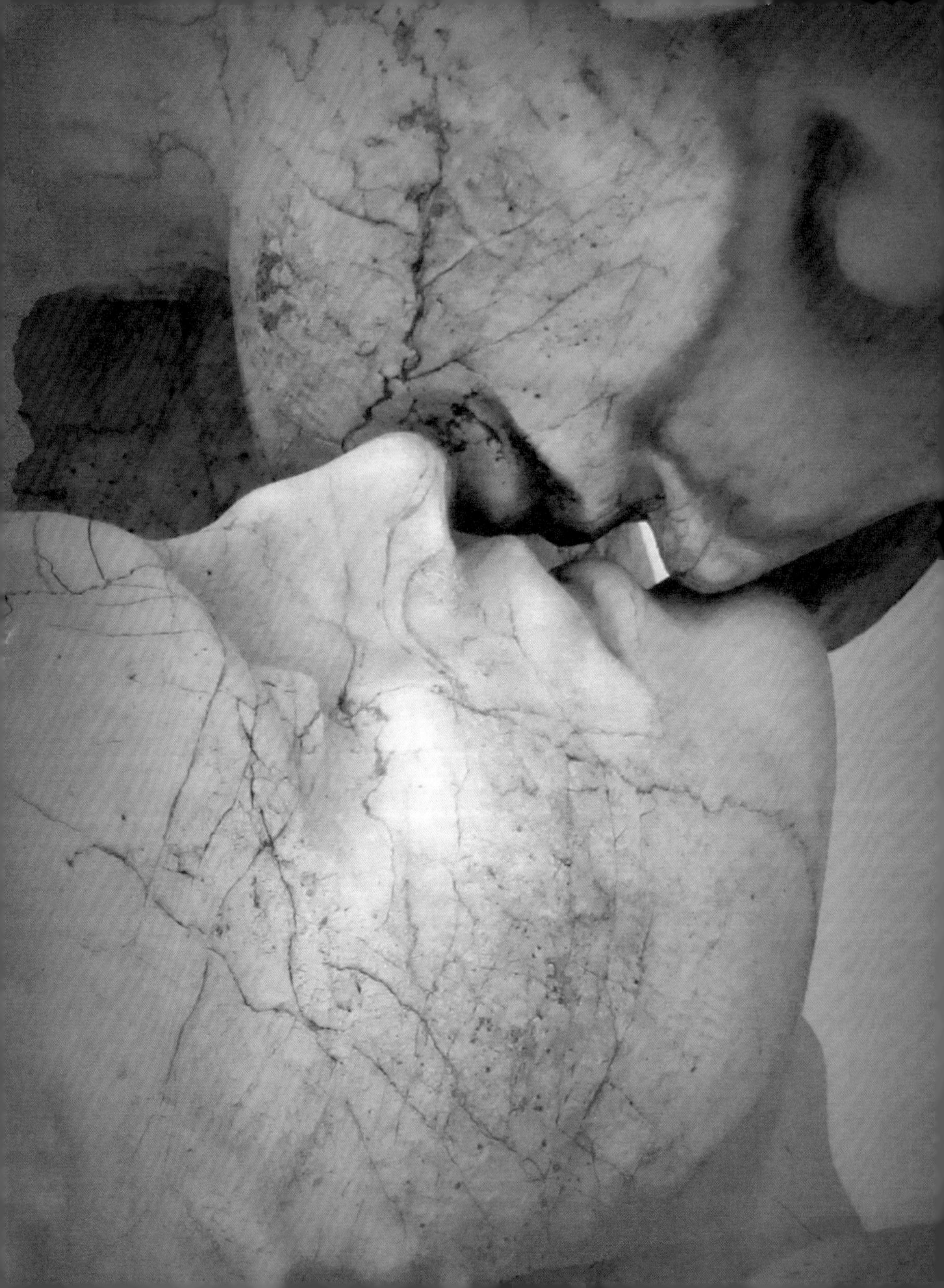

IN A HEART-BASED SOCIETY, HAVING ANOTHER LOOK AT SENSITIVITY

Most of us have too much on our shelves,
and we can see that having lots of belongings is definitely
not what brings us esteem.

*

And from a feminine and intuitive point of view, I look at the world and
I can feel what is actually happening, energetically.

*

What I see is a world based on taking, achieving status,
and gaining recognition.

*

SINCERE GIVING has to be real, not for show,
with no goal but to create a loving outcome.

*

So much is occurring because of insecurity.
People want to accumulate as much material gain
for themselves as possible.
So others will think they are rich, smart, gorgeous, or irresistible.
And that they're the coolest person in the room,
because of their fame or what they own.

*

I would LOVE to glamorize those who are the richest, smartest,
most beautiful in their SOUL,
because those are truly the coolest qualities.

*

The person who spends their life making the world a better place
is more alluring than those
that only want to make themselves look grand.

loving
capable
kind
worthy
giving
beautiful

TODAY IS THE BEST DAY

I woke-up, had my cereal and blueberries, and went for a swim.
The sun is shining and there is a lovely breeze.
Our dog is running merrily in the garden and the bright red cardinals are on the bird feeder.
I"m so lucky.
And I know it.

That"s worth everything to me, to have this tranquility and calm; to know that all is right around me.
Just to wake up and know that everyone is healthy and alive,
And each has the opportunity every day to enjoy life.

If only I could look at the expansive world and see that all is well.
As soon as people can relax a little,
maybe they will wake up to the fact that the world is already okay.
No need to tell other people what to do, or how to behave, or make yourself look great, or own more, or be more, or look different, or be different, or control other people.
Then there"s no reason to contest for MORE.

Everything is really OKokay, as long as we already know it and become our finest selves.
Live and let live, and let others be happy, too.

It all balances out when you"re open to the exuberance in your life.

Suddenly you wish all people well,
when you realize that we"re all living together on this incredible planet.

Compassion and caring, two of the most worthwhile qualities that you can have , make your life more valuable.

Without caring for others, your own soul can feel empty.
The constant chase of gratifying yourself can be very unfulfilling and boring after a while.

To bring some vibrancy into your life, try to making this world a better place, caring for others.

If you happen to come upon someone who is in the middle of a difficult time, a little friendship and tenderness are the best things that you can do for yourself, too.
Warm-heartedness to others is a gift to your own spirit.

A well of intrinsic joy, a different quality of joy, is so different from living on the internet, or buying new stuff , - as it really makes you feel good about yourself.
It"s an irreplaceable feeling that wakes you up, to knowing life is really good.

A FEW OF MY FAVORITE THINGS

A summer day in the shade of a tree,
a gentle wind, looking up at the blue sky
and fluffy white clouds.

Sounds cliché,
but is this not the most incredible of all?

❧

An afternoon, in time,
just being alive, breathing the beautiful air
and seeing the beauty of our existence.

❧

I love an open day, with open time, that you know is full of love.

Yet that day is rare.

❧

Our time might be given to tasks, responsibilities, work,
or even just sadness and confusion.

❧

So when there's a time that you delight in being alive,
luxuriate in those moments.

❧

Appreciate that time and place because you are happy and
in synchronicity with all that surrounds you.

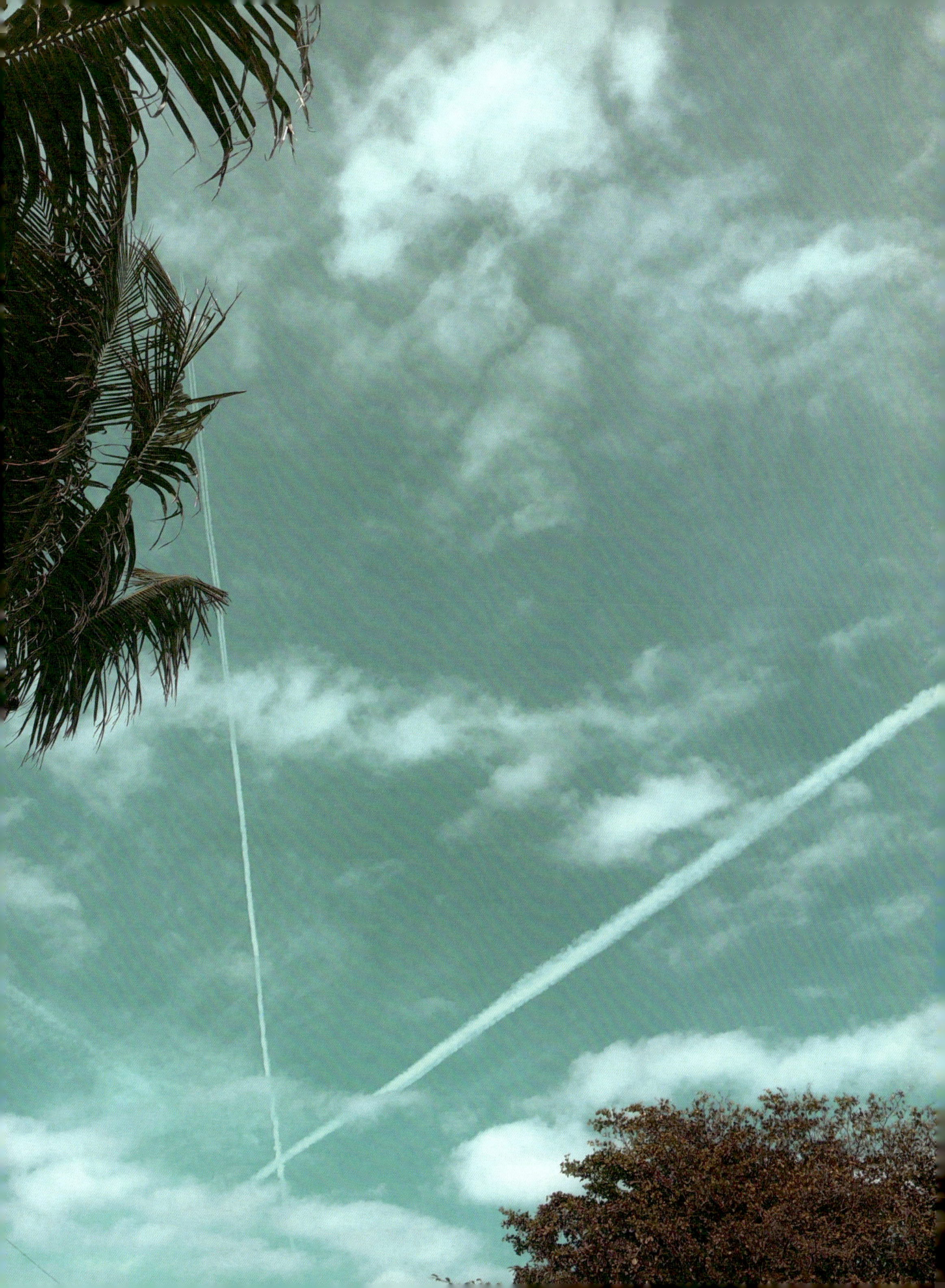

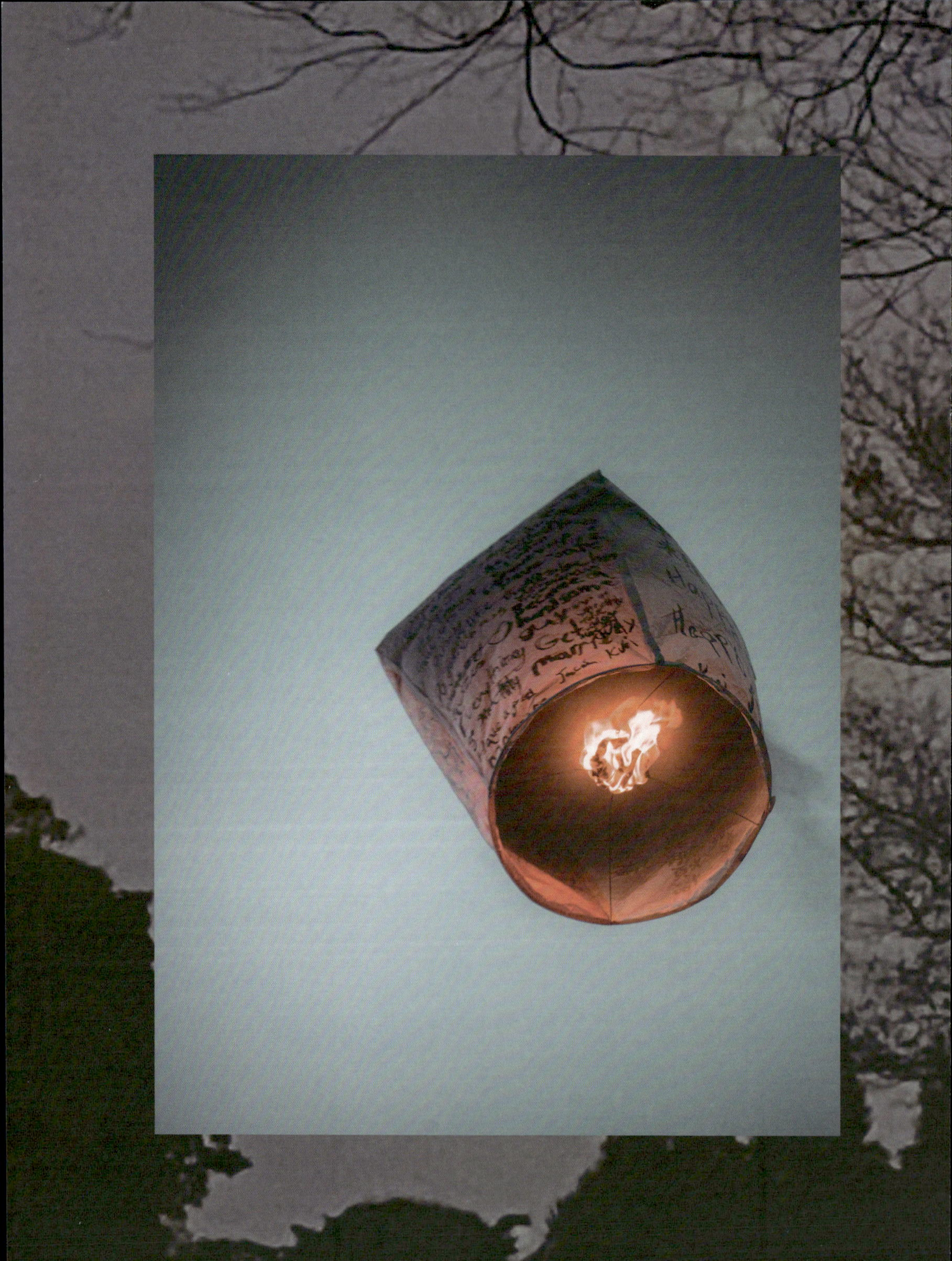

MY LIFE IS EXTRAORDINARY

I have been fortunate to experience so many extraordinary places and people, beautiful animals and special times.

Every day, I feel so blessed and lucky for the life that I am creating.

I have some regrets, of course, but not many.

I can see that everything surrounding me is a fresh wave of life, and if I'm smart, I will go with its flow.

All times have their value.
They are just moments coming to you and created by you, a dance.

If our eyes are wide open, we can see all that surrounds us, but it is not us.

We are ourselves, constantly choosing happiness, sadness, or fulfillment.

No matter what is happening around us.

Cherish your time, not what you have, or who you portray yourself as.

Share some "groovy wishes."
Someone once told my one hundred-year-old mother she was groovy. She LOVED that observation! She loved being "seen."

Believing now is a time to create something that all people really want.
A world full of love, happiness, and kindness.

I never understood why we're EVER living somewhere none of us wants to be.
Selfishness, sadness, illness, and loneliness.
Who wants that?

Yet here we live, year after year, day after day, seemingly stretching into eternity.

We all long for a life of peaceful happiness, and yet somehow, we continue along this trek of frustration.

We seem to be seduced by things that really have no intrinsic value, and we take for granted those things that are MOST valuable. Love and warmth and kindness.

With mindfulness, we can begin to wake up and see that what we choose to give importance to shapes our lives.

If we could pay more attention to the little everyday things.
And know how special and content we might feel, in recognizing their radiance.
Then we might stop putting aside life—hours and days and years—for an unfulfilling goal.

Something we just might discover much, much later on.

After we finally buy the Mercedes and see that we're still not quite as happy as we thought we'd be.
A bunch of metal isn't going to give you any love back—as good-looking as it might be.

I feel like I owe everyone that came before me, everyone that will come after me,
and everyone around me, to just say it out loud.

What this culture is valuing, what we spend our lives chasing, what we wish for and dream of is a fantasy.
It's never going to come true.

What money can buy, after food and shelter and education, is not real, will never satisfy you, will never make you happier than you can be right now.

Yes, we must buy food; we must have a home that costs money—clothes, transportation.
Yes, all those things need money to acquire in our world.

But all the rest: fancy homes, cars, expensive clothes—they will never do for you what you think they will do.
They will never do for you what a friend, a pet, some fresh air, and a walk will do.

All those things, which we have now, have so much more worth, than all the elusive things in life that we spend hours dreaming of and days working toward.

So relax and enjoy your precious moments. You have it all right this second.
Just open your eyes and hearts and you will see all that you have.

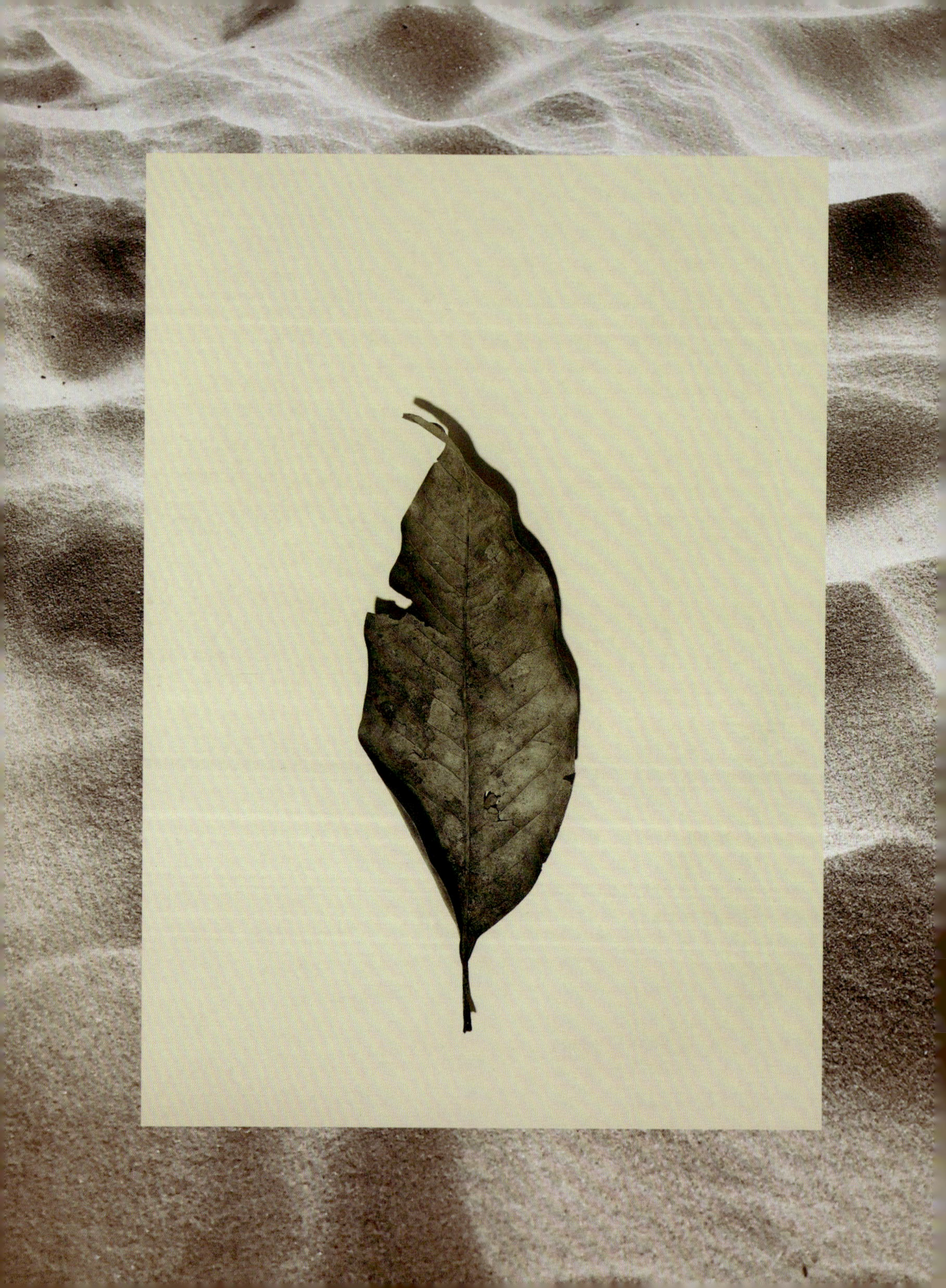

REFLECTONS ON AGE

I know what it's like to be old.

I've felt it and lived it and watched my mother move into her old age.

I know now that the body feels cranky, and the mind has holes in it.

When I was younger, I was so absolutely sure I would live forever.

That I, of course, could be the one to achieve immortality.

I had all these tricks—health tricks.

But now, as I age, I know for sure that we are merely mortal.

Our bodies have a clock ticking down to the final ebbs of health and vitality.

And now I know what it's like to sway between old age and youth,

one day good, the next a struggle.

I know that my life will end as I feel myself inching along to that finality.

Which, of course, I am smart enough to know is really the beginning.

When I pass on into forever.

Turn Around, Turn Around, Turn Around, and You're Old.

THINGS OF WORTH

Sitting around a campfire,
beach, living room
telling your truths to people
who really listen and
listening to their truths.

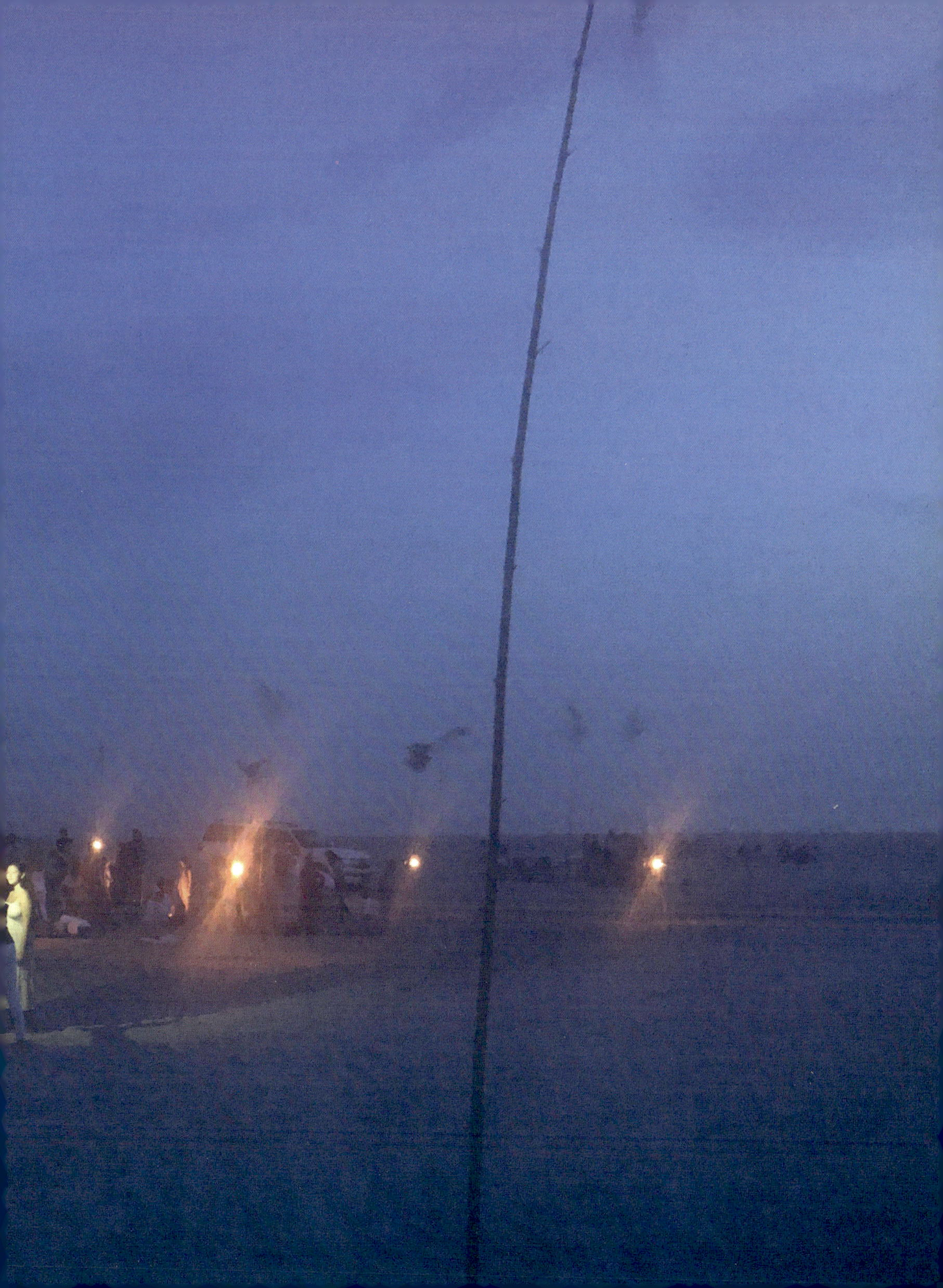

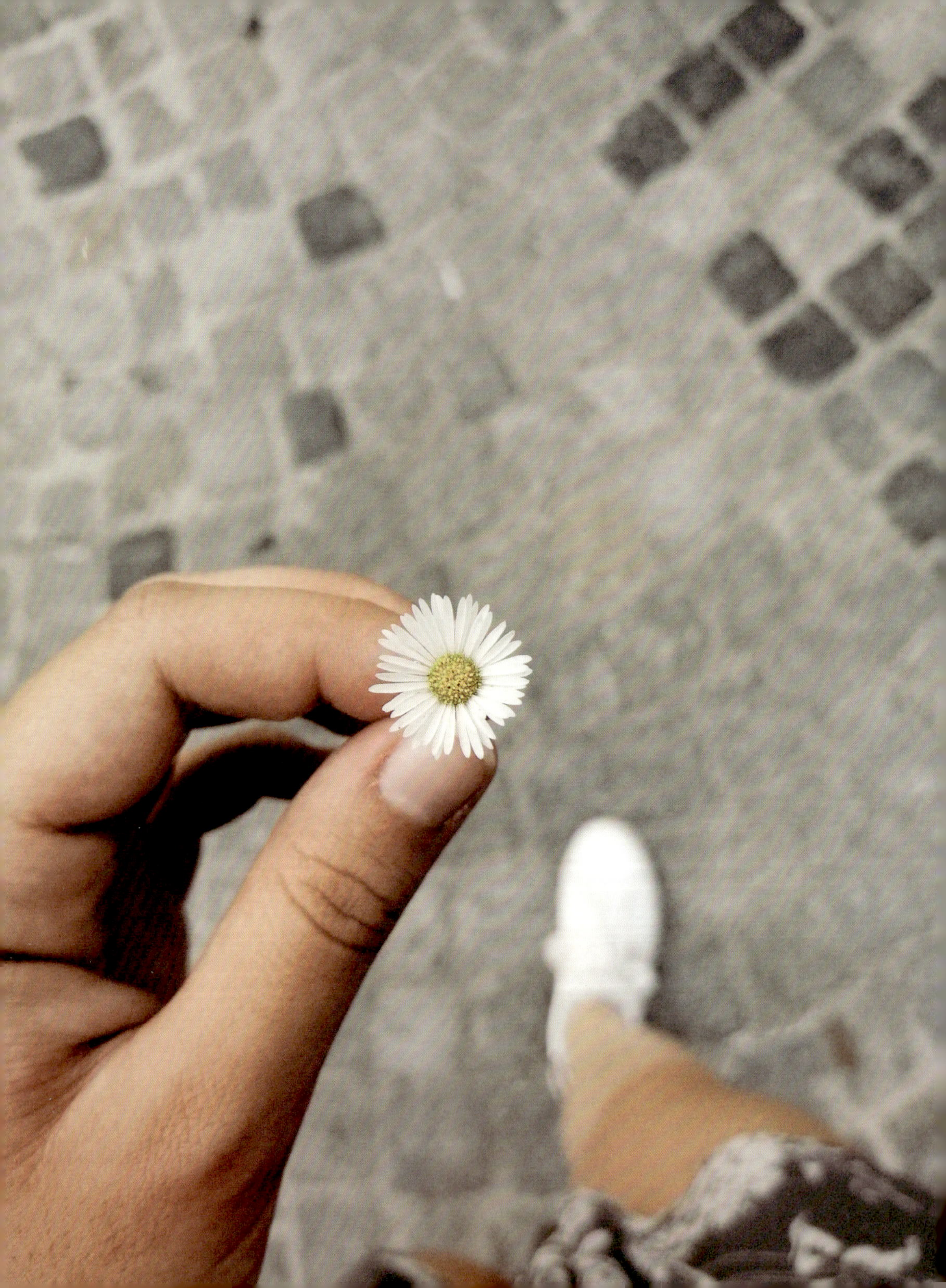

A MEDITATION ON WHAT'S IMPORTANT: A QUIZ

So here we go:

WHAT'S MORE IMPORTANT?

1.Me or You:
I guess it depends on who you're asking; I might say me, and you might say you.

2. Love or Money

3. Music or Silence

4. Family or Friends

5. Dogs or Cats

6. Up or Down/In or Out

7. Vegetables or Animals

8. Gold or Silver

9. Tea or Coffee

10. Yesterday, Today, or Tomorrow

11. Shoes, Bicycle, or Yacht

12. Birthday or Anniversary

13. The Moment you're In or The Moment You Wish You Were In
The answer is both. You see, everything has a different value to everyone.

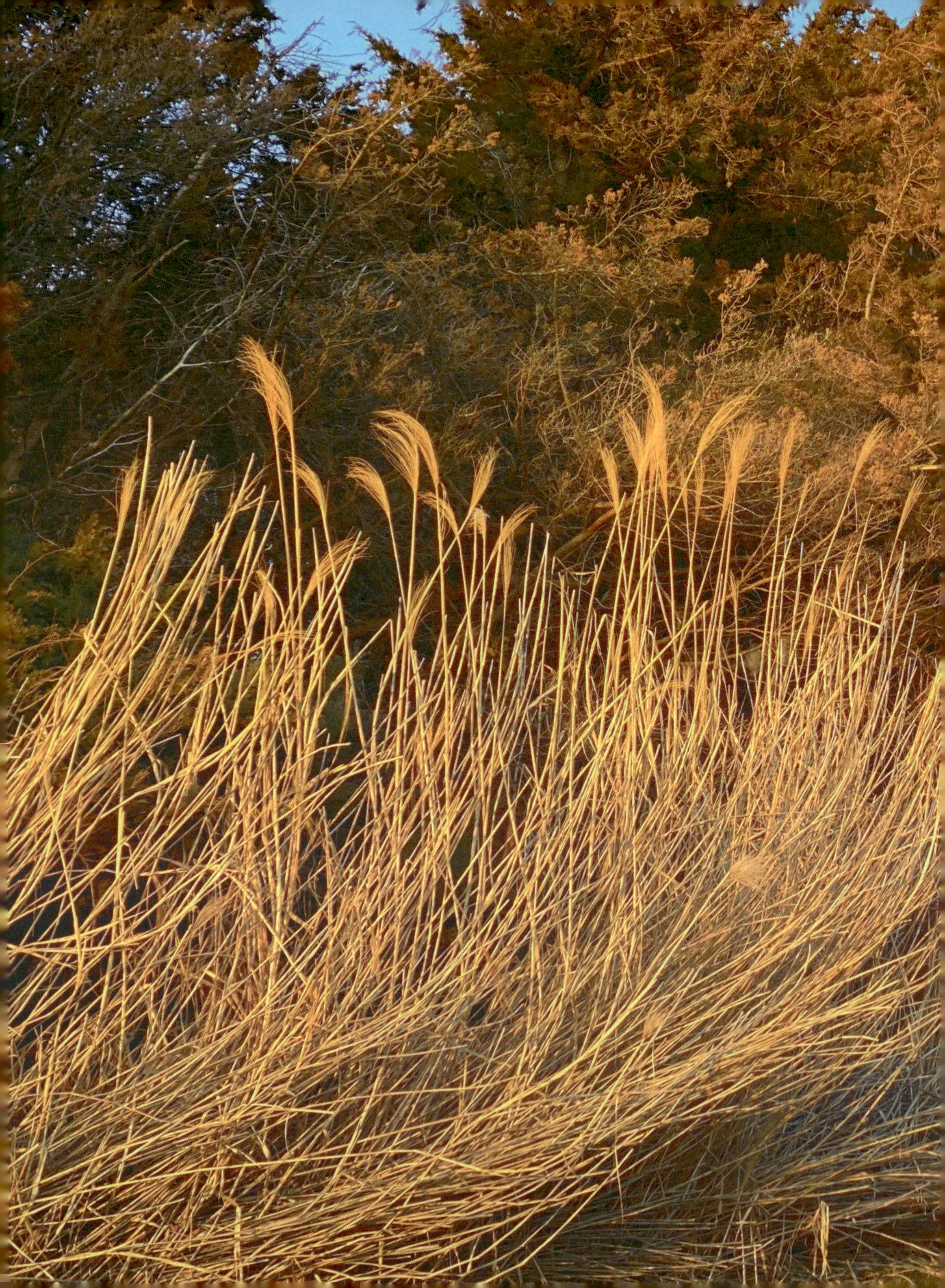

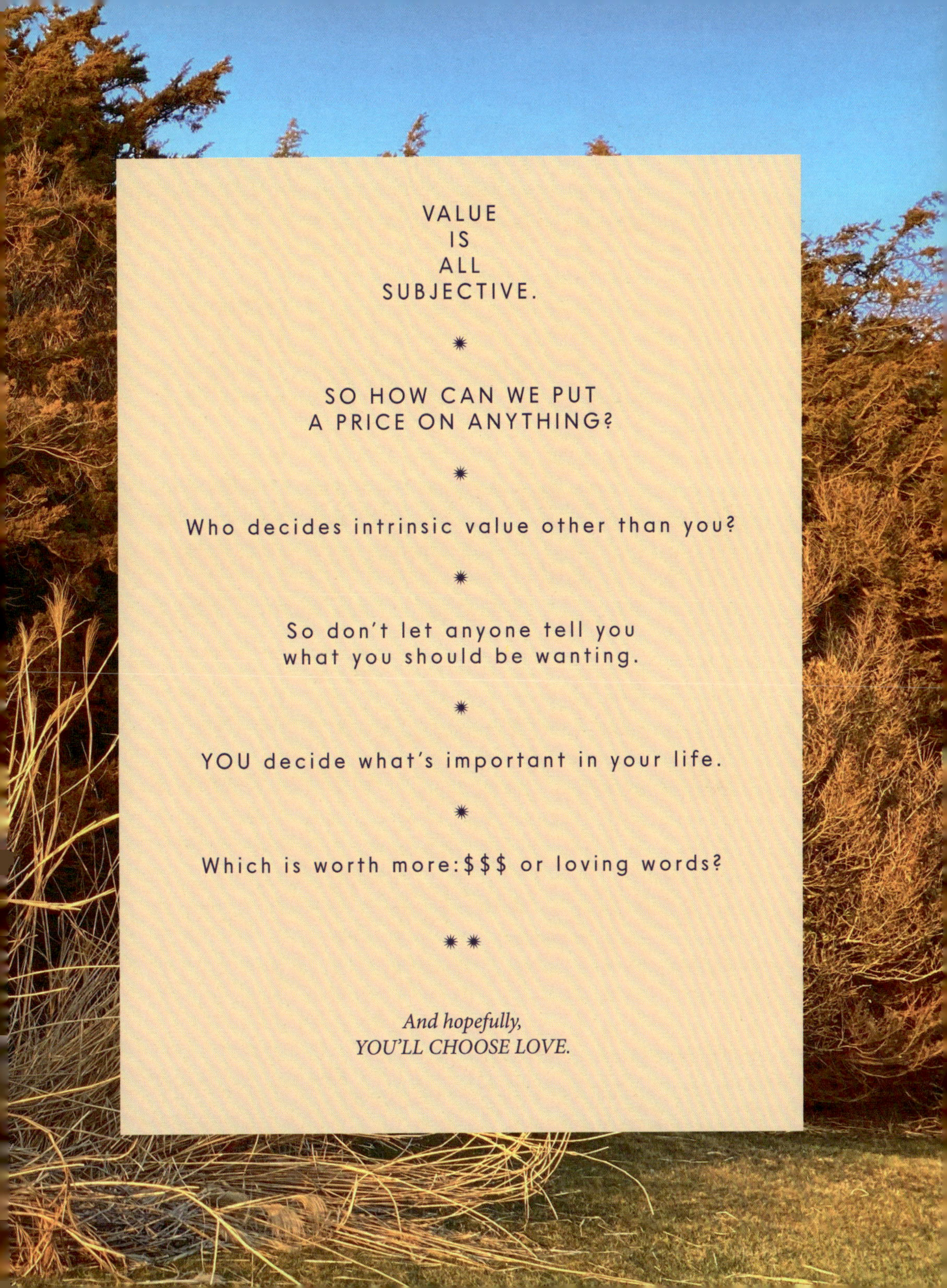
VALUE
IS
ALL
SUBJECTIVE.
✷
SO HOW CAN WE PUT
A PRICE ON ANYTHING?
✷
Who decides intrinsic value other than you?
✷
So don't let anyone tell you
what you should be wanting.
✷
YOU decide what's important in your life.
✷
Which is worth more: $$$ or loving words?
✷ ✷
And hopefully,
YOU'LL CHOOSE LOVE.

Don't be fooled ahead of time.

It's more fun to want something than to have it.

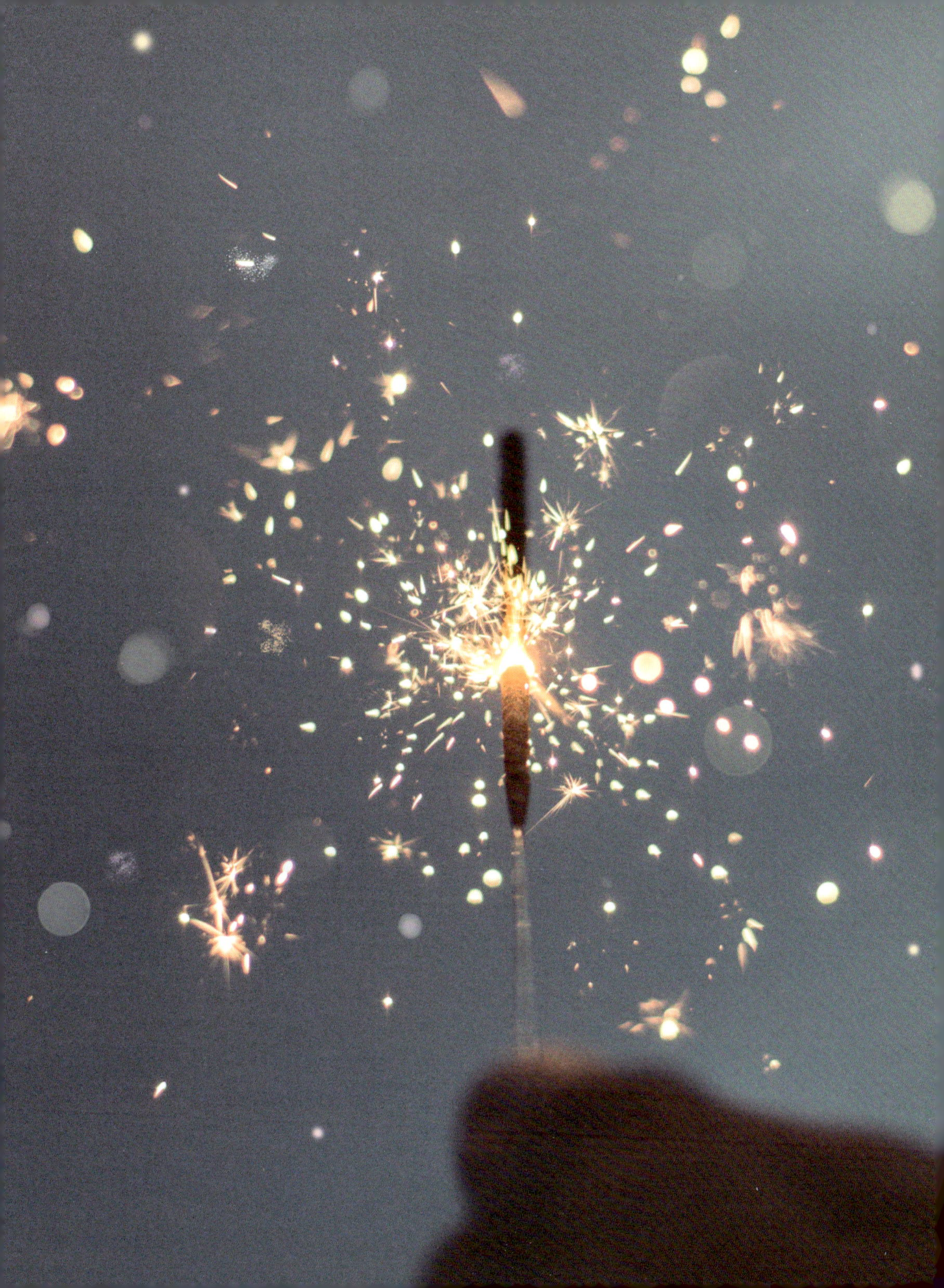

I'm watching the swan, watching Robert finally clean up our boat after much procrastination. Possibly as much procrastination as it has taken me to write this.

After innumerable trips to New York City and innumerable days of worrying about my Mom, I was ready to sit down for a summer of writing.

The story was about WORTH.

Everywhere I go, people seem to have things upside down.

They value things that are worth-less, like what they think people think of them.

So they buy, or save to buy, a new, fancy, status item people will adore them.

Some men who drive fancy cars can often be very unattractive; I mean lacking in stylish energy, kind smiles, warmth, a twinkle in their eye.

Men often feel if they drive a fancy car, it makes them more desirable.

An attractive man, to me, is warm, loving, honest, content, present, and funny....and no amount of cash can buy that.

But we continue to value the surface of life in this cultural dynamic.

Who's young, tall, well dressed, blonde, and famous?
Our culture is so young and easy to fool.

What's really a blessing is here, right now, for everyone to see—
If we could just see it—
Being authentic.

What's real is what's in the present moment, in whatever form it is taking.
That is the universe's display, just for you, and me, and all of us.

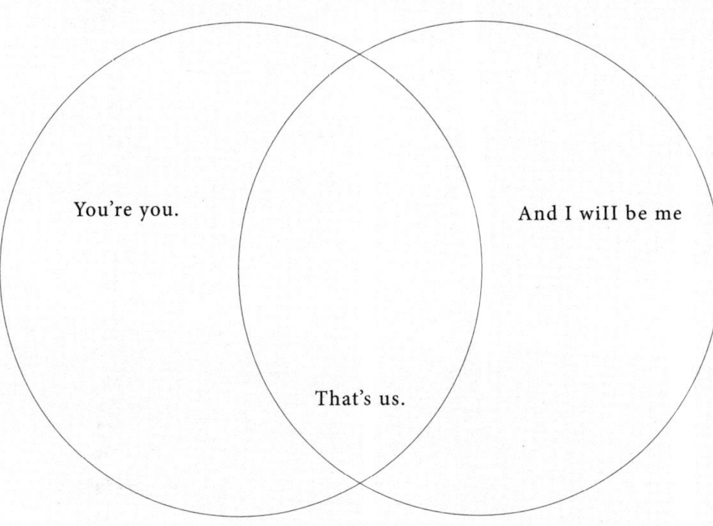

Soften hearts.

Hard-hearted when out for self;

I took that dimension out of my life.

Soft-hearted when out for others;

I like having a soft heart better.

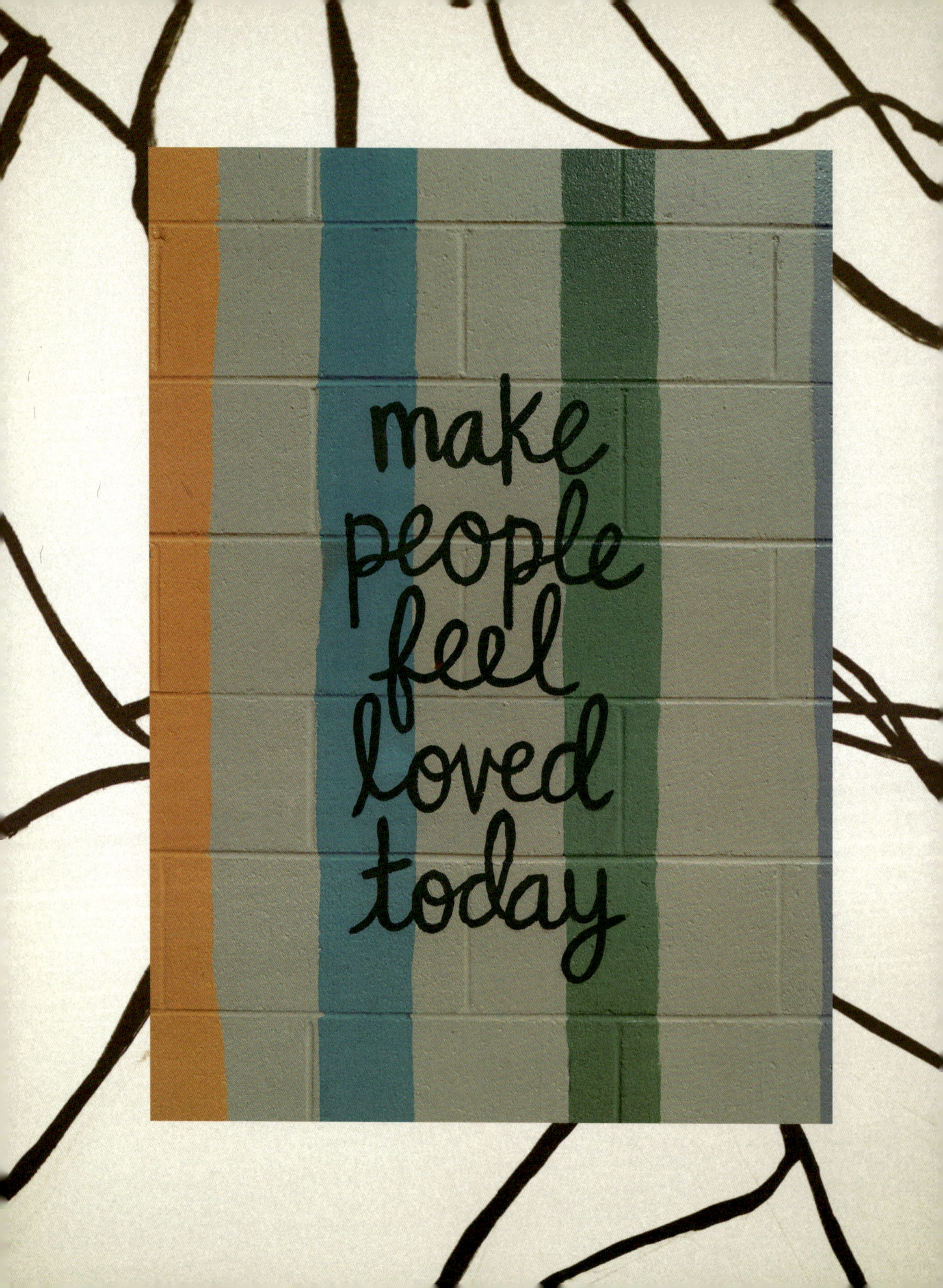
make
people
feel
loved
today

ART

I didn't know THAT before.

I was young then.

I just knew that I was.

Now I love to communicate to others,
by writing what I find to be meaningful.

Writing is sharing an experience with others.

And sharing that experience with myself, too.

The metronome of life sways back and forth.

Its frequency is what you perceive.
So do what you love. I love to be inspired.

I used to be plugged in;
now I'm unplugged,
listening to the sounds of my own existence.

The luscious rhythm of everyday life
is making me aware that every incredible
instant has so much worth,
as long as I am alert to its momentum.

I don't ever need to look further than where I am,
to own or claim something worthwhile.
All I need is here—the air, the light, the sounds,
the sounds of my breath—just being alive.
Although a nice meal and a good sleep are
essential, too.

Sometimes I have that awareness,
when I wake up on the morning of my birthday,
and suddenly I have this huge appreciation of
I AM ALIVE and living on this planet Earth, in
this house, with these people.
In this civilization.
I understand this gift of life.
But that feeling eventually fades into the everyday wants and needs and tasks and fears.

Now as I am becoming older,
I see obviously. Holding longer, the thoughts
of gratitude and the equal worth of
every moment.
NOT ONE MOMENT IS WORTH MORE
THAN THE NEXT.
All moments in life have value,
because they are being presented to you in a
second of time.
That is irreplaceable.

No moment is worth more than another.
Some might be more subjectively satisfying to
you at that time,
but fast-forward into the future.
That identical event may not give you exactly
the same satisfaction.

Such as a child playing with a favorite toy.
The charge of that toy may not have the same
level of appeal twenty years later.

So each second of time is to be valued for
what it is:
Life presenting itself to you in so many facets.

We just choose the facets of the moment we
wish to see.

Can you imagine how alive you might be, if you
could see contrasting perspectives at once?

That's an exciting idea.
To get beyond your own subjectivity and see
life for what it is.

All around me are people "chasing the dream."
They are already in a dream, actually, a fanta-
sy, about reality.
Reality, to some people, is the physical exis-

---

tence of food, sleeping, and shelter.
And to others who have achieved those basics, it is fancy shelter, fancy food, fancy transportation, looking good, success, showing off, sexuality and making yourself look better than others, but all that is often insecurity.

Because, if one is really awake,
one can clearly see that every living thing and everything in existence has its own unique personality.

Not ONE thing in this world is more valuable than anything else, whether it be animals, people, or things.

Who are we to proclaim valuation?

I'm saying it again: when you really need something, that is when you see it's merit, whether it's a jet to visit family or a simple lunch.

Things are only worth something if you value them.

Children playing with toys are not just cute—

Those toys are Valuable to them.

Teenagers hanging out with friends are not wasting time—

Those friends are Valuable to them.
Adults enjoying life and nature are not slacking—

but finding great value in the Beauty of Life.

Beauty is indeed in the eye of the beholder.

How can I convince someone who's spent all their life acquiring wealth that they may not really be wealthy?
Such a Shakespearian tragedy.
Maybe it was a great ride, the challenges, the respect, the risks.
Maybe it was big adrenaline, lots to show off, people groveling, fame.

Sounds good to some,
But it wasn't EVERYTHING.
Because everything was already here to start.
You were just too busy giving your time to the chase.

So now you're a little older, you HAVE it: Right?
You have it all?
Every moment is better, every day is glorious?
Right??
Now that you have it all, life is just about perfect?
Because wealth has brought you health, love, friendship, and peace, right?
No worries, mate!

So why do we put so much value on accumulated wealth?

More than we need for everyday living
and contentment?
Why don't we value applying that wealth to helping others, making a world in which we all want to live?

I'm not talking about rules and regulations and limits surrounding wealth,
Not Marxism or communism.
I'm not talking about progress in tech
and science.
I'm just talking about intelligent and compassionate and sane living.
Common sense sees what really has value
and appreciates it.

It's kind of wonderful to share with you what really has meaning.
I can't believe that so many people still feel that glitter and showing off expensive belongings matter and are not just empty.
Fun, maybe,
but not worth a lifetime of labor or yearning.

Fashion is fun, of course. I appreciate
brilliant design.
But natural beauty, good health, and loving kindness are more attractive,
because they're real.
Style is personality,
not always something to be bought. It's how one carries themselves.

Health and vitality from exercise and nutrition are worth so much more than looking unhealthy and old
from all those attempts to hang on to money or status.

Kindness and humor radiate from people's eyes!
Selfish charisma radiates, too, but the love, light, and twinkle in your eyes is quite dim
by comparison.

Generosity and gentleness to others is the key to so much of the happiness that money can't buy.

So if you're smart, why not aspire to a life
of contributing,
rather than the life-dampening chase of money, power, and control?

Why spend your life putting the light out in your eyes, when you can live the biggest, fullest life imaginable by doing something great
for others?

It's amazing to me,
watching people chasing more money than they'd ever need, just for the dash.

Toasting a bottle of champagne to their lack of insight and compassion, and drinking vodka to their pain.

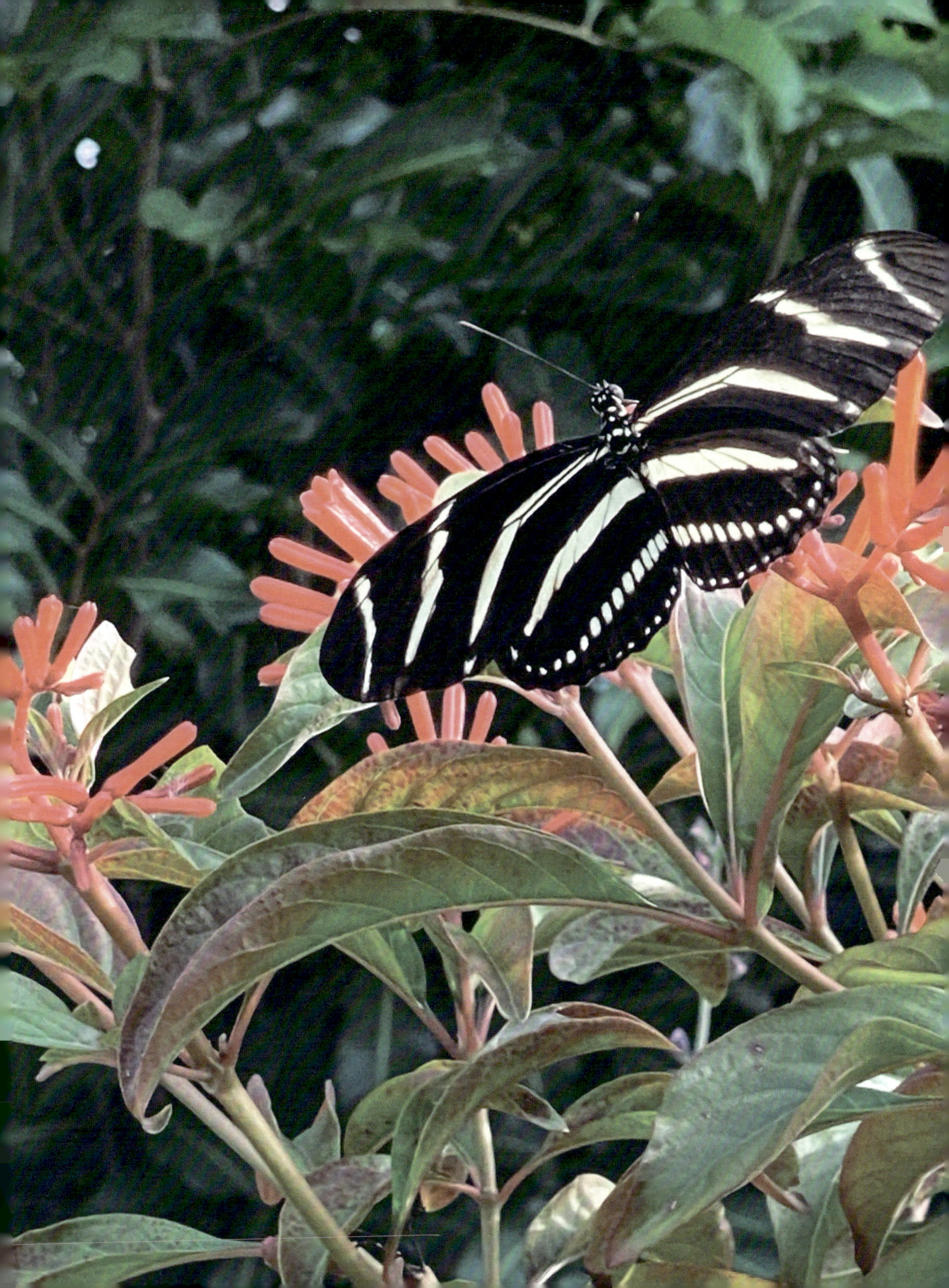

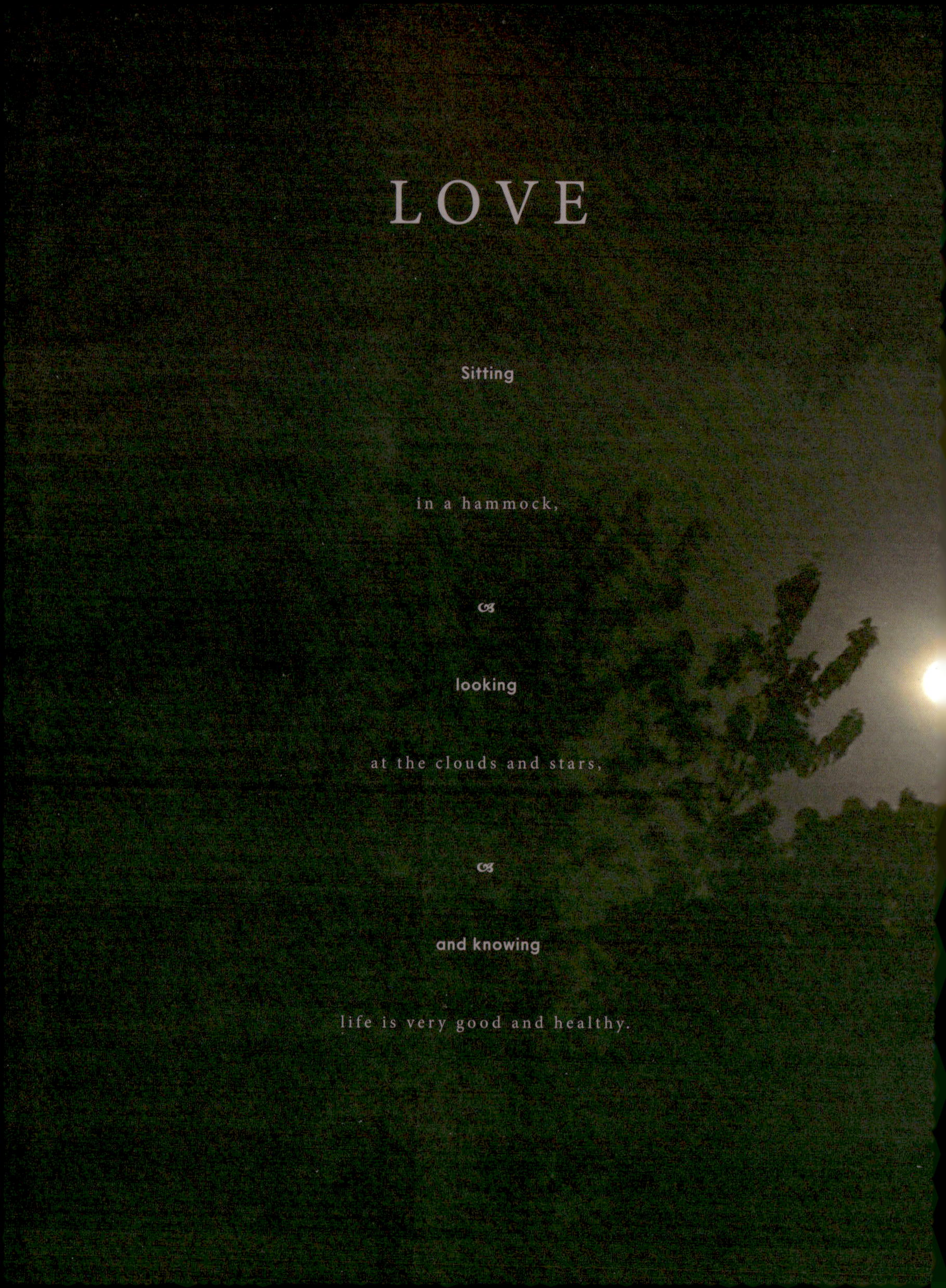

LOVE

Sitting

in a hammock,

ꝏ

looking

at the clouds and stars,

ꝏ

and knowing

life is very good and healthy.

As the world became more social, as in social media, I became much less social. . . .

CREATING a template that the next generation takes for granted. . . .

We are spinning the reality.

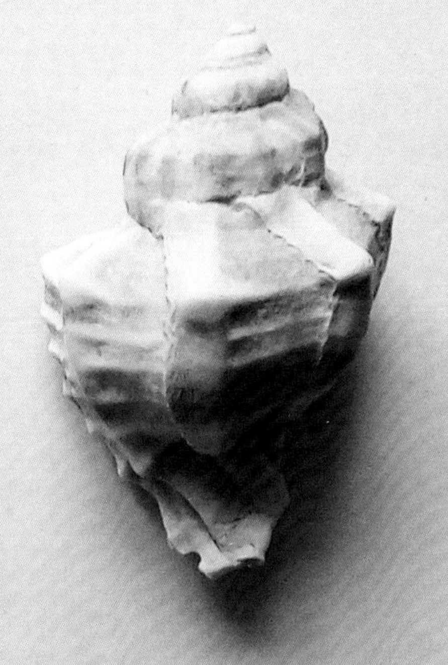

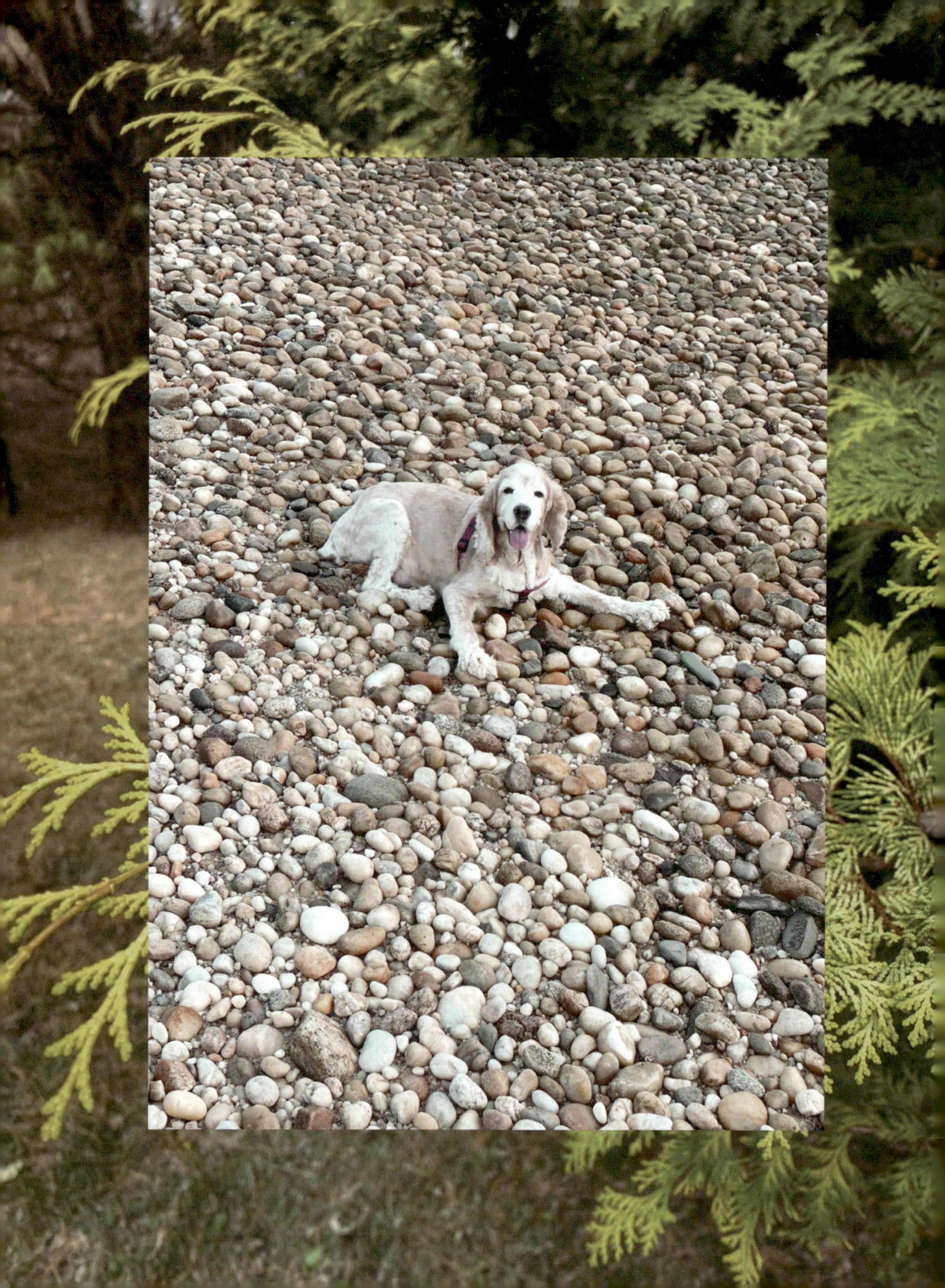

FRIENDSHIP: WHAT IS IT REALLY WORTH

Some people are really good at being a friend.

What does that mean to you, when you need a friend?

Yet how much are friends paid for their expertise or that particular job qualification? Nothing, of course, because we can never put a monetary value on friendship.

Nurturing a heart is worth more to me, if necessary, than someone who is making a fortune on Wall Street.

Yet I know a few stellar friends that are without funds.

I DIGRESS.

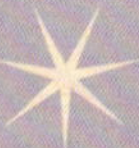

Digression = A Diversion
(New Oxford American Dictionary)

An activity that diverts the mind from serious concerns;
a recreation or pastime.
Something intended to distract someone's attention
from something more important.

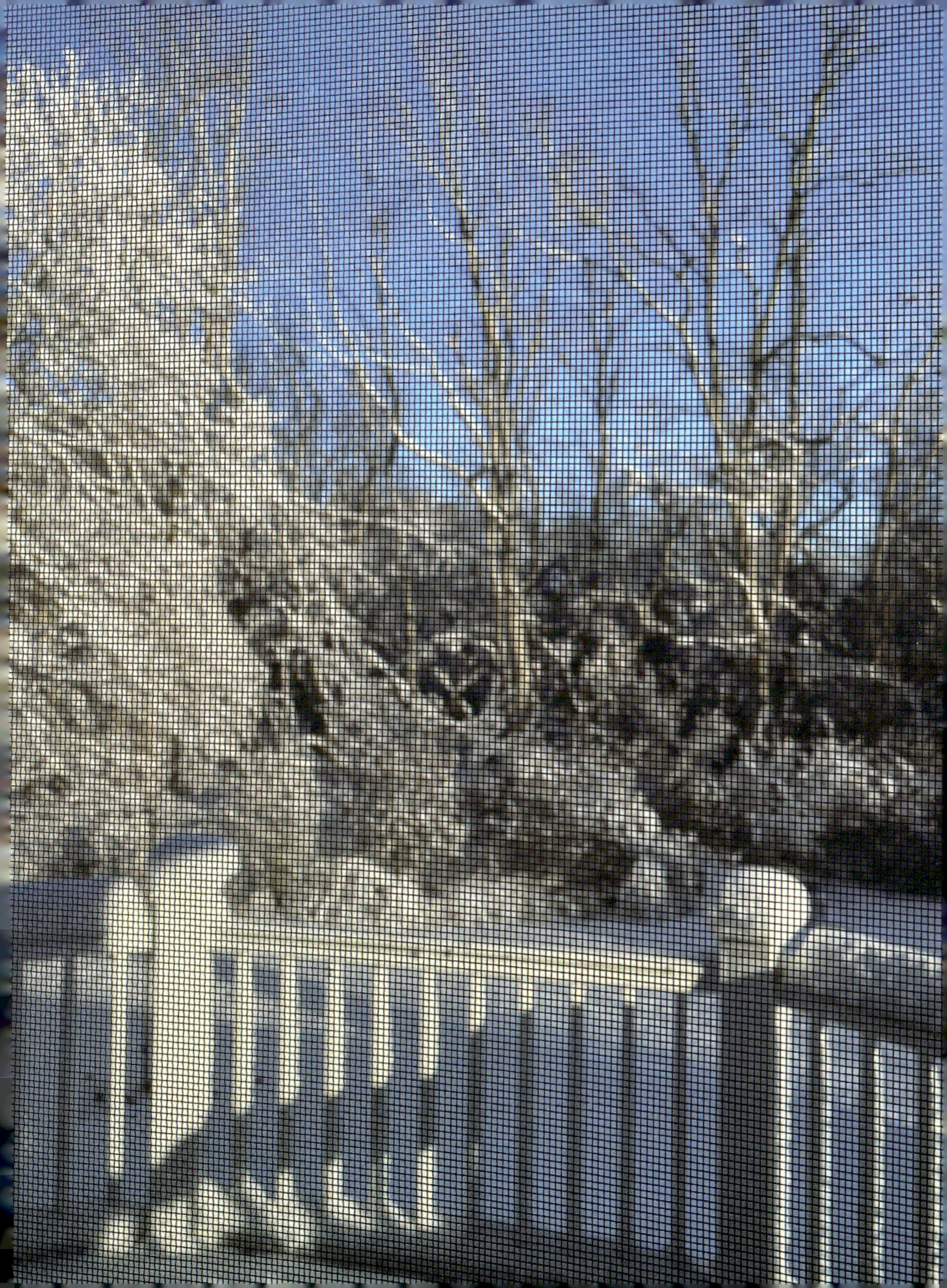

THINGS OF WORTH

Giving my days away like chocolate.

ଓ

Go ahead, have one; it's just one of my days!
How many days do we have in life anyway?

ଓ

What's more important: a day spent in fresh air, sunshine, and laughter,
or a day with a grudge, an annoyance, or anger?

ଓ

Living all the wonderfulness of each nanosecond
is a life full of joy, beautifully lived.

ଓ

Nothing-nothing-nothing is important or potent enough
to take our joy away from us;
And if we should slip,
loving the moment is easily found once again.

ଓ

You can always try listening to Louis Armstrong singing
"What a Wonderful World."

ଓ

I did just that when I first arrived in my hotel room.

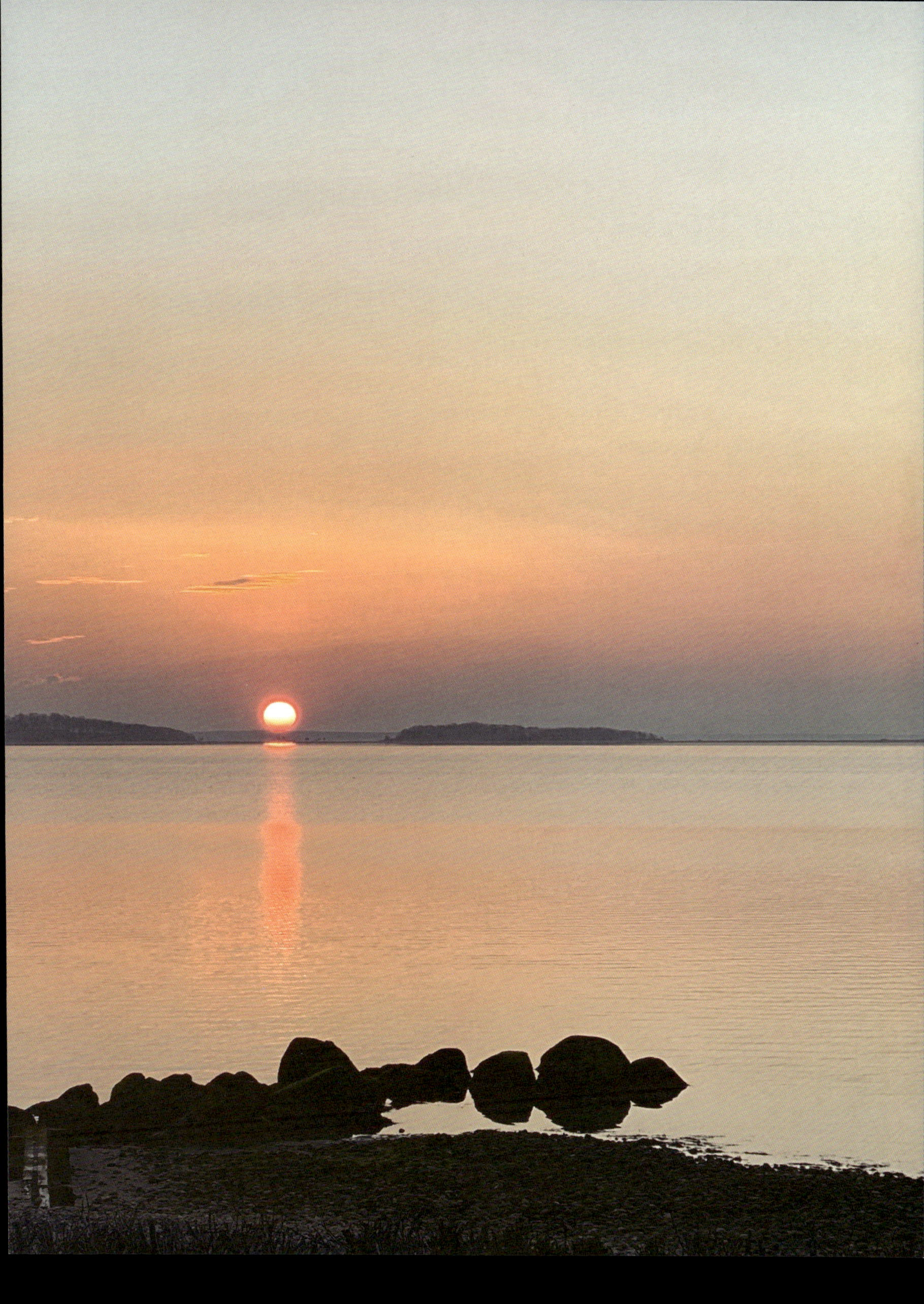

WORTH-LESS

The well-dressed person on an airplane
who sat next to me and can't really be bothered to say hello.

ෆ

Or look up from their phone when I greet them in a friendly way.

ෆ

No thanks.

SOMETIMES

WHEN I AM TRYING TO GET THROUGH A FLIGHT

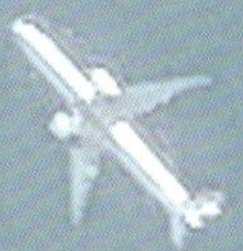

I really don't like flying.

I buy a bunch of gossipy magazines and dark chocolate
in an effort to totally distract myself through the trip.
That's just how I feel trying to go through a stressful time.
Life lately has been feeling like one long stay in the emergency room.
Peace and tranquility aren't as available as earning money sometimes.
Contentment should just come easily to us,
as wealth should be considered as peace and happiness.
So much time feeling frustrated; no reason unless we make it so

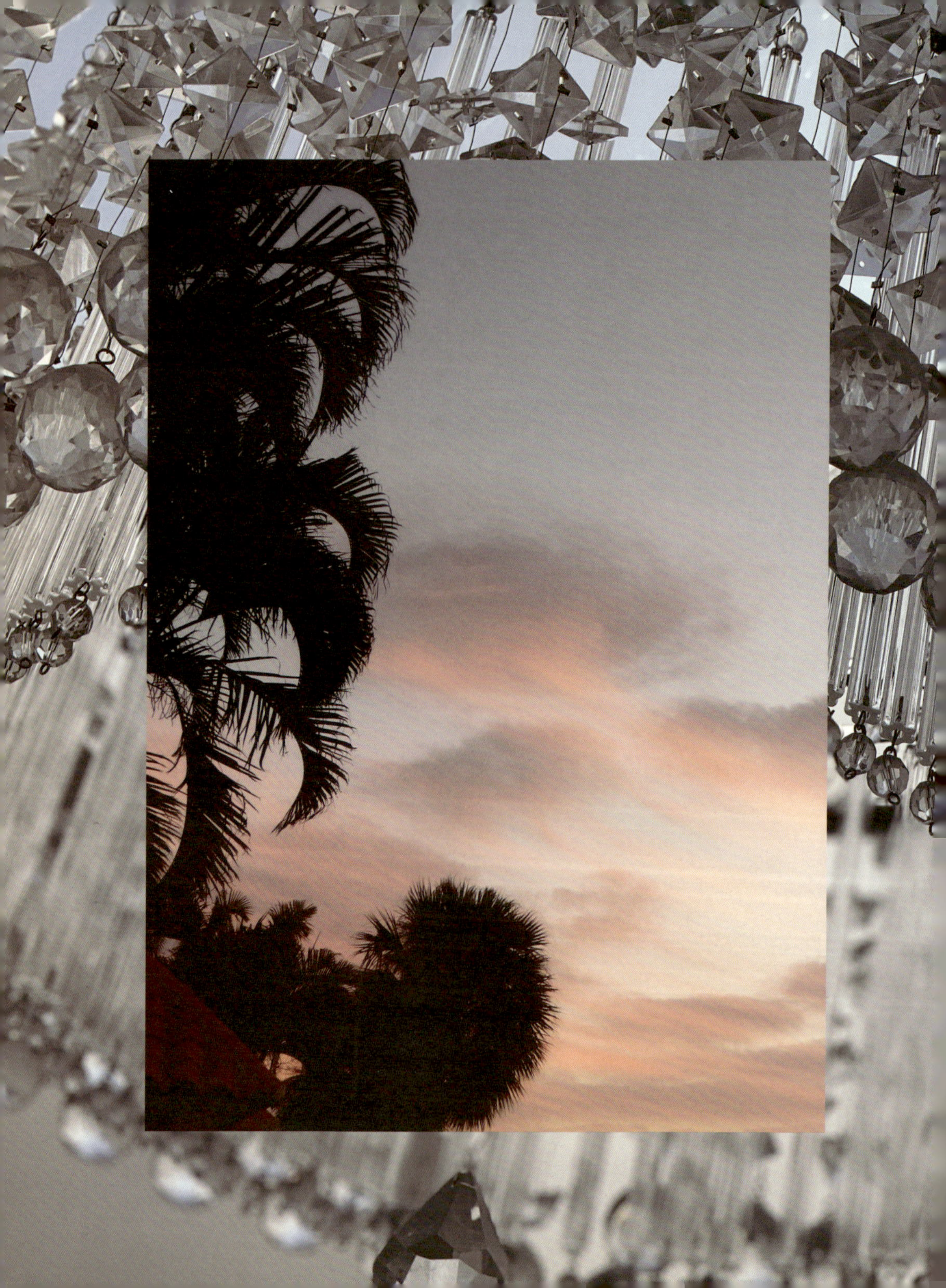

HIGH LIFE, COMMERCIAL INTERVAL

Five Days at the Beverly Hills Hotel

True Story: On Virgin Air, on route to the hotel, I sat beside an incredibly sensitive, blond, stringy-haired Viking, who found it excruciating to even reach into his pocket to get out his credit card to buy a film, because it might disrupt his Universe, it appeared. Across from me, a young actress/dancer with sunglasses, hat, and an aura of having been much photographed.

On arrival at the hotel, given a tour of the gorgeous suite of a room (an upgrade) by my new best friend, the front desk manager, I tipped him incredibly well. He so understood me, and I could be funny around him. That lasted all of fifteen minutes.

Dressed in what I considered to be a Beverley Hills outfit—cashmere sweater with some ostrich-ey feathers on the shoulder and tight blue jeans, with cool jewelry and high heels—I pondered how much effort and money people put into their appearances, often to be just looked beyond and ignored. Although sometimes it does pay off.

What are we looking for and spending a lifetime selling? Acknowledgment from strangers, for validity for our existence? And the extent people especially go to, here in Beverly Hills.

Odd assortment of people at the dinner table. Tom Cruise bodyguard, into anti-aging and exercise, from France. Trustfund ex-party boy, still living in his mind at Studio 54, buying Cristal champagne for the table. Italian mid-level designer with a nice smile. Young Asian, smart hedge fund guy; nervous. Military-looking guy with a baseball cap, who spends the evening texting.

They all invite me for a drink, and I do succumb to a taste of Cristal, although I don't really drink.

Bodyguard tells me I look like a young Rosanna Arquette in *After Hours.* (I don't. Must not be a good night. And unlike most LA girls, I'm wearing my glasses.)

Girls come and go, and the Asian guy is fixated on a famous hedge fund guy at the next table, who is sitting with his bodyguard and is worth billions and looks like Greek Mafia, in a low-cut V-neck sweater and bare chest.

I become curious, too, as he seems more accomplished than this crowd that I have fallen in with temporarily. He does not make eye contact. Must be my glasses . . . or he's not into Rosanna Arquette.

We find out about a book signing in the other room and all wander in to receive very high-end goody bags, with a book and products. I speak with Dr. Nicholas Perricone about telomeres, to live a long life, as he has just spoken about anti-aging.

He is skeptical and has a deep suntan.
He gives me his email address, as we are both in Florida.
And I take photos of the bodyguard with the doctor on his iPhone, as he apparently eats strawberries every day and so is into health, too.

The party guy is busy trying to get goody bags for two girls he met in the bar.

In the lobby, I see a famous writer that I know from New York, who is intensely speaking with two guys. He appears not to notice me, as I wait for a break in their conversation to say hello.

New York fashionably can be just so much more dismissive and de rigueur, unless, of course, you're perceived as being an aristocrat, wealthy, or having star power. Hello, New York.

Good night, Beverly Hills.

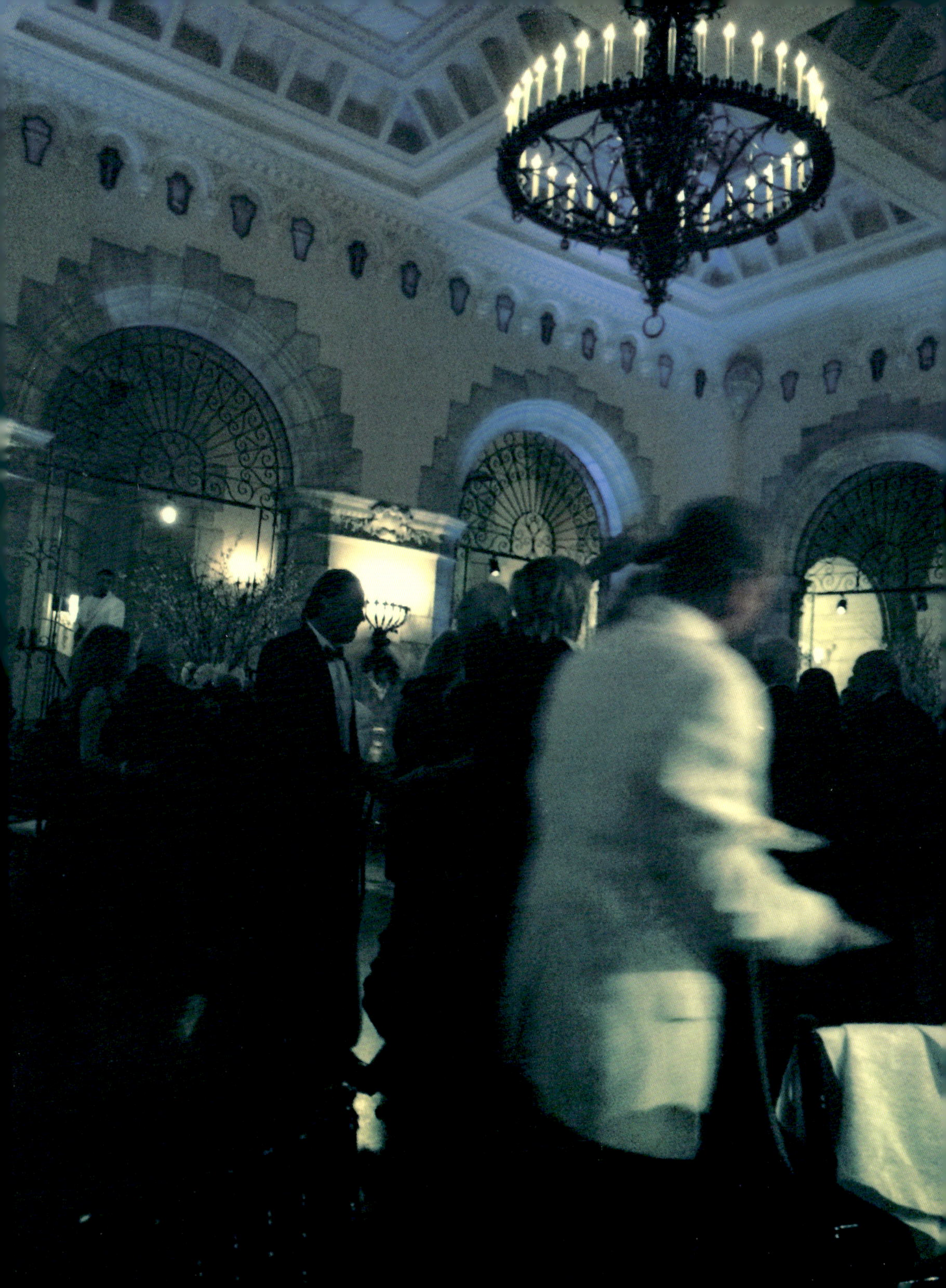

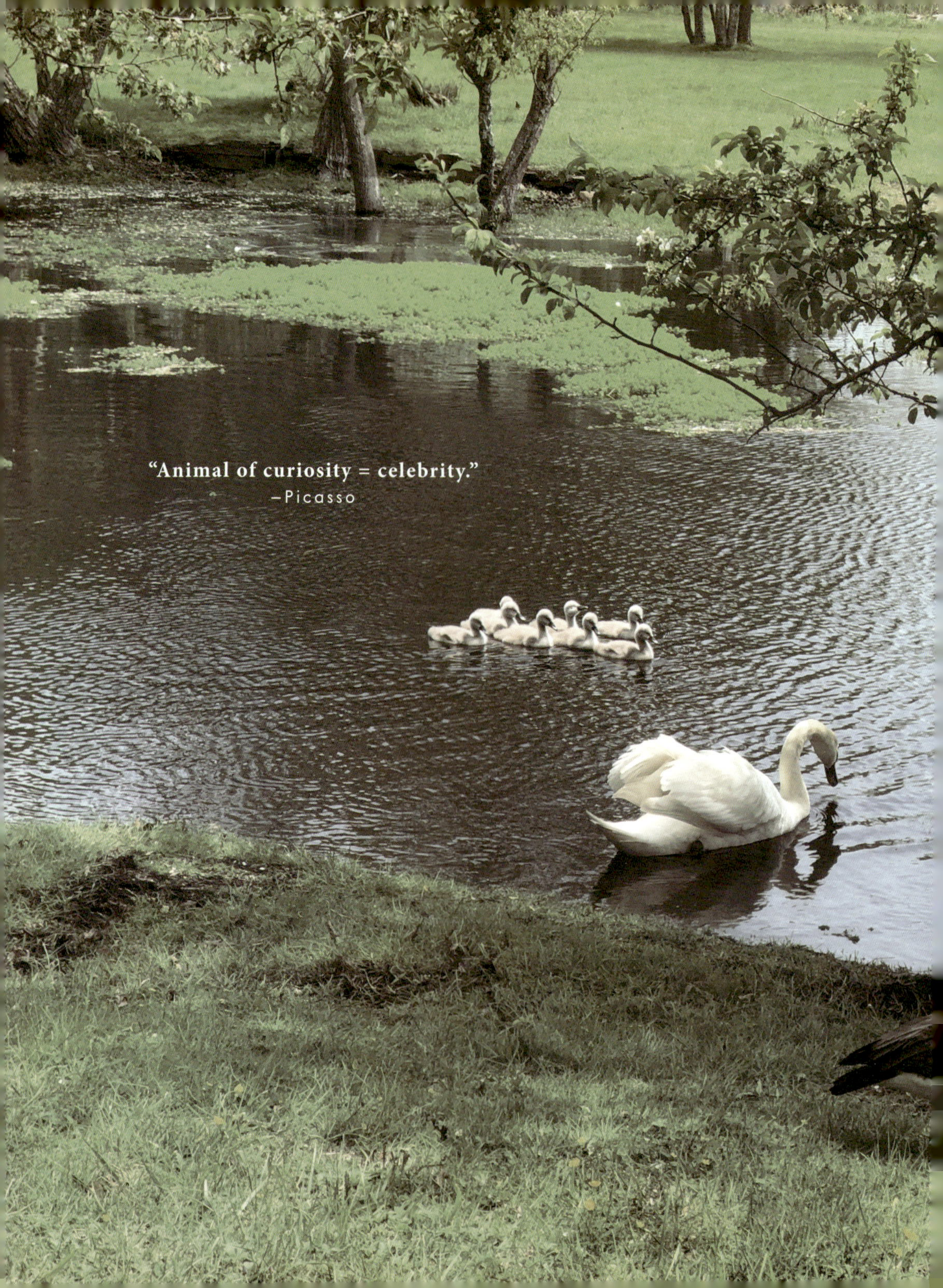
"Animal of curiosity = celebrity."
–Picasso

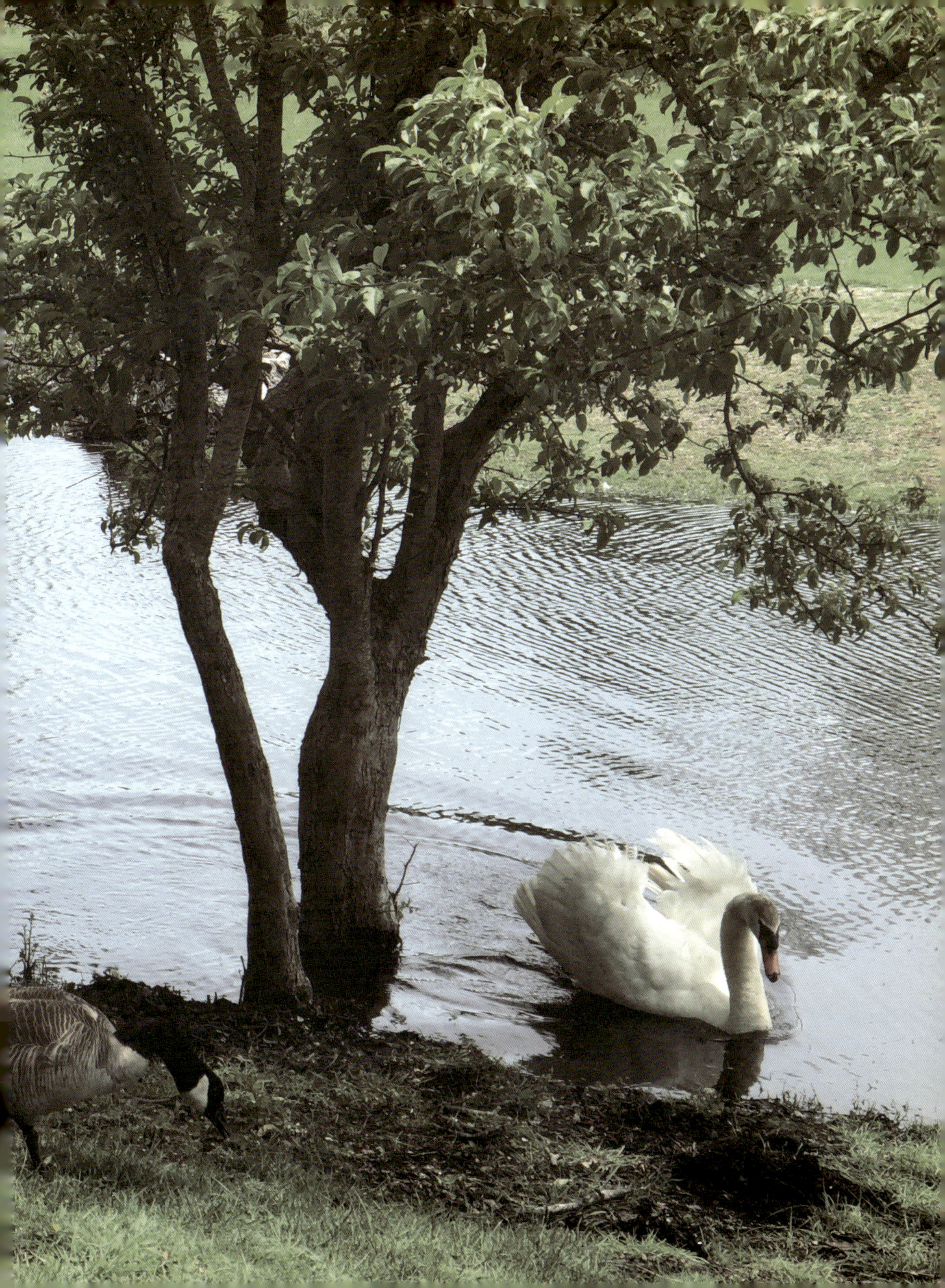

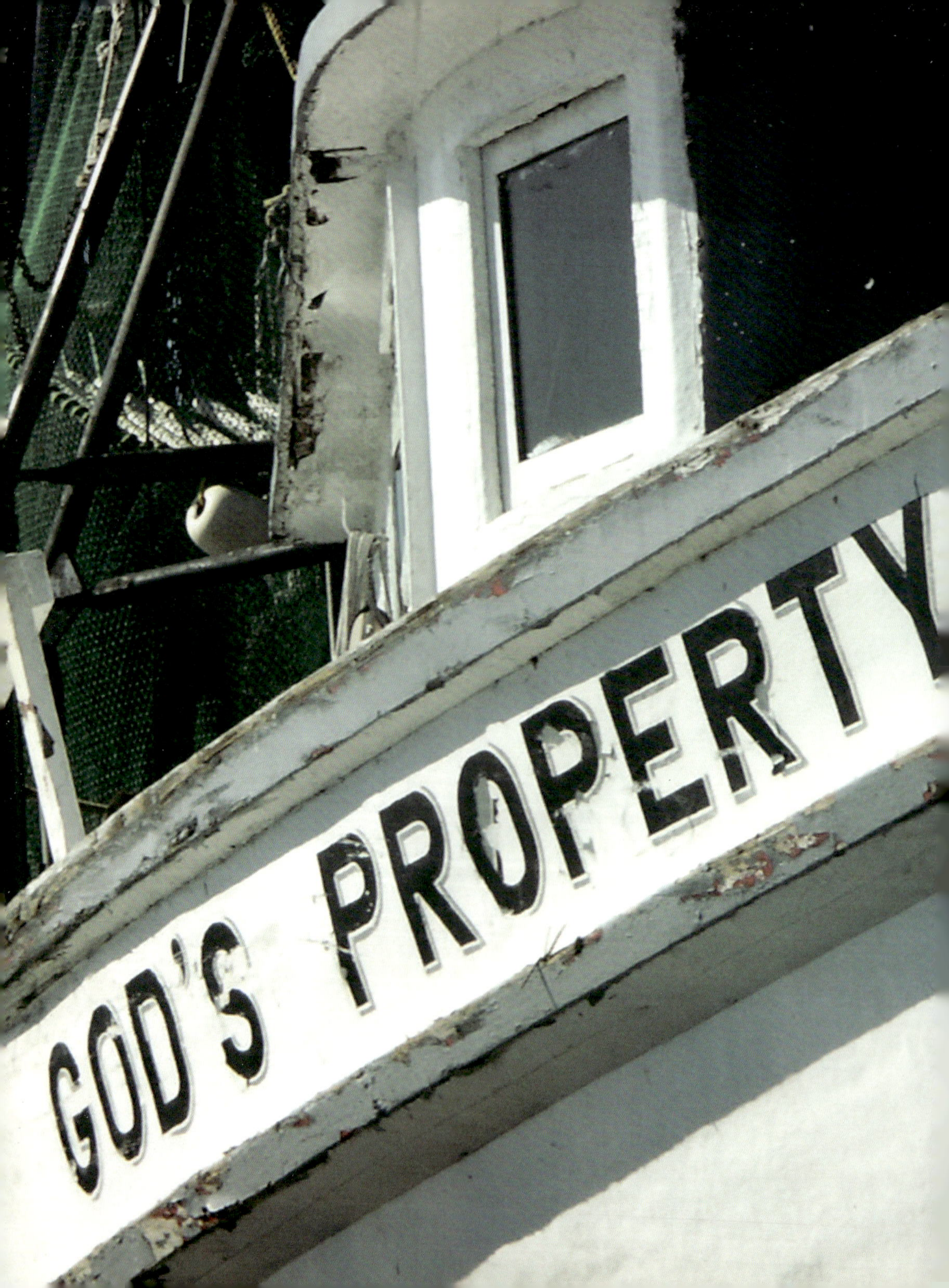
GOD'S PROPERTY

Animals are content

Animals live in harmony with nature
and so they exist in the vibration of this planet.
That's why animals are so precious—
because they are living life's truth.

Animals are hyper-alert in the present,
but cannot comprehend a bigger world and its laws.
They are fully immersed in that moment.

Although, when an animal is vicious,
it's hard to imagine harmony.
We are all evolving on this planet.
Faster and faster.
All life is created from energy,
and we must respect all aspects of life.

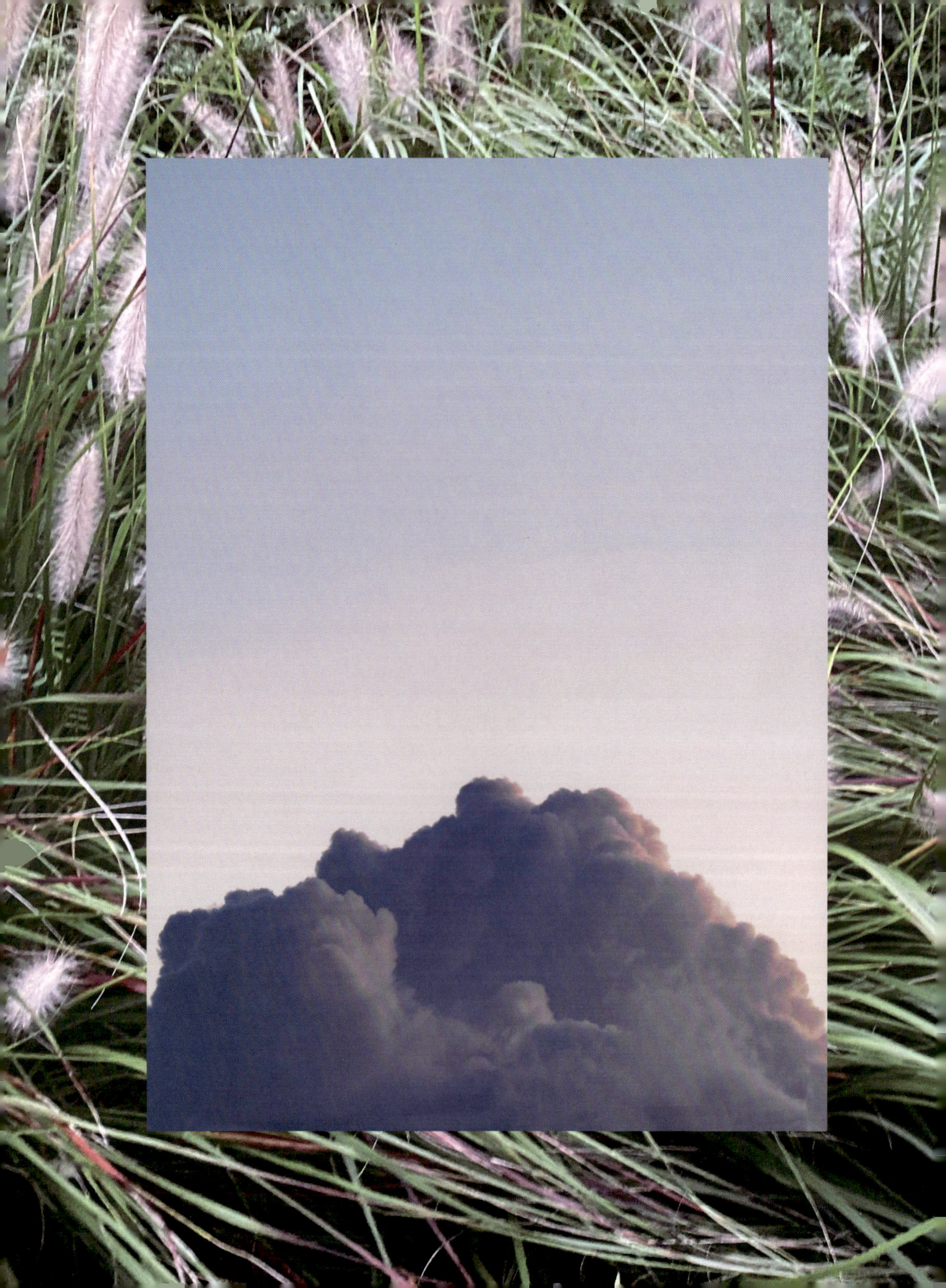

CULTURAL MISUNDERSTANDNGS

Even within individual cultures there can be huge misconceptions.

Because there's no stamp written on someone's forehead that shouts that they're famous or from a wealthy family or are brilliant or worth paying attention to or whatever you're looking for.
You need the ability to see others for who they truly are.

Money can't cure misunderstandings or loneliness. It is possible to find temporary companionship by taking someone out for dinner or drinks. But you can't buy joie de vivre.

When you really communicate from the heart, you're not lonely anymore.
You feel great.
When you feel good, you want to do good.

EVERY DAY SHOWS UP

That's the way of Fate.

Sometimes it's more exciting to desire something than to acquire it.

Because most economies are not heart-based.
They're established on endless excessive success.

But truly:

Things only come to you if they're yours.

So which is worth more?

Paper money or paper with words of wisdom?

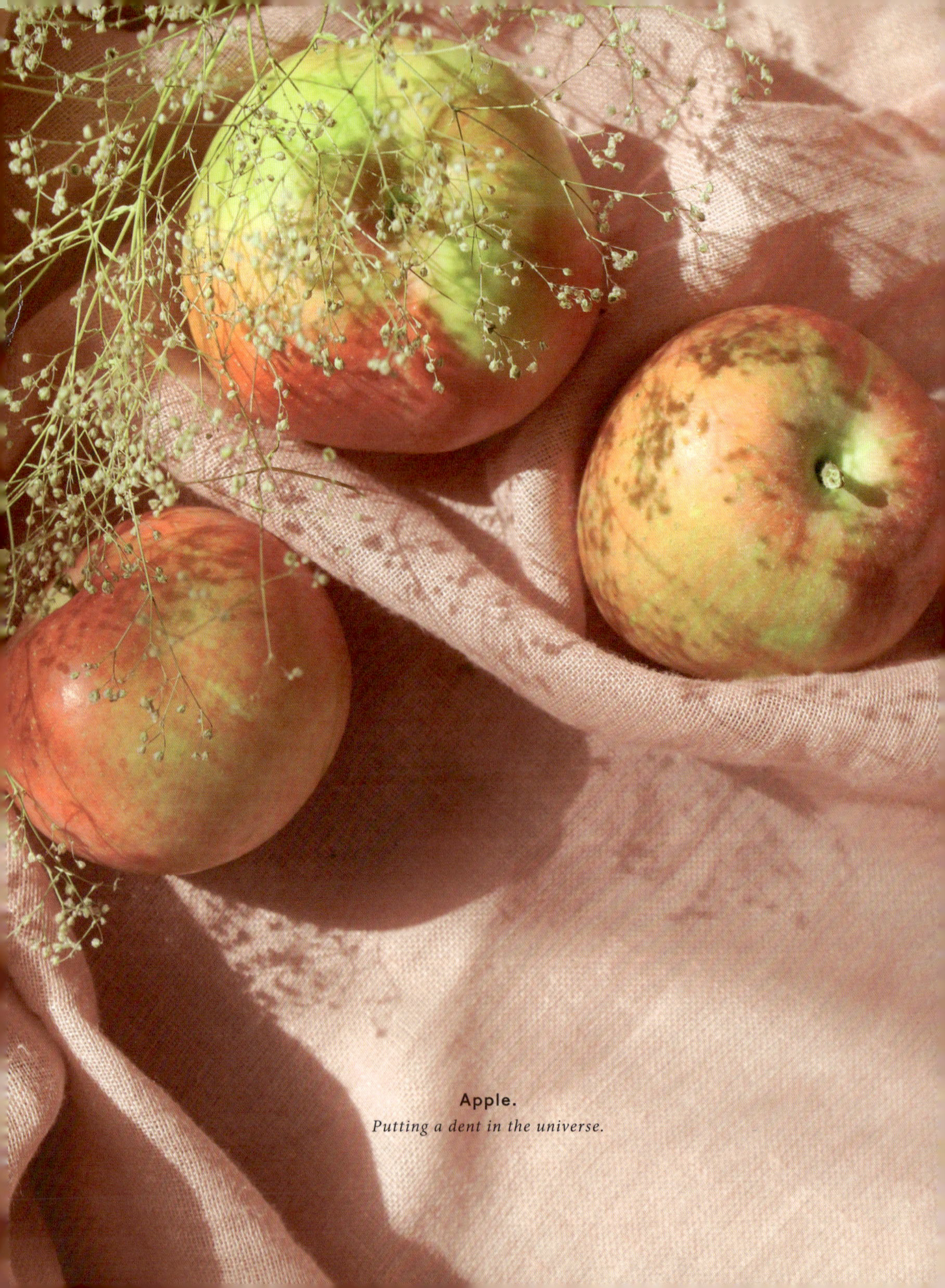

Apple.

Putting a dent in the universe.

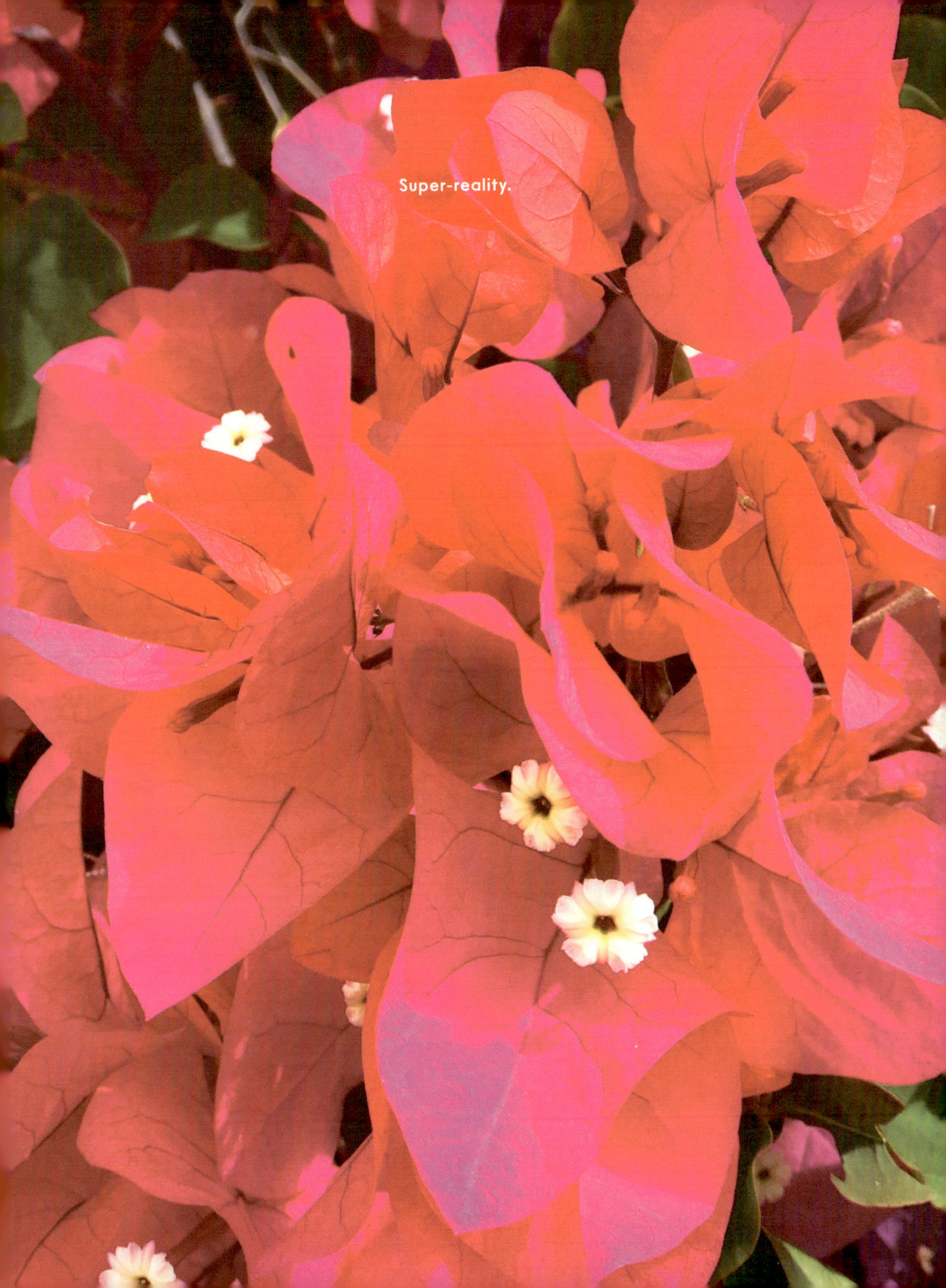
Super-reality.

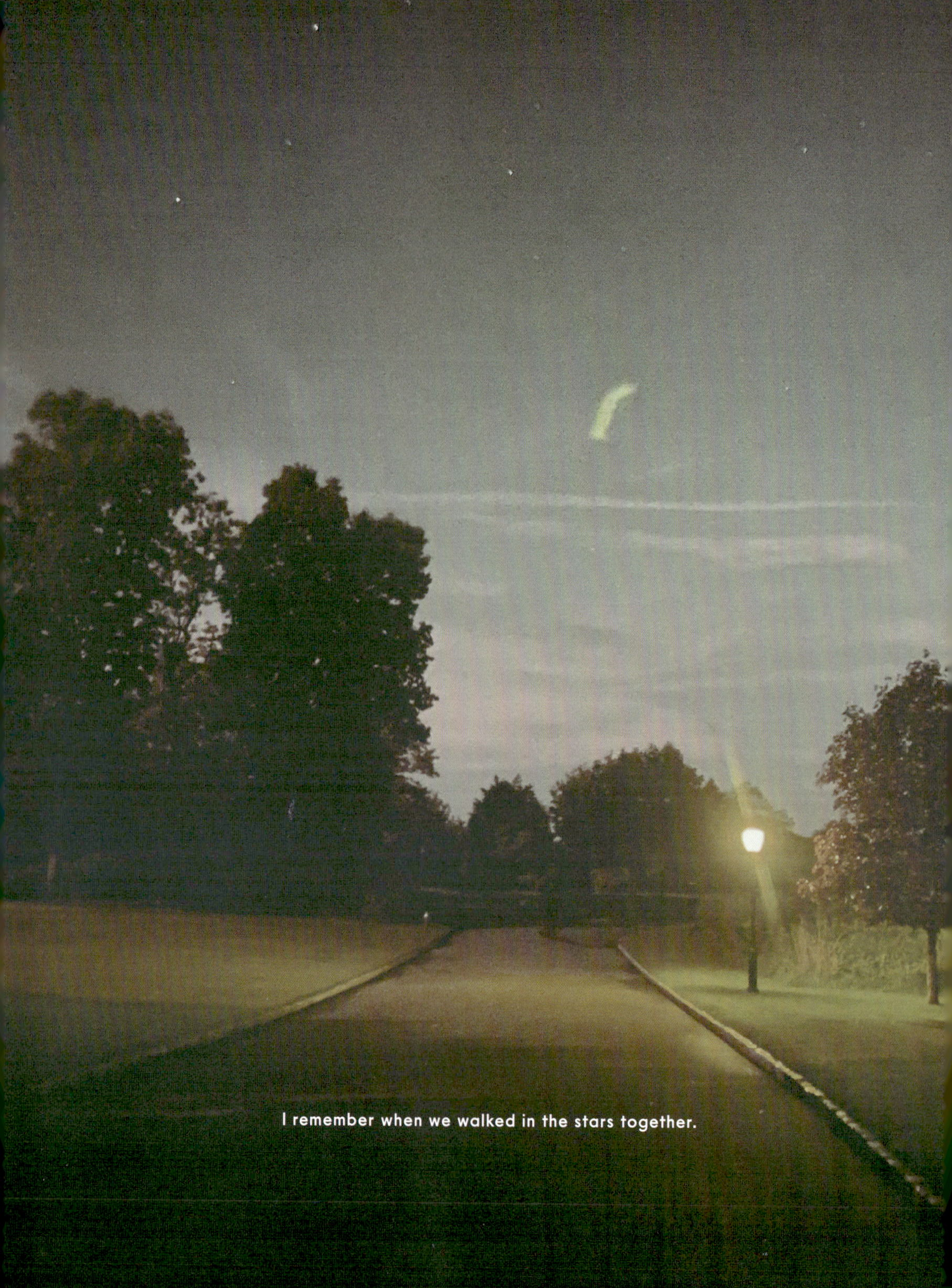
I remember when we walked in the stars together.

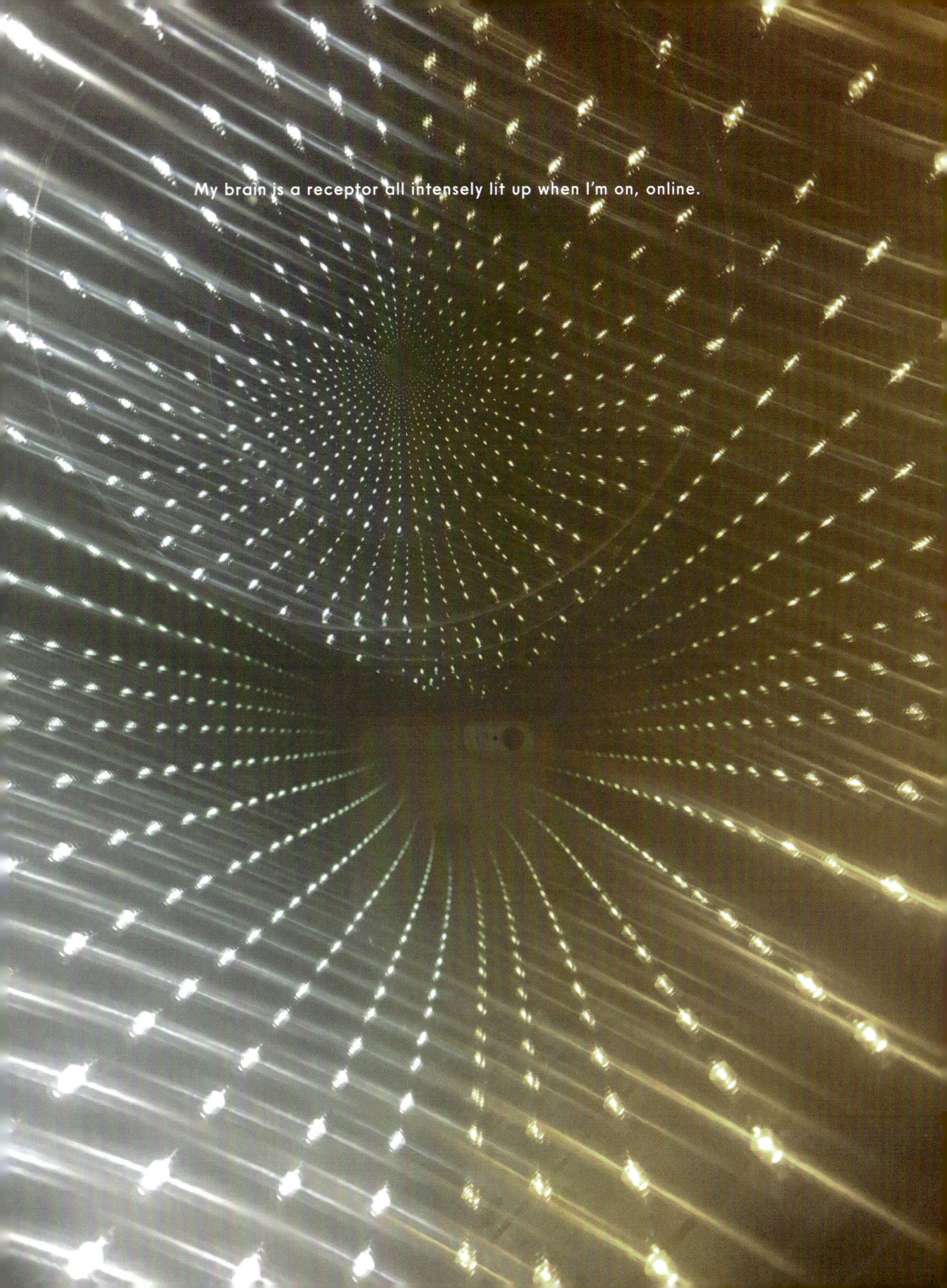
My brain is a receptor all intensely lit up when I'm on, online.

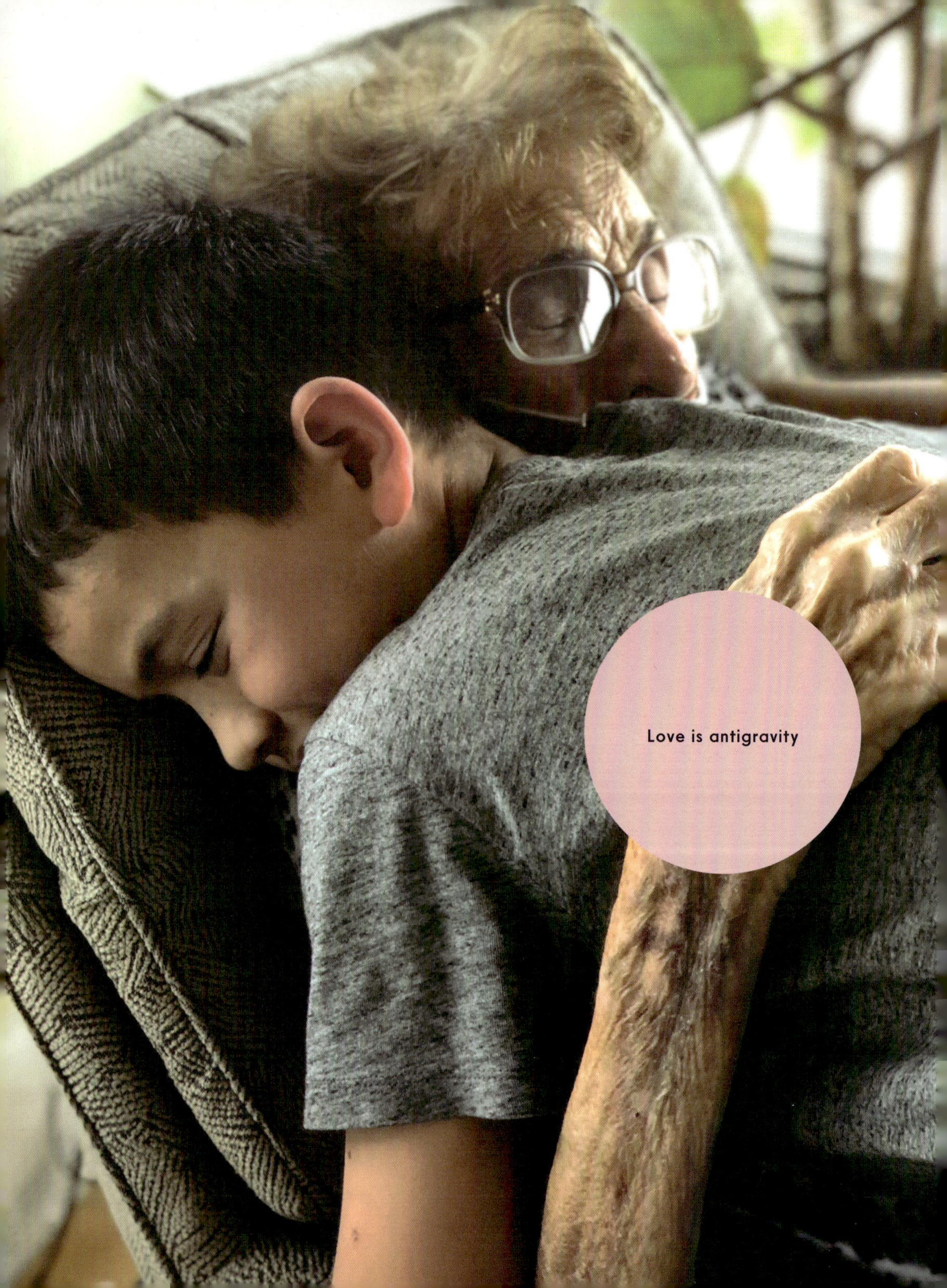
Love is antigravity

I'm imagining all the people on the planet—everyone, with all their small aches, huge pains, and unparalleled sadness, realizing the possibility of regret, in their last moments of life.

All those people who might be hurting or feeling for others' difficulties—all those people, which might include everyone on this planet.

Everyone going on strike, like a union might, if the conditions were not up to fair standards.

The whole population of the Earth going on strike, saying "ENOUGH!"
"We've had enough!"
"No more!"

I guess not much would happen, if we went on strike, because to whom would we protest?

If we put that much energy, focus, and belief into stopping all the crazy challenges that affect us . . . might they resolve?

I can imagine an end to all pain and sadness, and yet I wonder if we'll ever let it go.

Then we can live on this planet together in simultaneous loving radiance and balance.

Caring about our healthy selves and all those around us, near and far—in other words, living in warmth.

THIS IS MY MONEY

Love on a summer's day. What's better than that?

✹

Swans, red cardinals, ducks, yellow finches, hummingbirds, and lilacs.

✹

Your beautiful dog running,

your beautiful children running,

a beach,

a meadow,

beautiful shade trees,

gentle sounds,

gentle light.

A vivacious and vibrant afternoon.

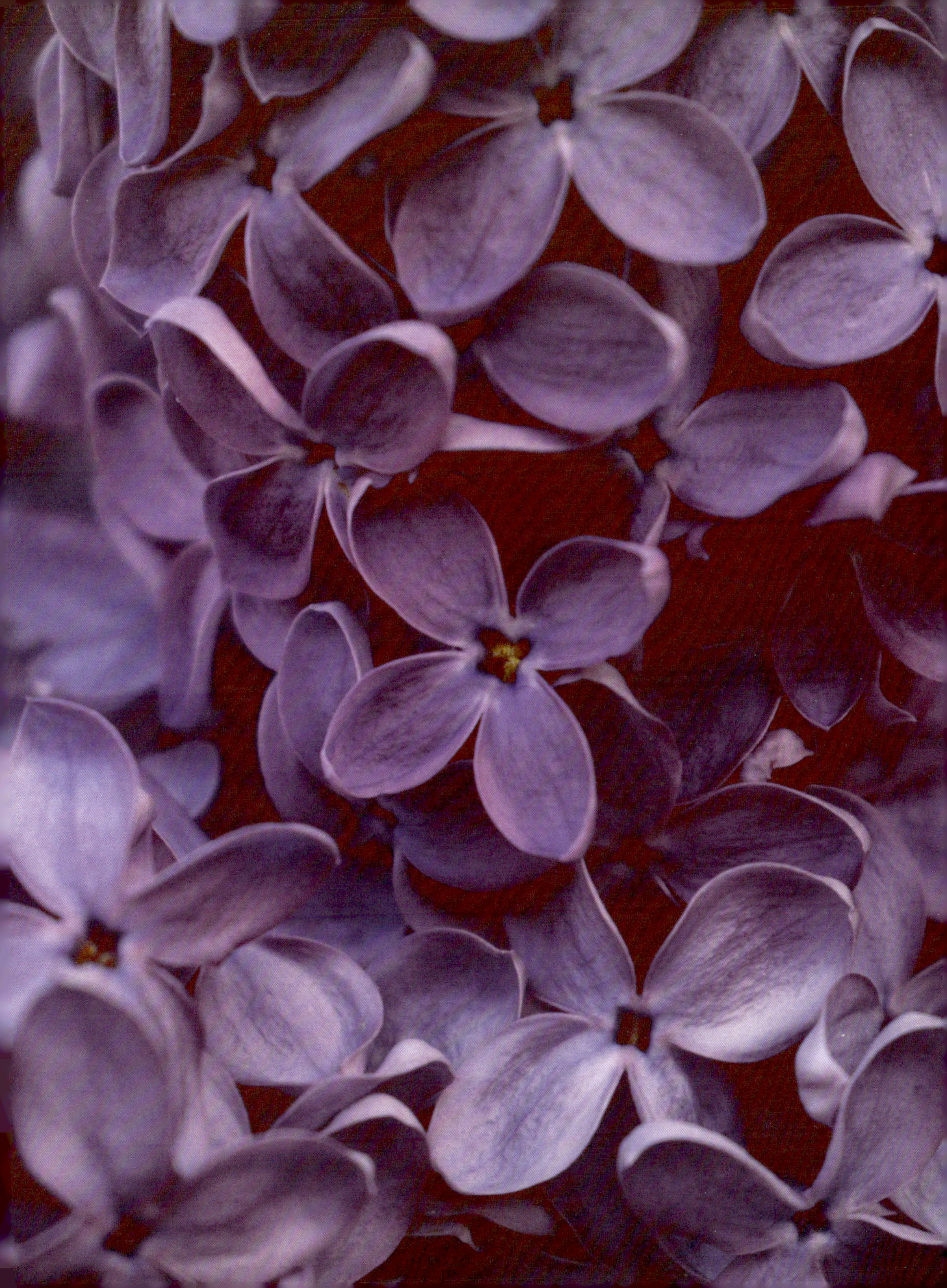

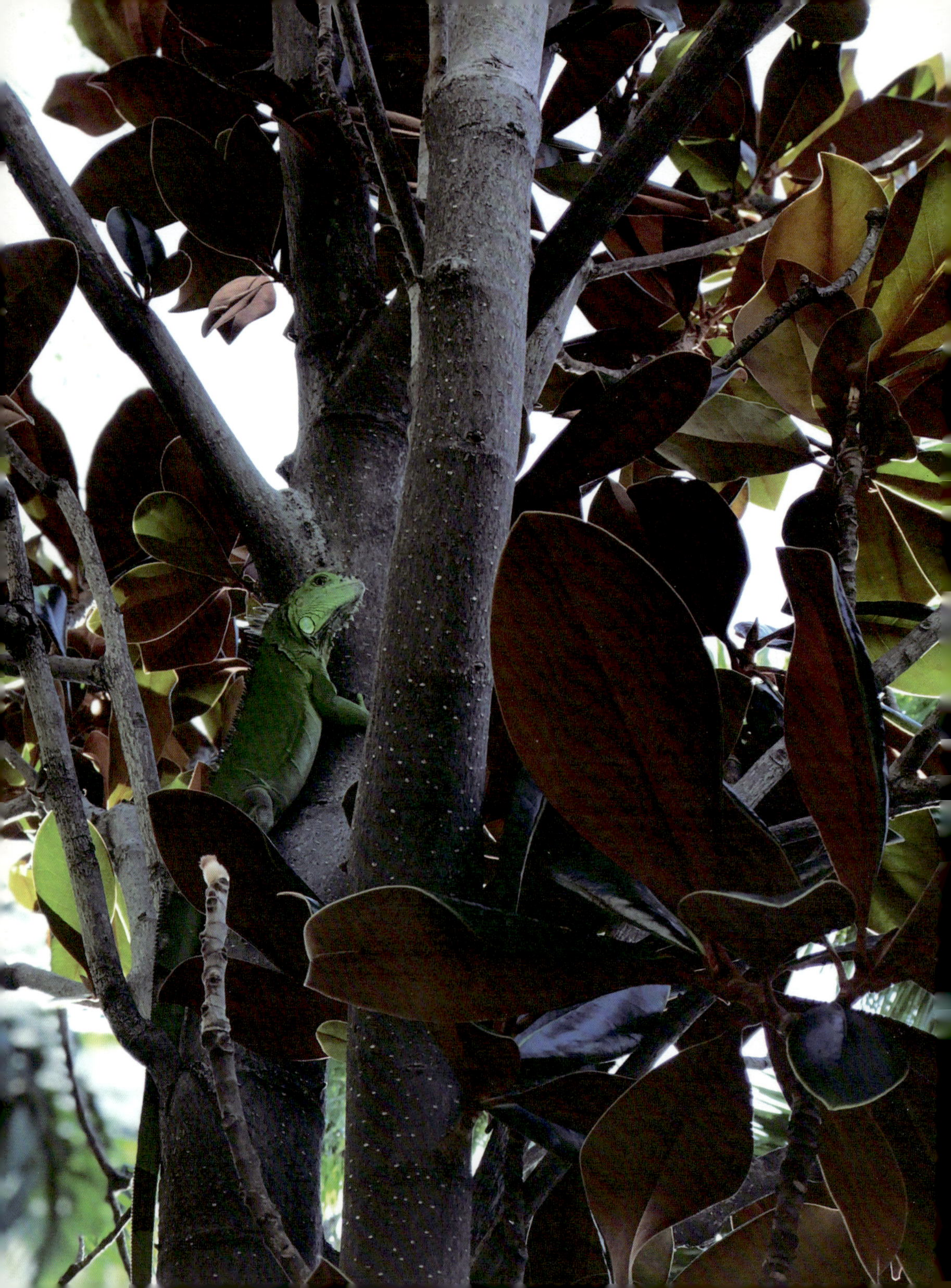

MY BIRTHDAY VISITORS

Two great blue herons on the ocean.

One emerald lizard on a tree, in a courtyard behind me.

Three monarch butterflies in our garden.

A dove in the same garden as above.

An egret flew right over our courtyard.

Muchos geckos.

All in the days leading up to my birthday.

I'm still lucky enough to be sitting by the water.

I'm watching the warm breeze blowing through the bull rushes and the seriously quacking ducks, flying just above and in front of me. The swans gliding about, on the gentle rhythmic ripples.

And now more ducks, the air alive with the universal energy of life.

And I'm trying to be in the present moment of now.

But I can't help thinking, just how very lucky, how very lucky I am.

That I am not sitting in some lonely room, some crowded bus, some constrained space of an airplane, or even in a prison cell.
How I can breathe the clear air, turning into the clear breeze. And hang out with the animals.

And be alive in this time on this earth.

And look up at this sky and know all is well here at this moment.

I can't think of anything that I would rather experience than this.
Sitting on my rickety green chair, which my husband sweetly painted for me.

Even appreciating that the owner of the jet ski, which is parked somewhere too near to me, is not around and all is quiet.
I am not disrupted now, just for his or her satisfaction.

Now sitting here, I have to muse on the possibility and even probability of a good life.
With good food, and good moments, and a deep sense of joy of life surrounding me.

I am lucky beyond words, to find this awareness

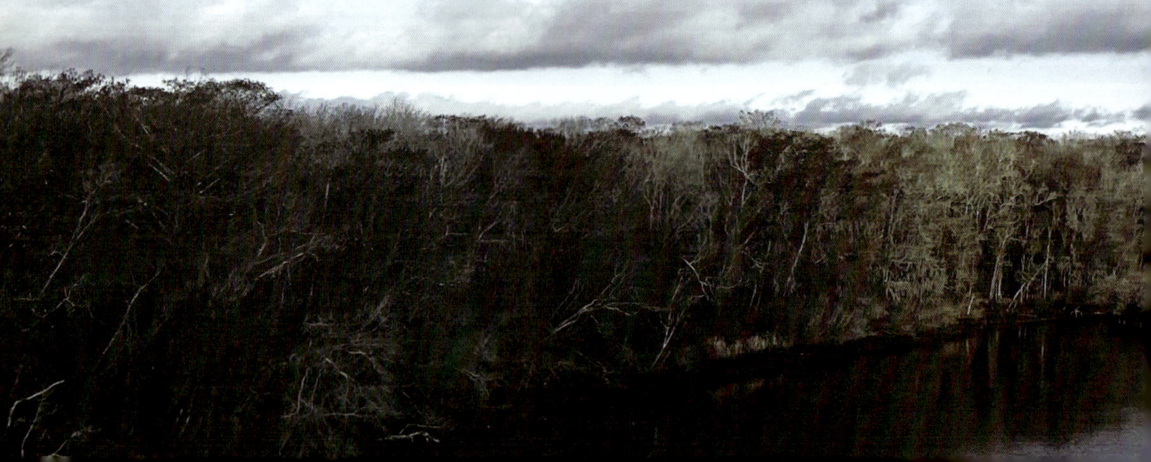

of the beauty of this world that we all share.

And to be able to tap into and attract the love that surrounds me.

And to know that in the quiet, there is a great sense of peace.

Today is a very special day, because it is a day that I have seized the moment for writing.
I have managed to find a hidden spot, without too much noise to concentrate.
And I can try to convey my thoughts to just tell you all—Hey! What we are often crazy about is a myth, not based on anything real.

Buying something fancy, looking a certain way, having a big house—just looks really unimportant to someone whose eyes are opened to the subtleties of life.
It's like waving a red flag in front of a bull. If you're not a bull, who needs a red flag?

Sharing with you how much love I have for this very special moment that will never repeat itself exactly.

How precious this is; every sound, every feeling, every breeze, every cloud, every bird, every tree, every friend, every love, every delicious taste of fruit, the music in the distance, the grass under my feet, the dirt under my feet, the sidewalk carrying so many lives, all sharing this extraordinary experience of life on this planet, knowing what we have all learned, so silly not to live what we truly know: that happiness feels good, it's easy to choose to be happy, and that choice is free and direct.

And it's right here, now.

So why waste life, very precious time, yearning for things that can never be more than things? A fancy house, car, jewelry, never will have the power to make you feel better or happier if they

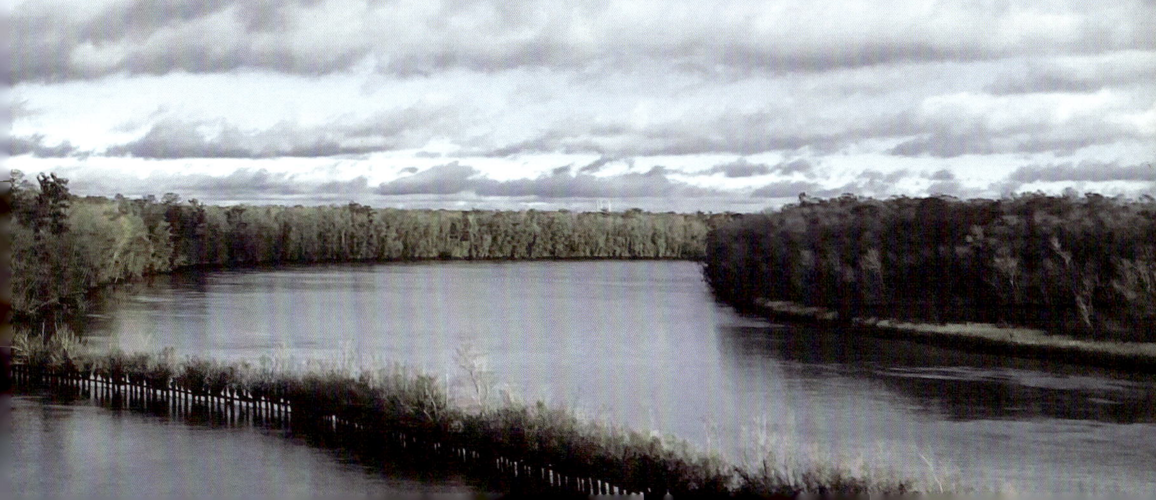

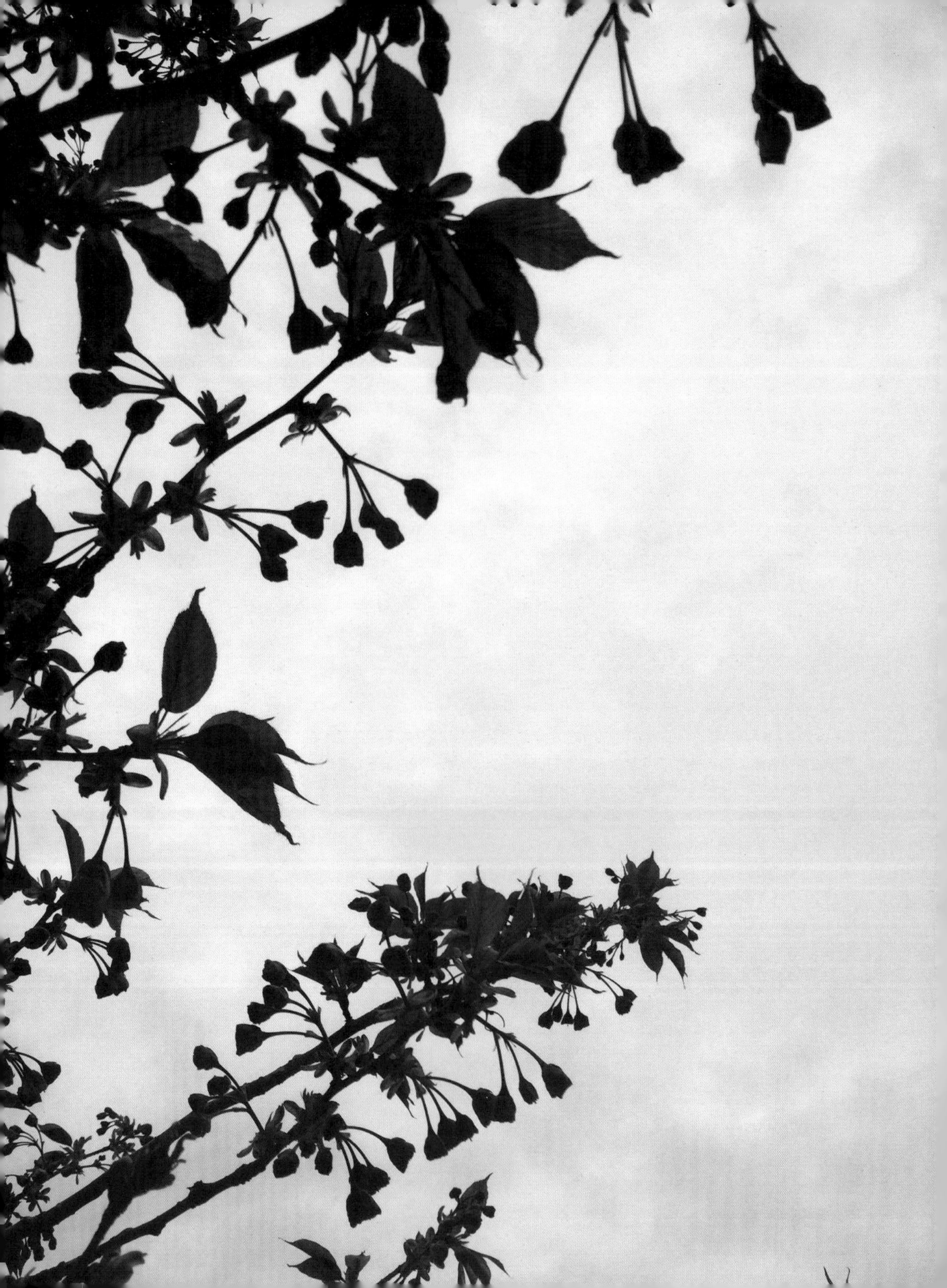

are empty—they are just in the realm of things.

And as soon as you acquire them, right away you know that the important element of possessions is to remember the circumstances of when you bought it, the memories attached. The crucial part is to not waste all that precious time, precious life, yearning for things that are just an illusion, have not the power to make you truly happy.

For me, sitting on this rickety chair can do that.

Breathe in the beautiful day, and if you're lucky enough to have a sunny day, that's a bonus.

Because when the desire for all these myths falls away, so does their power.

And so is born a new time of complete happiness just because.

No suffering to acquire what you can't seem to afford, no sadness in who you're not, just a pure life, without the image of what life could be like.

If only that was real in our experience. Because that reality is in the beauty of the moment.

Nothing you can ever buy will bring you that kind of vibrancy.

If I could have a Cartier watch or today, I'll take today.

Because no possession, pretty as it might be, will ever bring me the dynamic magic of this day, breathed deeply, and lived fully into my very cells.

The Grand Illusion: That which is not.

You choose.

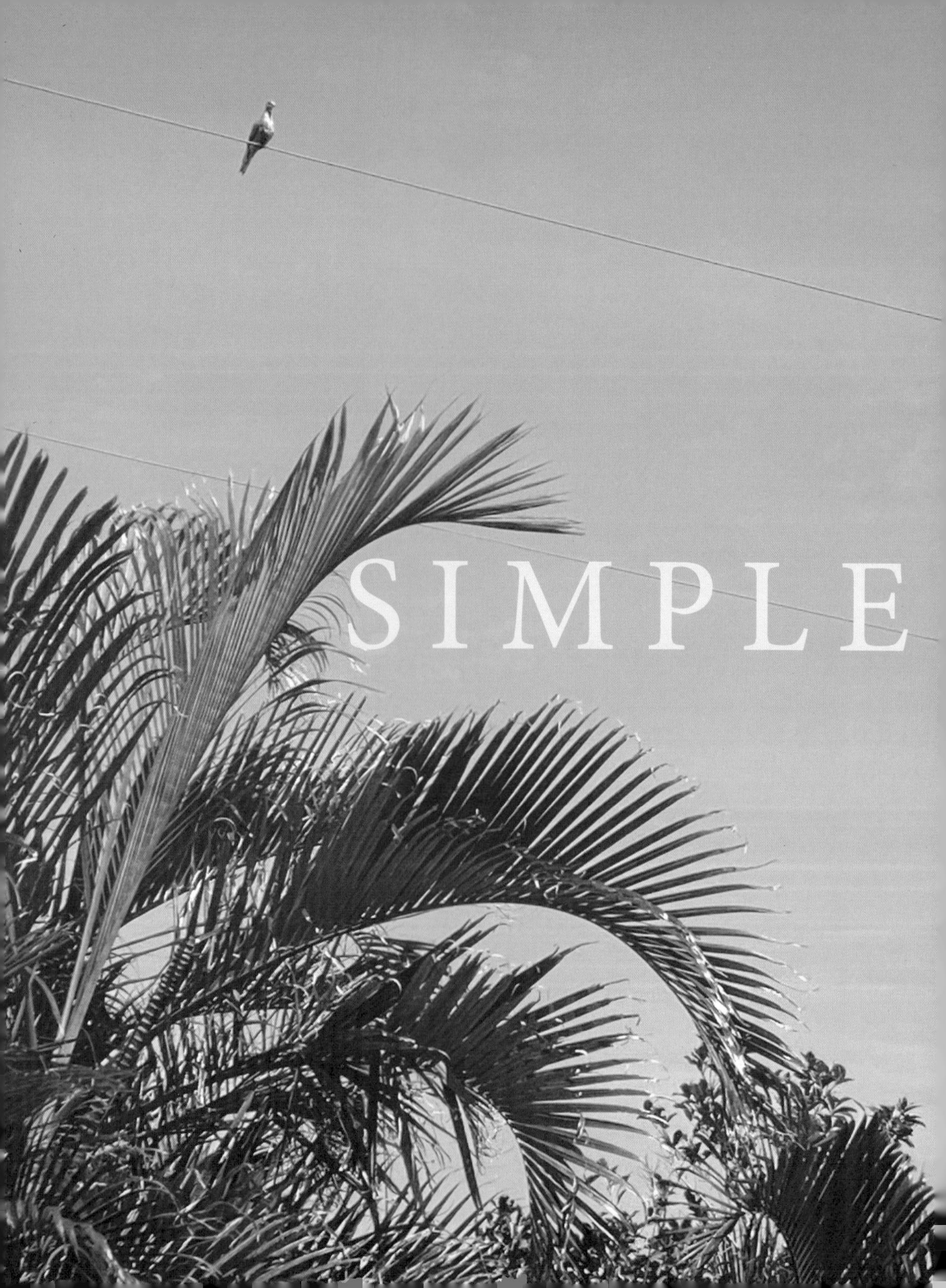
SIMPLE

TRUTH

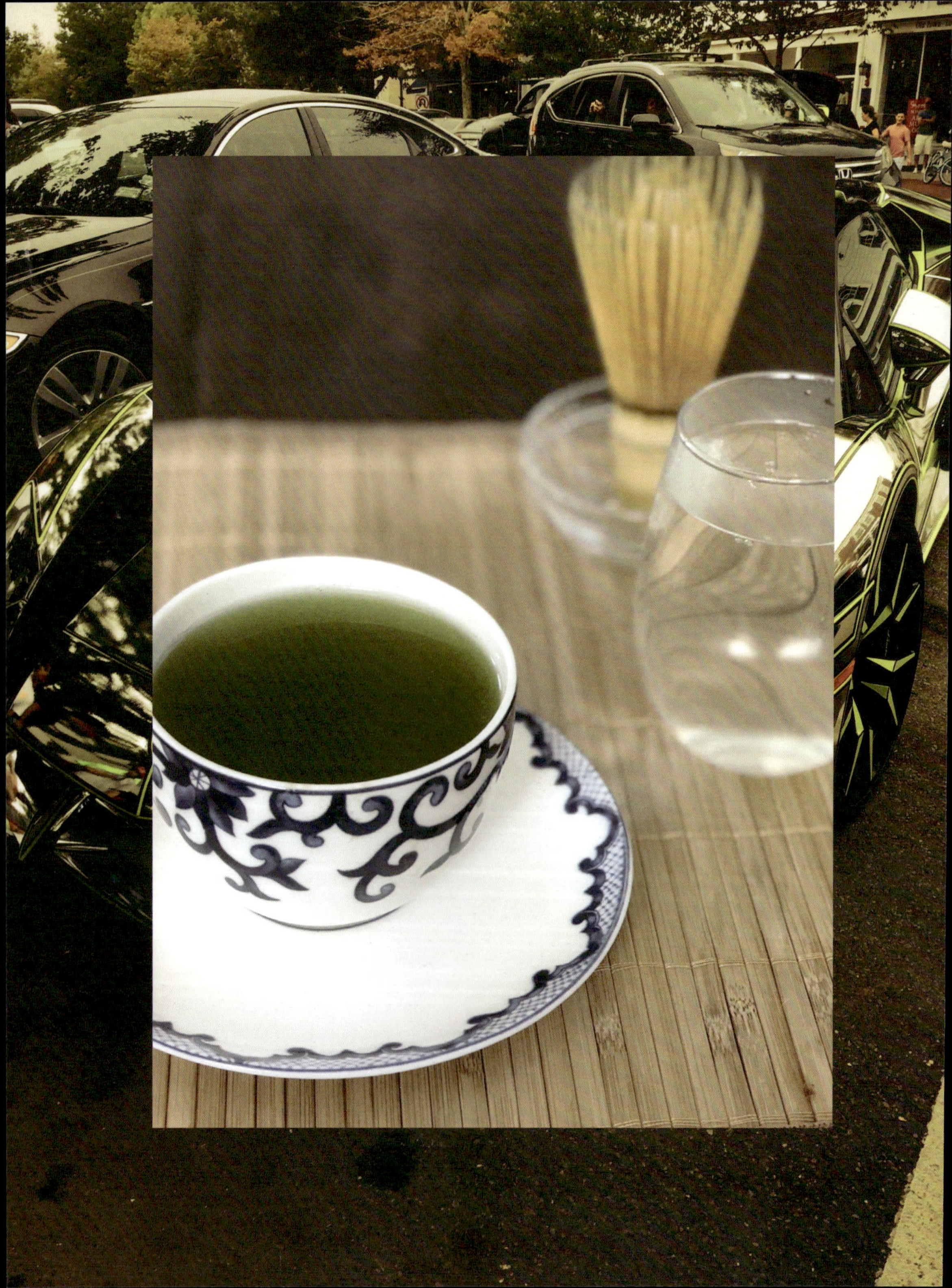

BENEFITS

Car or boat? Moving around.

Boyfriend/girlfriend/partner? Seduction, sexuality, connection.

Husband/wife/spouse? Companionship, sexuality, growing.

Wedding ring? Sharing a life.

House? Warmth and shelter.

Tent? Close to nature.

Hammock? Gaze at the sky.

Beach chair? Gaze at the ocean.

Water bottle? To carry your water.

Water? Quench your thirst.

Cup of tea? Warmth

Coconut? Hungry on a beach.

Truffles? Delectable.

Pet? Loving animals.

Towel? If you're wet.

Toothbrush? If you don't have one.

Hat? On a sunny day. . . .On a cold day.

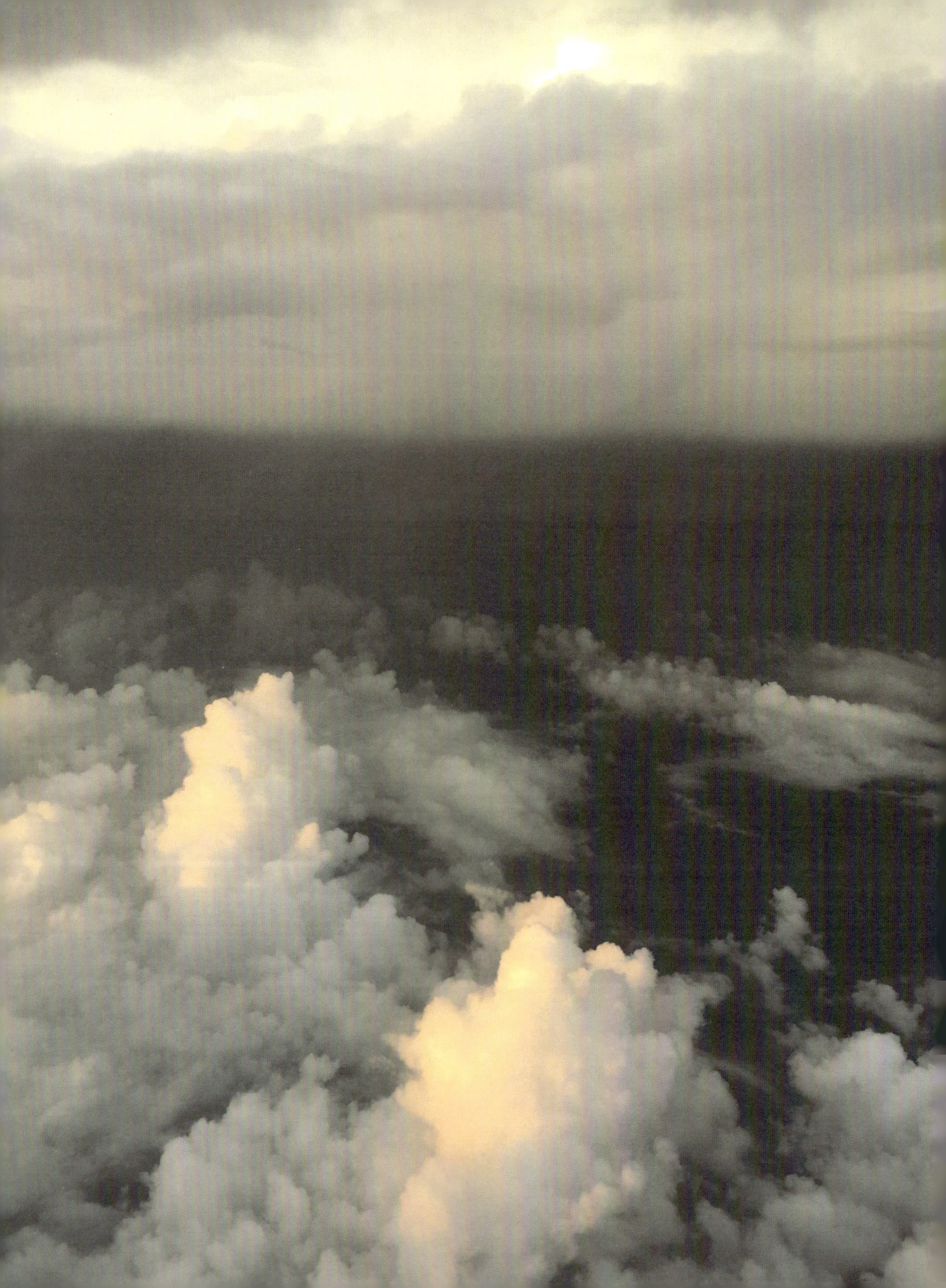

ENERGY SENSITIVE

I'm living in light.
As in, "I'm Living Light."

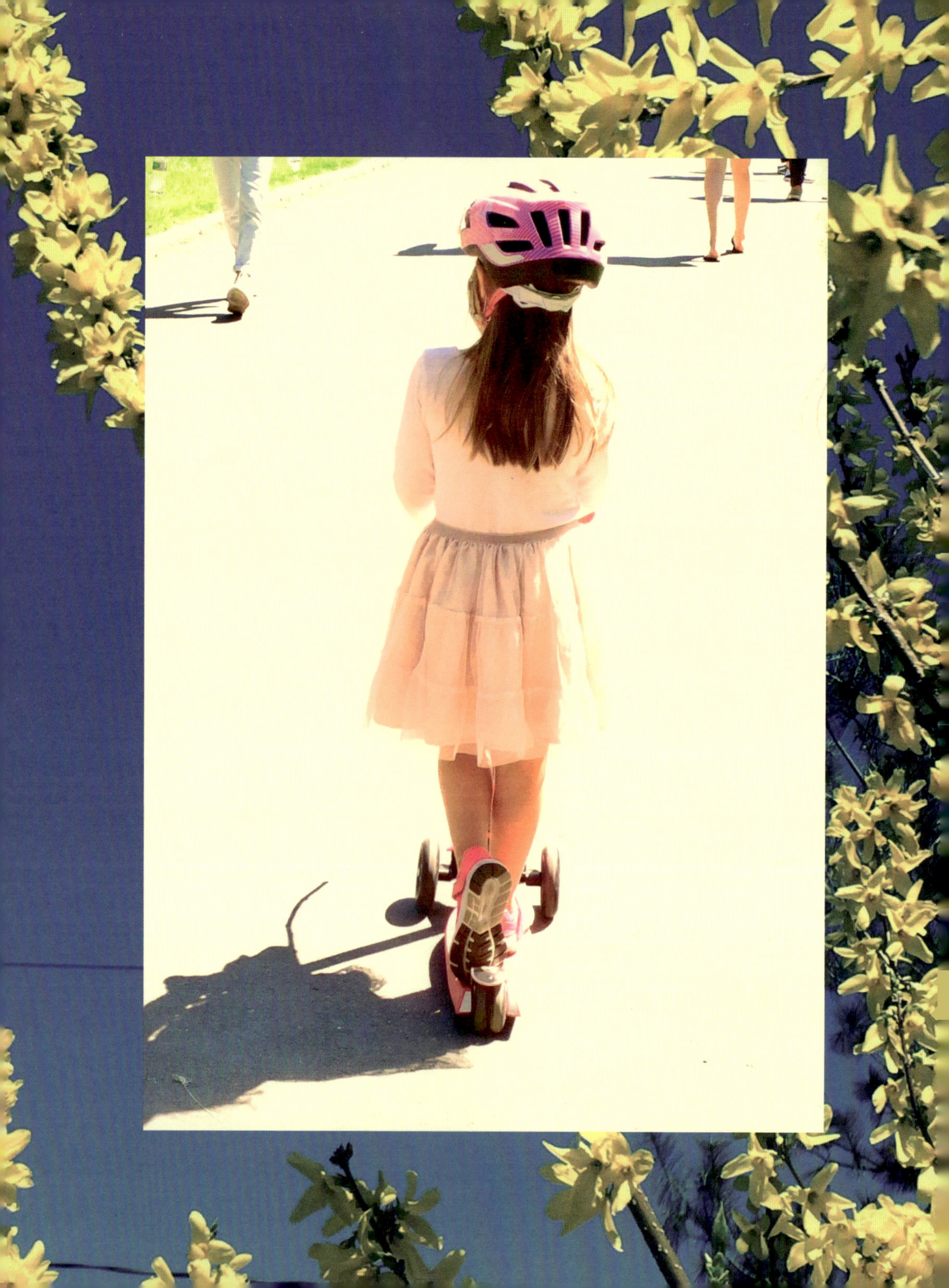

FEELINGS

Sometimes I feel like her wholi-ness, all my
friends and family, needing to be healed.
Lots of effort: Continuously sending out positive
intentions to the planet.
Yet it makes me feel so delighted, wishing
people well.

Not wishing people well is terrible, leaving you
empty and horrible.

Wishing happiness, success, and to the Earth,
peace and health, is marvelous—causing you to
feel absolutely, extravagantly fantastic.

*

With the free wind blowing through your hair,
you're young and you don't care.

*

Aliveness is wide open, yours for the shaping, anything is possible.

*

Experience is coming down through you and surrounding you,
and you're breathing life in and out.

*

Liveliness is everywhere, and in your heart,
you can feel the yearning of the universe for all of life.

*

And when you're no longer young, this all still true.

*

For life is always life, one and the same, for all of us.

*

If you take away all the facades....

*

We could all sit down together, in front of a big, bright, beautiful fire,
over a good meal, and talk about the wonder of it all.

*

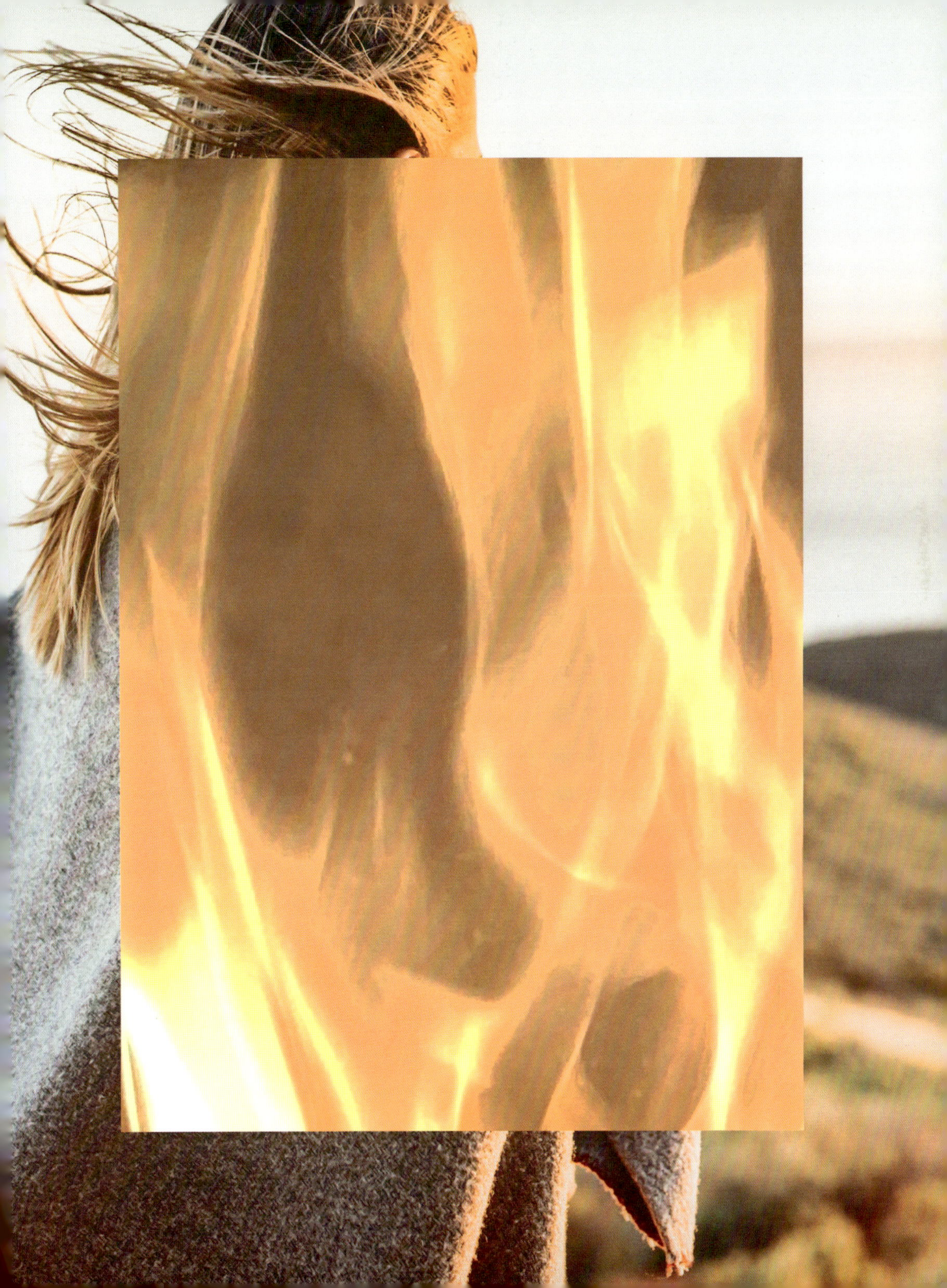

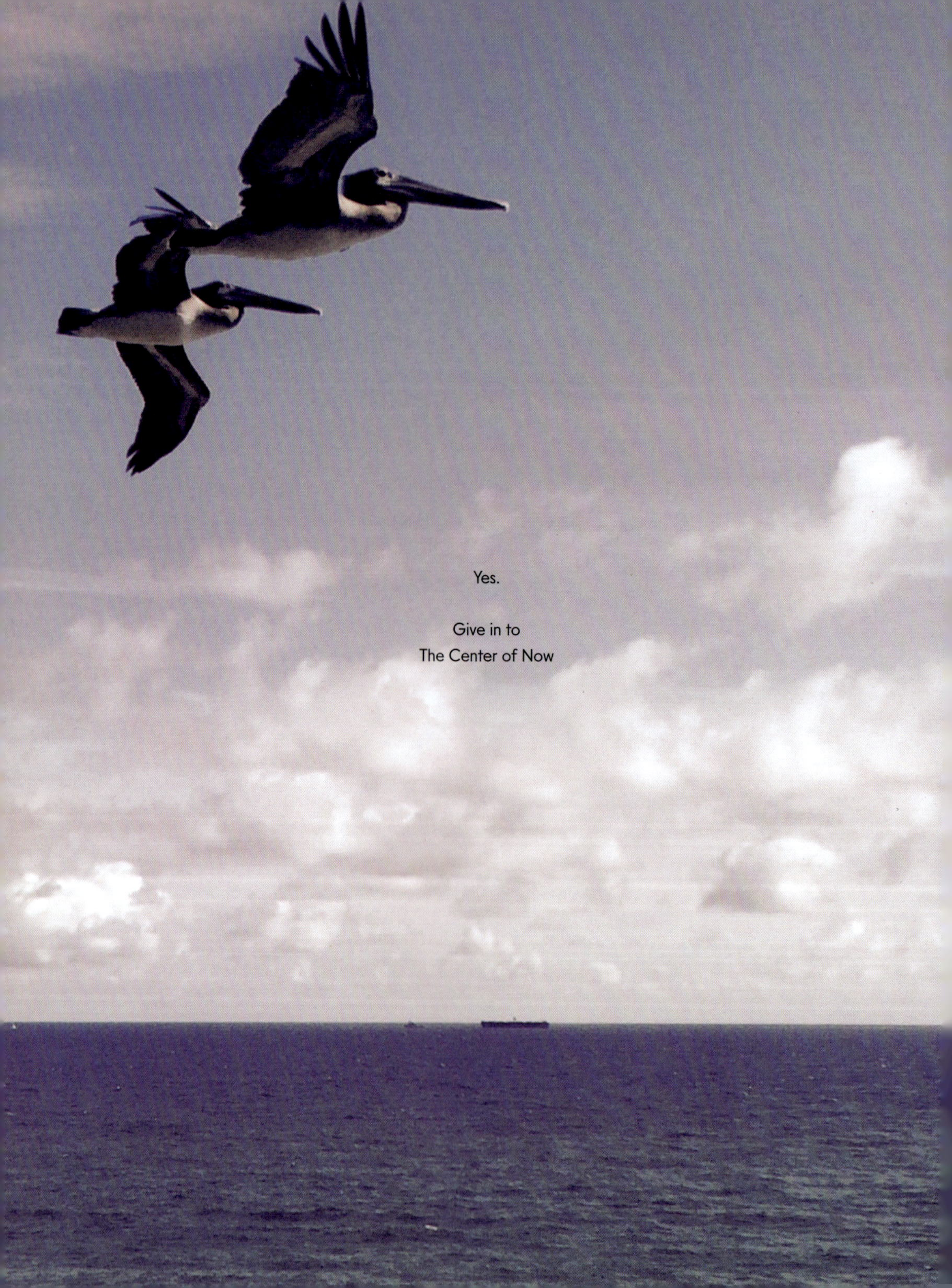
Yes.
Give in to
The Center of Now

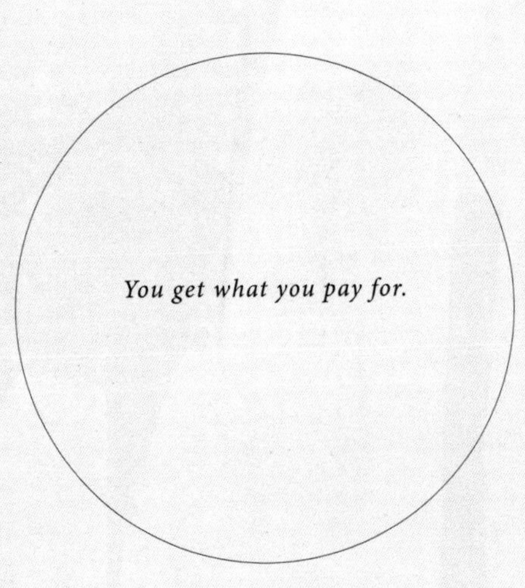
You get what you pay for.

Looking at a person's room,
full of possessions, you have no idea what items
have more value to them than the others.

It's purely subjective.

Everything, when shining an individual light,
is equally precious.

Radiating with its own particular vibration
and energy.

Who is to say which one is more important?

The universe sees all of us equally—
all things and all beings have their
own unique assets to greatness.

The cardinal of happiness just
flew past me—full speed!

I did get a glimpse of him, with his shimmering
red feathers and his fleeting presence.

I can just imagine hanging out with him
for an afternoon by a sparkling lake,
with a light summer rain,
sheltered under a big umbrella.

The sun coming out, and then
a rainbow in the sky; the cardinal on his way
and me feeling pretty happy.

Lucky we had the umbrella,
and so lucky to meet the cardinal.

(And I could have done it
without the umbrella, too!)

These aren't really short stories.
These are places that I've actually been.

Sometimes with Positive People,
sometimes not.

I like to read and see movies.

That means, of course,
having my thoughts managed.

But sometimes I just like to freeform,
lying in the sun.

Someone should invent clear windows
with sunscreen.

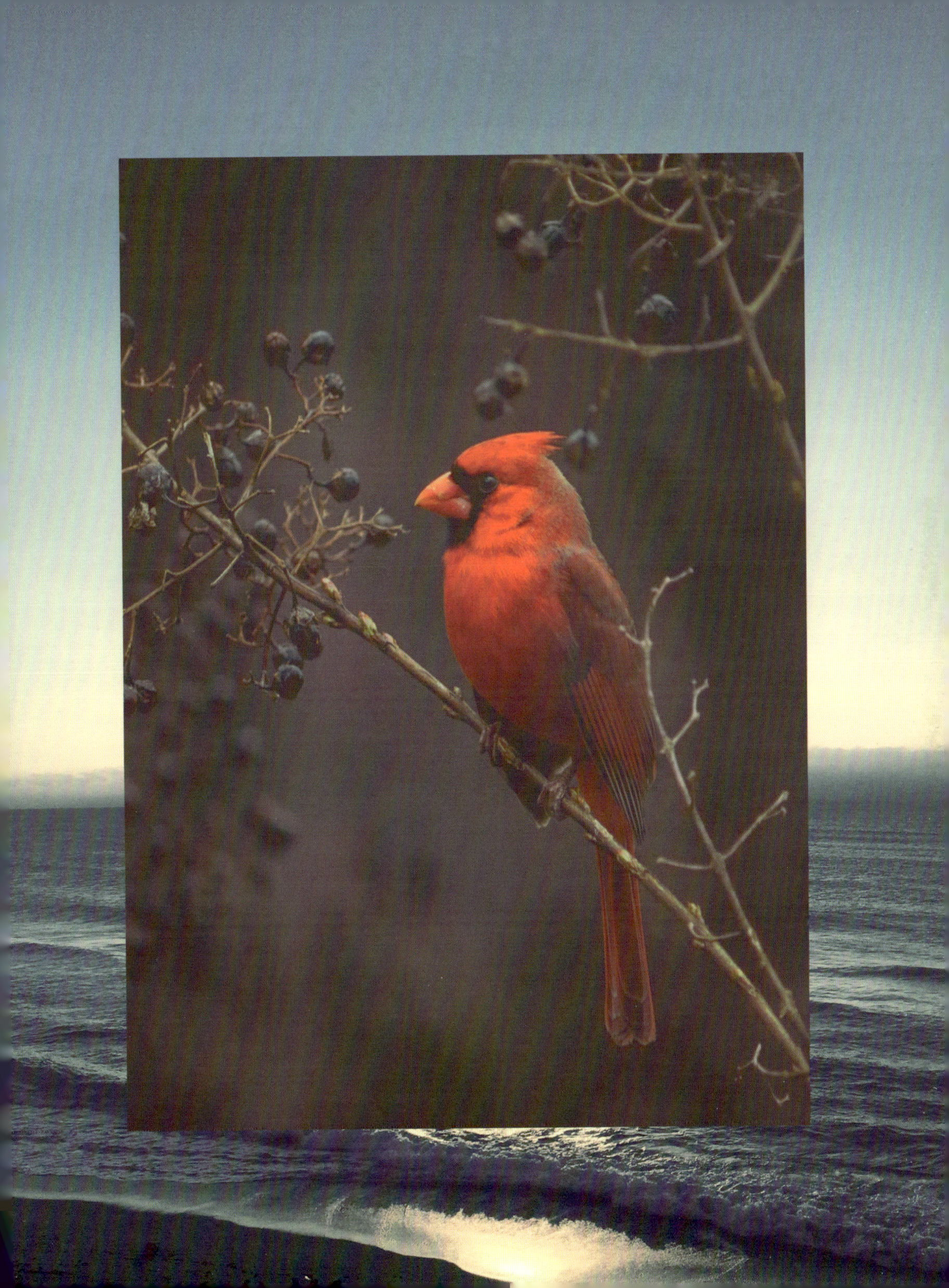

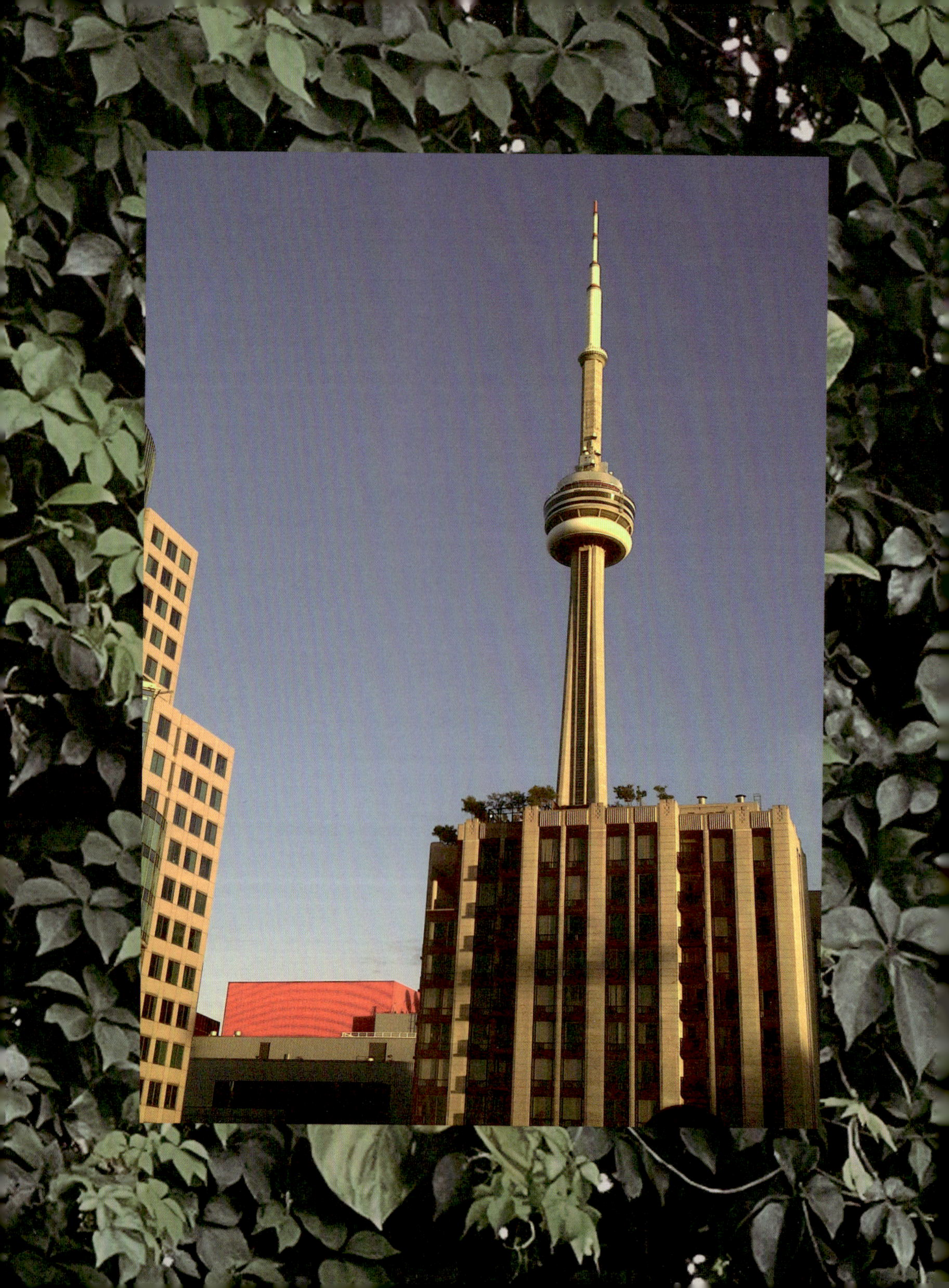

BUYING TIME

Something you need when you really need it.

Like a sweater if you're cold. A phone charger. A safety pin. A mop for cleaning your house.

YOU KNOW WHAT'S TRULY IMPORTANT.

And Money can't ever buy a cure for loneliness.

You'll see when you're old. Try buying time.

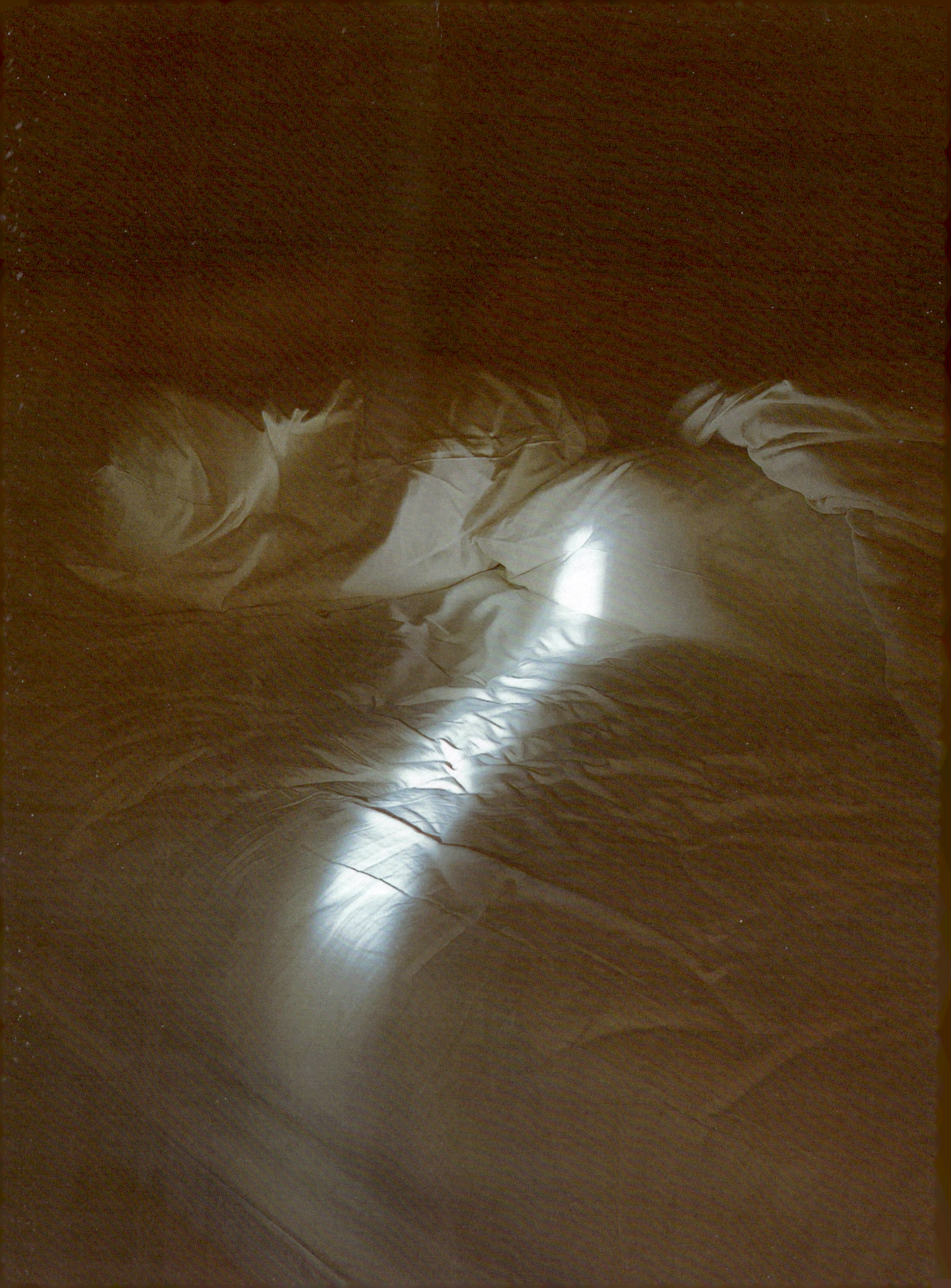

Sleep is worth a lot.

Our best sleep usually comes with peace of mind.
And peace of mind isn't on sale.
It's earned by kindness, generosity, and tender feelings for yourself and what you've achieved.

Integrity/Honesty/Character

Who you are. Just like a warm embrace in the night.

Robert, my husband, played James Taylor as we sped out of Water Mill.
Escaping the big hurricane that was expected to arrive later today.

We"re on our way to Woodstock, New York, and what was amazing, was that Sweet Baby James was my music on my way to the Art Students League in the town of Woodstock when I was in my late teens on my way to the adventure that was becoming my life...."So was the turnpike from Stockbridge to Boston.""

Remembering that feeling of aliveness and amazing energy as I traveled to my sparkling destiny. And here I am now, escaping the next storm to the same music.

Driving along the Cross Island Parkway, I was reminded of a dream that I"ve had over and over about a house on the side of a cliff or hill, overlooking the Hudson River, or some kind of water, just near New York City. And right here, there were some houses that nearly fit that description.
Just like that house that was mine in my dream.

The jazz DJ that Robert"s playing on the car radio, has just played an old Joni Mitchell song., "Carrie, the wind is in from Africa, last night I couldn"t sleep. It sure is hard to leave you, but it"s really not my home. "M, maybe it"s been too many years since I"ve been scrambling down in the streets, I"m getting used to those clean white linens and that fancy French cologne." "

I can see that this hurricane is surprisingly taking me back in musical time.

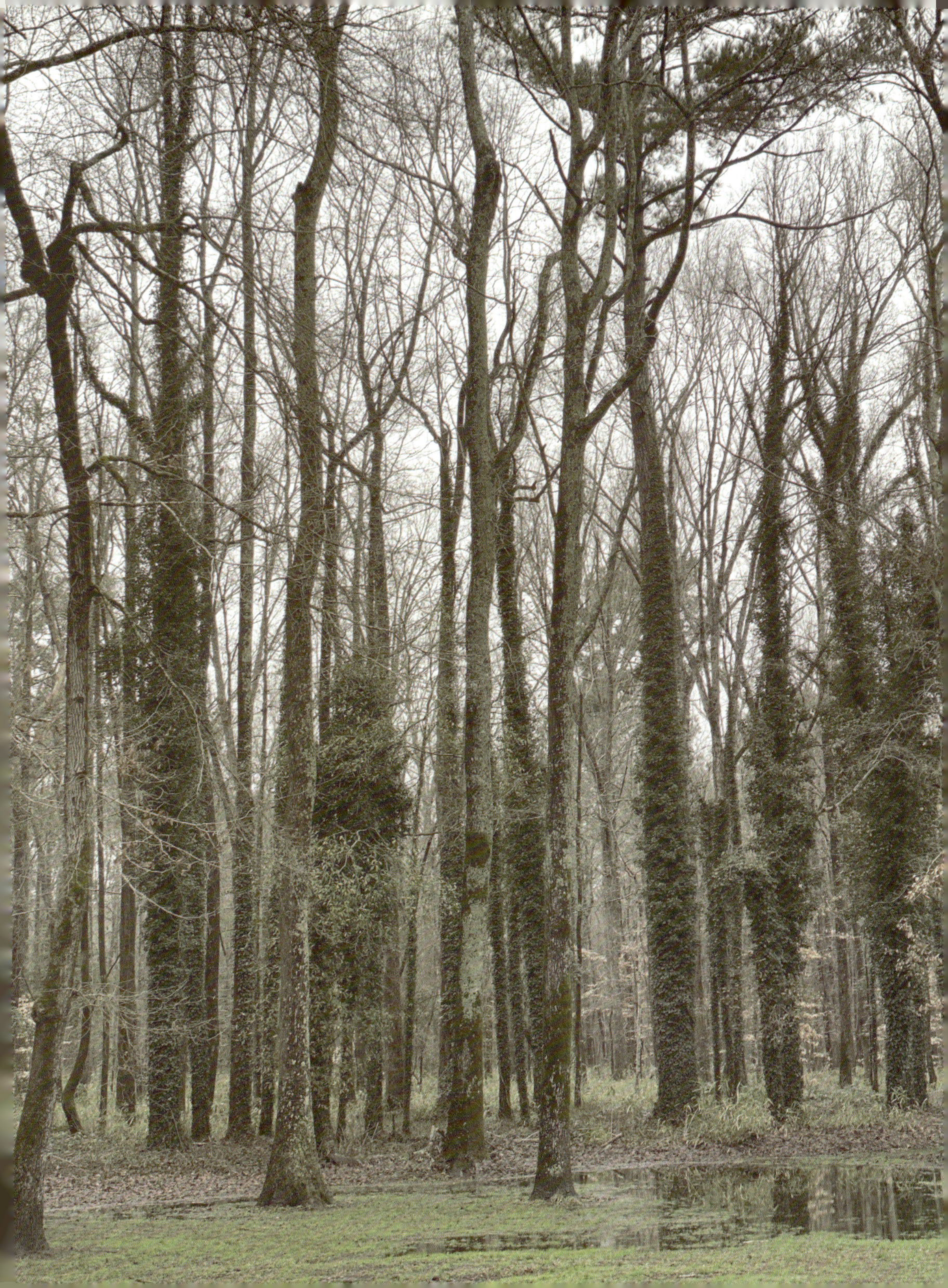

MAY THE
WHOLE WORLD
HAVE SOME
SUNSHINE
IN ITS SOUL

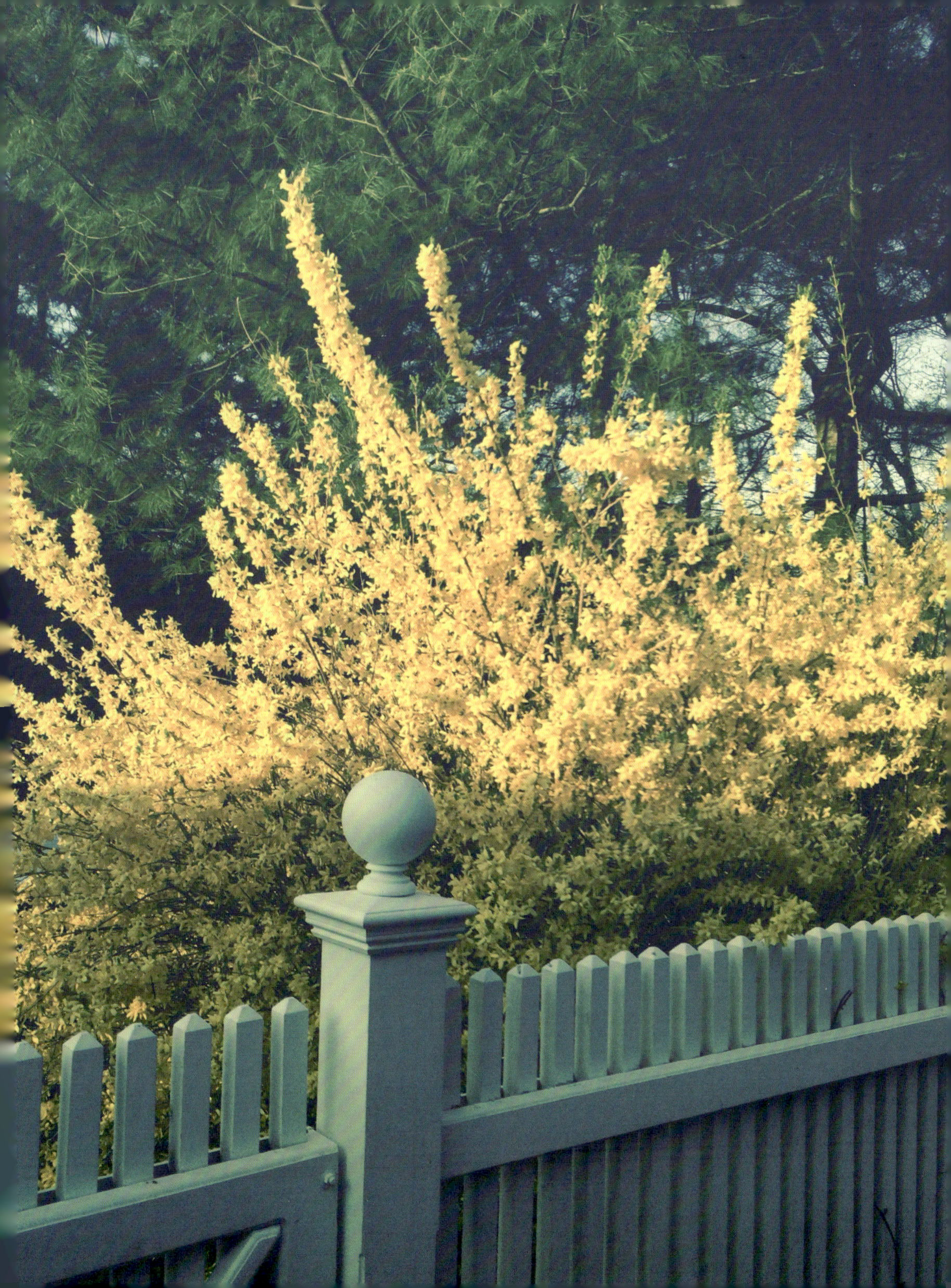

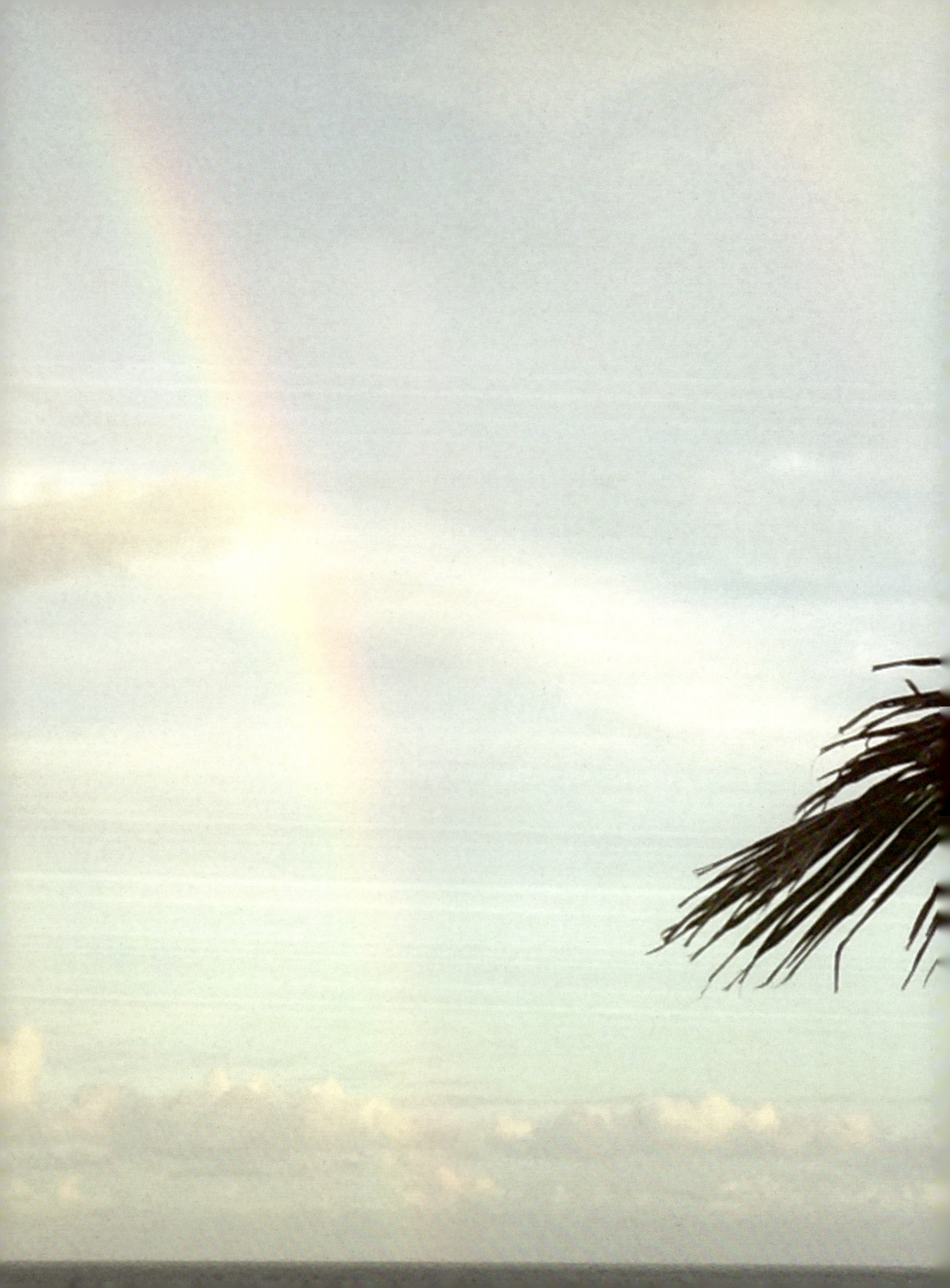

Open yourself up,

so the light can shine inside of you.

Shake away the density in your body.

Connect to the beauty of each day.

Essence backup. . . . That's how we live forever.
That's How God structured the world. ?? YES.

For a sense of accomplishment, and to feel proud of yourself,
it's important to help others.

So many affairs that you might want to have with life,
to make this world a better place for yourself, others, and those to come.

As far as the eye can see, that's the main reason to be alive—
making things better for everyone.

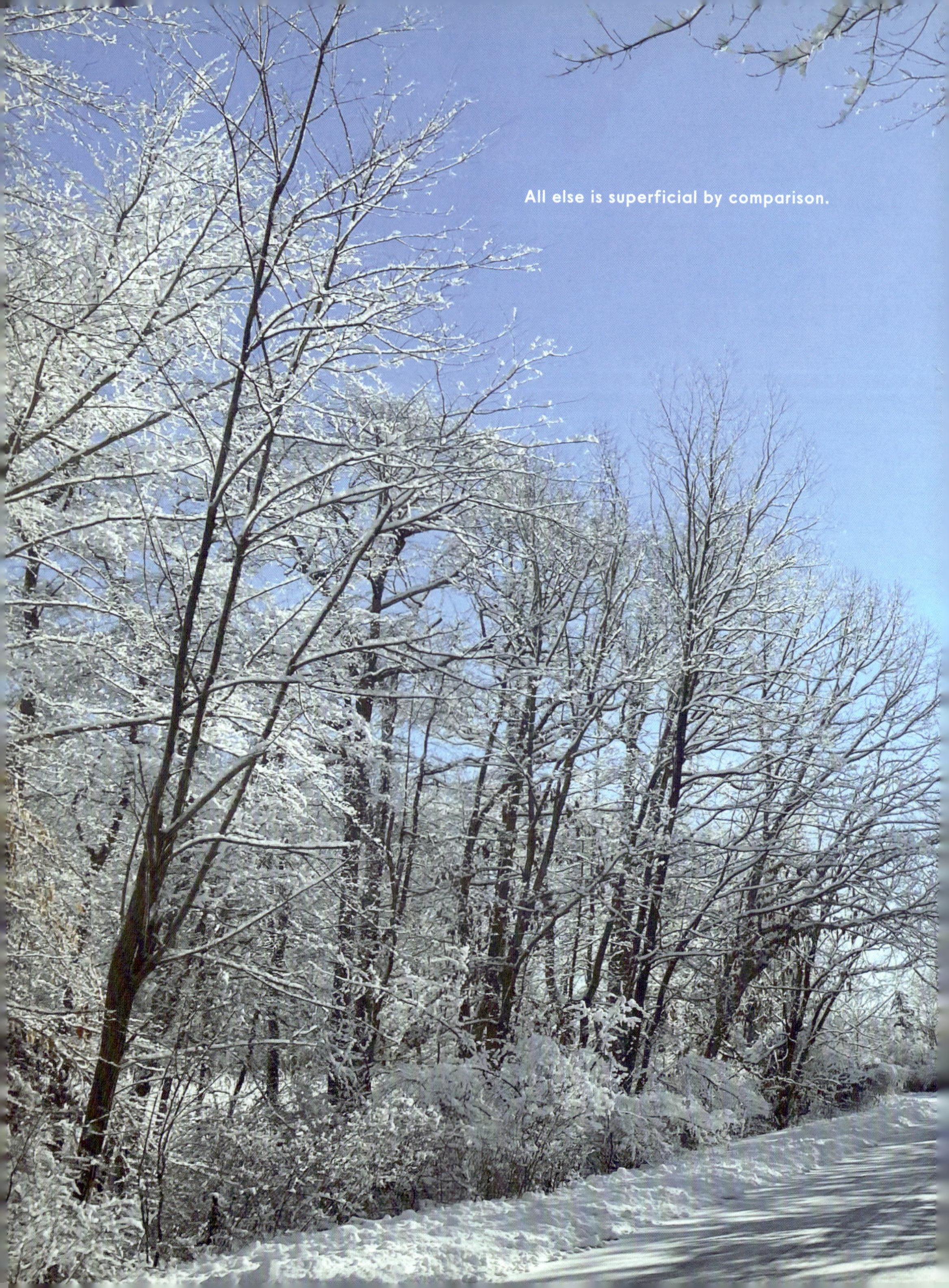
All else is superficial by comparison.

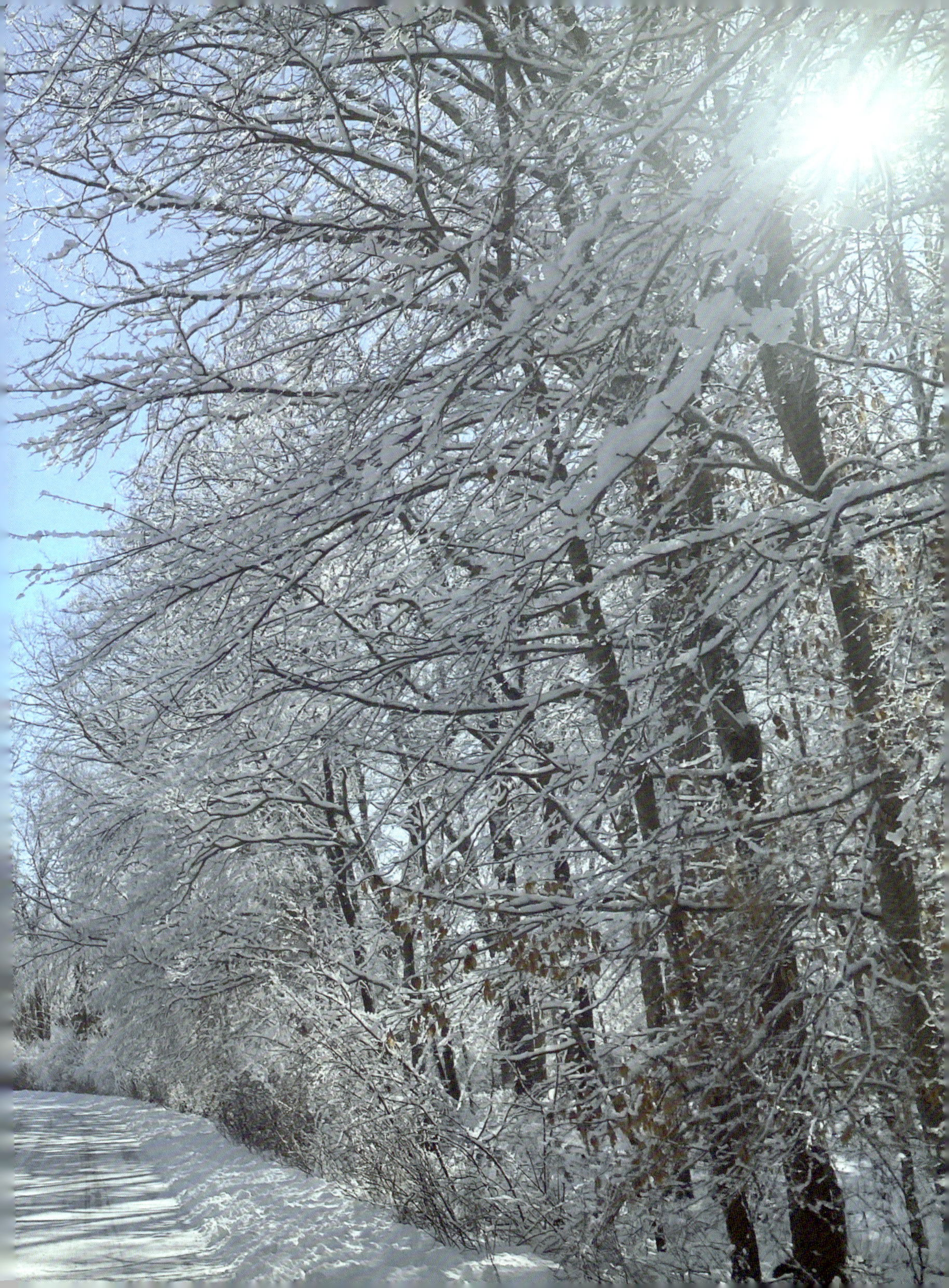

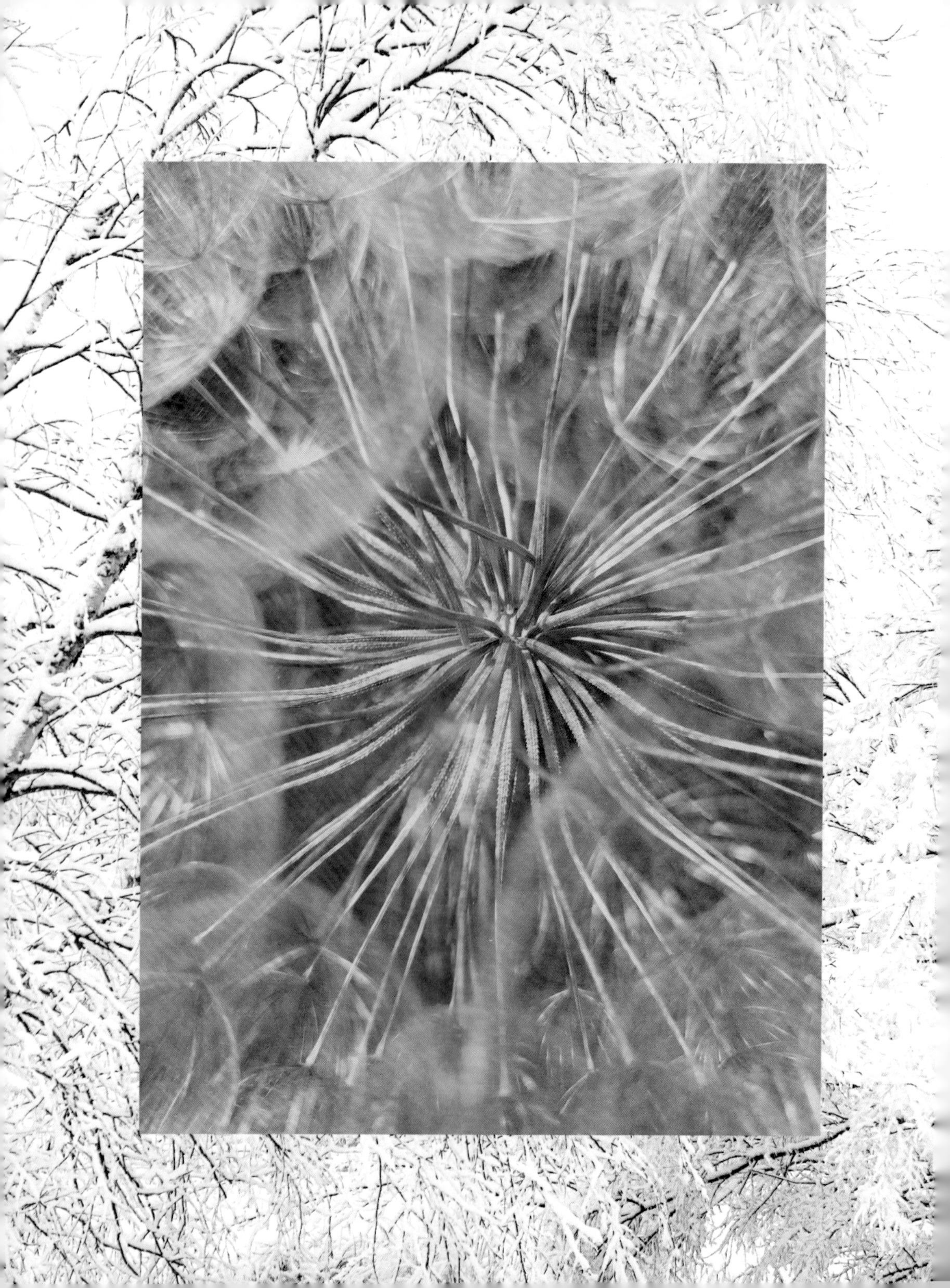

WILD INNOCENT

That was me growing up.

I wanted to go everywhere and
know everything.

And I did.

Completely, with a sense of deep morality and
consideration for others.

As I was taught,
by extensive reading and listening and knowing.

Now I can take all of that
and sit down and write about it.
You have to live it to know it to write it.

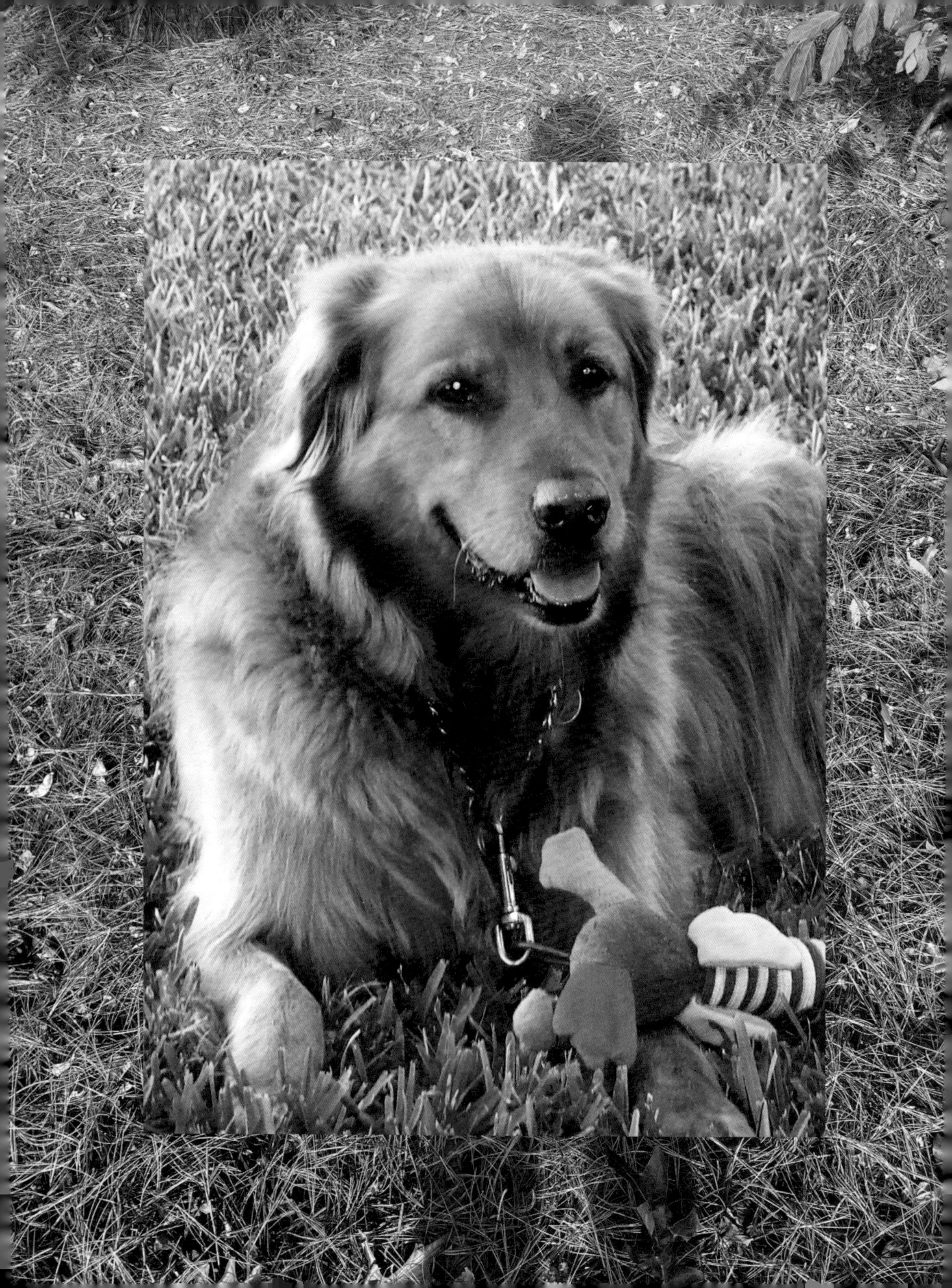

Robin Baker Leacock grew up in Toronto, Ontario, Canada, and currently divides her time between Sag Harbor, New York, and Palm Beach, Florida. She has directed and produced five films, all of which have been viewed widely at film festivals and on national television (PBS) in the United States. These include *I'll Take Manhattan,* which follows a group of Native Americans reclaiming their land in Lower Manhattan by taking over a Wall Street building; *It Girls,* about young and older women's creative energies, especially in the world of fashion in New York City; and *A Passion for Giving,* which discusses the power of giving instead of taking. She directed and produced the documentary, as well as served as director and producer, on the film *Stella is 95,* which features her charismatic Mother and explores the wonders of growing older; as well as *Stella & Co.,* a romantic musical comedy documentary about aging, again featuring the author's Mother and her friend, neighbors, and peers. She is also the author of *Mortimer's: Moments in Time* (G Editions, 2022), a retrospective in words and pictures of the noted watering hole for the local and international society crowd in New York City's 1970s, '80s, and '90s.

Robin lives with Robert Leacock and, until recently, their dog Luca, although she often thinks of her golden retriever, Bubbles.

CREDITS

Photography by © Robin Baker Leacock

All other © Christophe Von Hohenberg, pp. 91 | © Robert Leacock, pp.78 | © unsplash: © Andrea G., pp. 106 | © Andres Perez, pp. 102 | © Anne Nygard, pp. 92 | © Annie Spratt, pp. 80 | © Arfan Abdulazeez, pp. 140 | © Bas Glaap, pp. 98 | © Bunny, pp. 56 | © Clarence E., pp. 74 | © Clay Banks, pp. 114 | © Cristian Escobar, pp. 111 | © David Clode, pp. 60 | © Diogo Fagundes, pp. 42 | © Harry Cunningham, pp. 16 | © Ian Schneider, pp. 48 | © Ilja Frei, pp. 123 | © Jeppe Hove Jensen, pp. 35 | © Jon-Tyson, pp. 174 | © Jose Ignacio Pompe, pp. 46 | © Marek Okon, pp. 78 | © Margarita Zueva, pp. 151 | © Marina Marchyk, pp. 194 | © Martina Bombardieri, pp. 94 | © Max Bender, pp. 20 | © Mikita Yo, pp. 23 | © Muhammad Saushan, pp. 152 | © Nathan Dumlao, pp. 114 | © Olesia Bahrii, pp. 87 | © Raul Angel, pp. 102 | © Sacha T., pp. 101 | © Severin Candrian, pp. 46 | © Sincerely Media, pp. 94 | © Sofia Ornelas, pp. 83 | © Tamas Tuzes Katai, pp. 30 | © Timothy Dykes, pp. 171 | © Tyler Nix, pp. 167 | © Valery Rabchenyuk, pp. 74 | © Zoltan Tasi, pp. 124

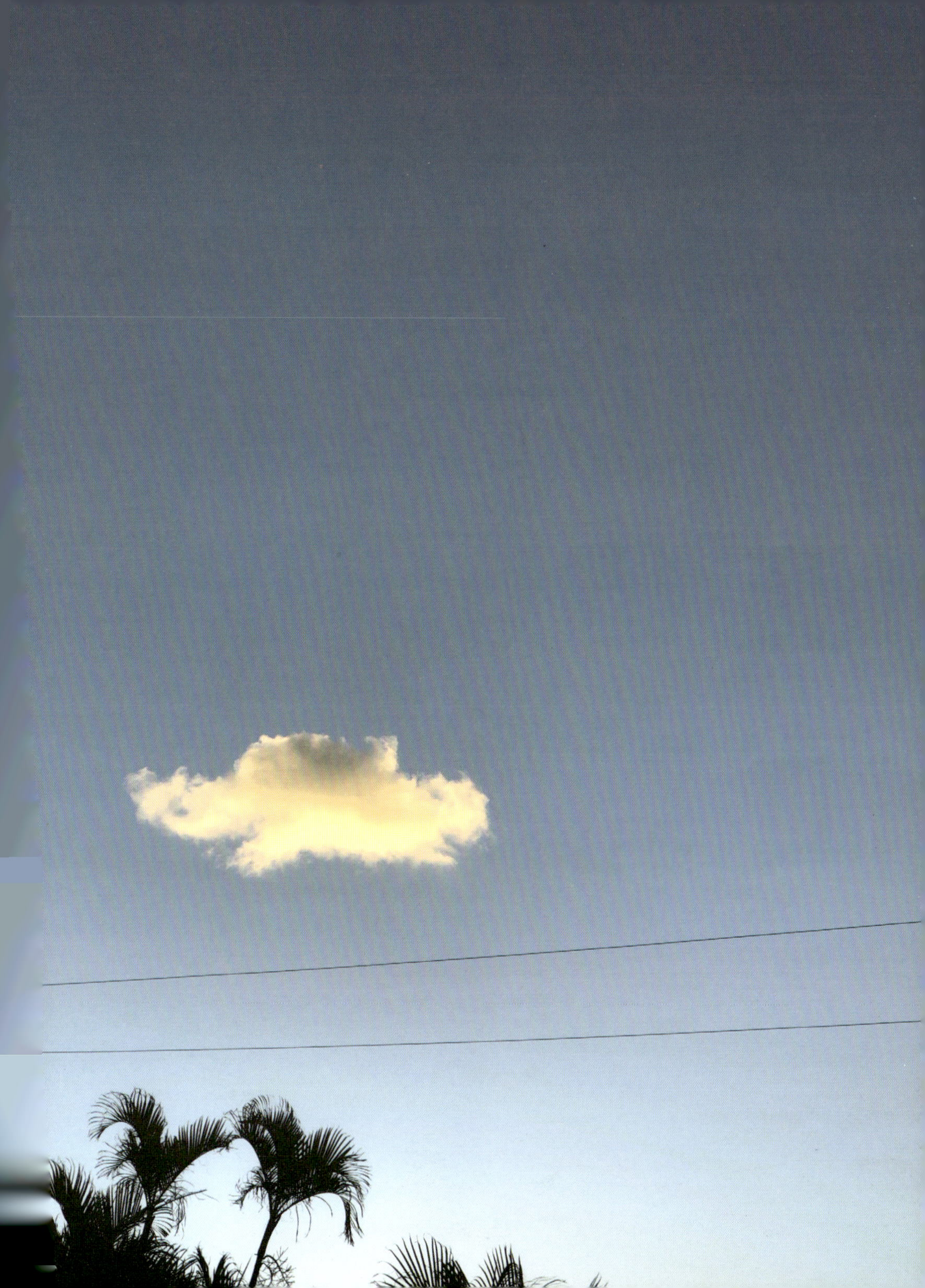

It's your lucky day now
It's your day
It's your lucky day now
It's your day

When you think straight
Straight, clean, and simple
And no matter what you may do
It''s all coming right back to you

Yes, it is.

From "Sing High, Sing Low",
Music and lyrics by Brent Titcomb

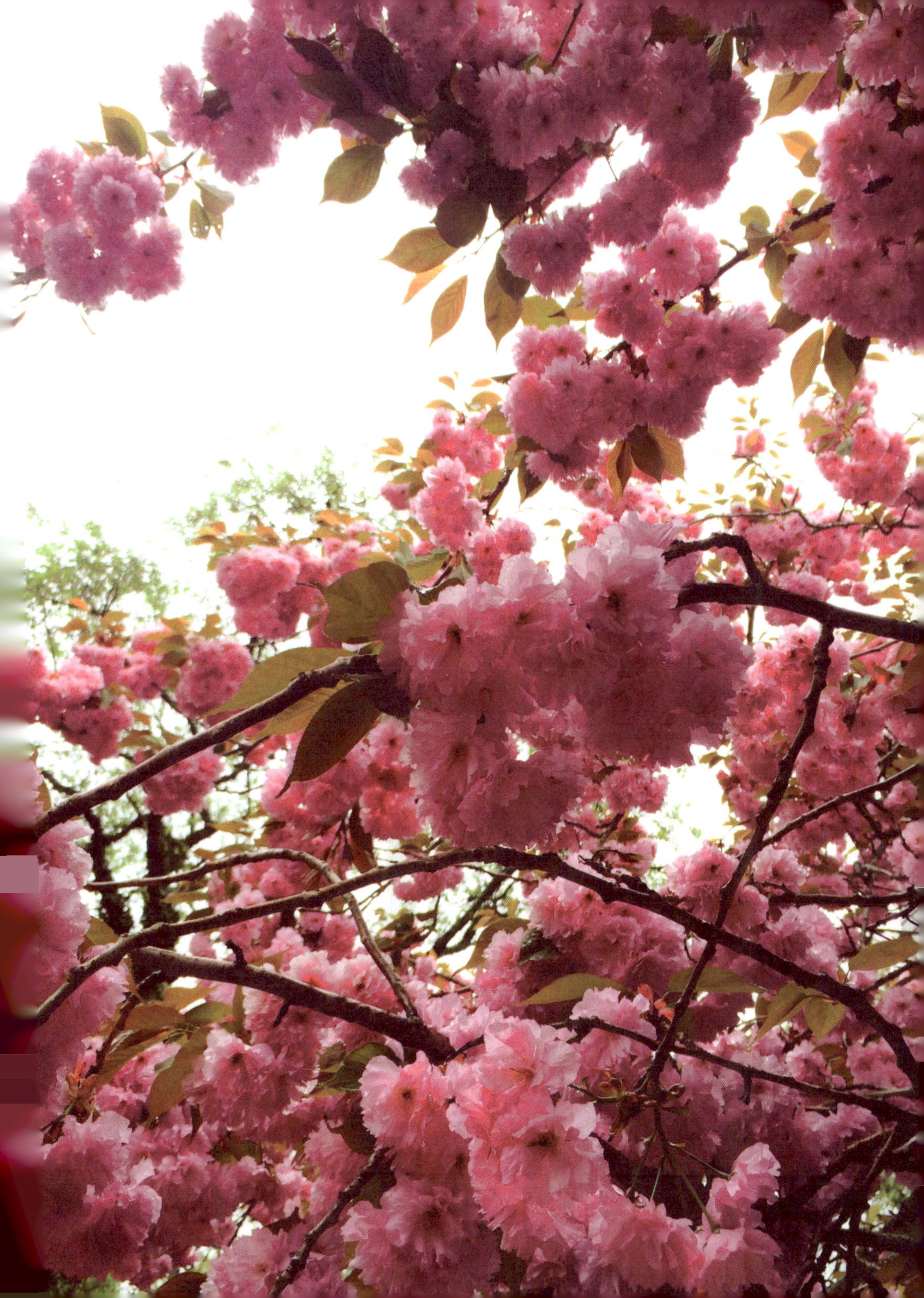